PSYCHE AND SPIRIT

PSYCHE
AND SPIRIT

readings in
psychology and religion

edited by
John J. Heaney

PAULIST PRESS
New York / Paramus / Toronto

Library of Congress
Catalog Card Number: 73-83810

ISBN 0-8091-1786-X

Published by Paulist Press
Editorial Office: 1865 Broadway, N.Y., N.Y., 10023
Business Office: 400 Sette Drive, Paramus, N.J. 07652

Printed and bound in the
United States of America

99683

Contents

PREFACE 1

I

IMMANENCE AND SELF-TRANSCENDENCE

1. THE PHENOMENON OF RELIGION 7
Sigmund Freud

2. REACTION TO FREUD 19
Paul Ricoeur

3. CONSCIENCE AND SUPEREGO 33
John W. Glaser, S.J.

4. C. G. JUNG AND RELIGION 57
Regina Bechtle, S.C.

5. REACTION TO JUNG 83
Martin Buber

6. HUMANISTIC RELIGION 91
Erich Fromm

7. RELIGION AND PEAK EXPERIENCE . . 97
Abraham Maslow

8. RELIGION AND
   MIND-EXPANDING DRUGS 109

   *Walter N. Pahnke, William A. Richards
   and Huston Smith*

9. TRANSCENDENTAL EXPERIENCES
   AND MEDITATION 125

   Roberto Assagioli, M.D.

10. THERAPEUTIC MEDITATION
    AND CONSCIOUSNESS 139

    Thomas Hora, M.D.

11. MARTIN BUBER'S MEDITATION
    ON THE I-THOU RELATIONSHIP 151

    Patricia B. Heaney and John J. Heaney

12. THE SELF IN EASTERN
    AND WESTERN THOUGHT 163

    W. Norris Clarke, S.J. and Beatrice Burkel

13. PENTECOSTALISM: THE SPIRIT
    AND THE COMMUNITY 175

    Charles de Celles

14. PARAPSYCHOLOGY:
    SURVIVAL AFTER DEATH 193

    H. Richard Neff

II

SELF-TRANSCENDENCE AND ULTIMATE MEANING

15. MAN'S SEARCH FOR MEANING 213

    Viktor Frankl

16. MEANING AND EXPERIENCE 225

William James

17. MEANING AND ACTION:
THE BLONDELLIAN SPIRIT 237

John J. Heaney

18. GOD AND THE DYNAMISM
OF THE MIND: KARL RAHNER 253

Joseph Donceel, S.J.

19. THE THEOLOGICAL SIGNIFICANCE
OF EXISTENTIALISM AND
PSYCHOANALYSIS 261

Paul Tillich

20. MEANING, PURPOSE
AND THE UNIVERSE 275

L. Charles Birch

BIBLIOGRAPHY 305

Preface

This collection of readings is designed for courses in religion or theology in which the center of interest is contemporary psychological insight into religion. The readings have been chosen largely on the basis of my own teaching experience. Ordinarily, the use of such a collection is enhanced by the presence of a teacher who will situate the excerpts within the context of an author's overall thought, although the book may also be read on its own merits. Ideally, one should make an in-depth probe of a few particular authors by reading some of their original work in its entirety.

Most of the bibliographical references include annotations which indicate special problem areas, thereby enabling the reader to pursue his specific focus of interest. The bibliographies have been selected not only according to quality but also with a view to the availability of texts. Wherever a paperback edition is available, this has been indicated.

The readings may be divided, roughly, into two parts. The first part, Chapters 1-14, centers in general on the phenomenon of self-transcendence in man. The second part, introduced by a chapter of transition (Chapter 15 by Viktor Frankl), includes five approaches which propose a philosophical-theological grounding of the previous data.

Part I begins with Freud's analysis of transcendence (God, the Father image) as a projection mechanism which operates as a protection against cosmic anxiety. The mystical "oceanic feeling" is seen as an infantile regression to an early state of life. In Chapter 2, Paul Ricoeur picks up Freud's analysis. While he rejects the non-theistic postulate, he finds in Freud's theory a purifying solvent against infantile religion and unhealthy inhibition. John Glaser, in Chapter 3, demonstrates the need for a clear distinction in psychoanalytic thinking between conscience and superego in order to liberate man from unfounded guilt feelings and to allow him to grow toward a mature conscience.

1

In Chapter 4, Regina Bechtle, S.C., presents an overview of Jung's theories. Here we see the unconscious as a rich reservoir from which flows the revelation of the God-image and the ego ideal. In Chapter 5, we see Buber's reaction to Jung's theory which he believes leads to the "I" but not to God as the Absolute "Thou." Chapter 6 contains Erich Fromm's presentation of religious transcendence as humanitarian religion free from authoritarian control, and as a projection of man's highest self. As we continue to survey the phenomenon of self-transcendence, in Chapter 7, we consider Abraham Maslow's comparison of psychological peak-experiences with religious experience, and we learn that such experiences are needful for human growth, prescinding from the reality or non-reality of a personal transcendent goal.

In Chapter 8, Walter Pahnke and William Richards compare the self-transcending consciousness attained in some drug usage with religious experience. The authors underline the importance of future research into methods of attaining self-transcending "religious" consciousness by chemical means. This is coupled with a caution by Huston Smith that such religious experience does not necessarily make a person religious. Roberto Assagioli, in Chapter 9, suggests certain meditation techniques for arriving at self-transcending wholeness.

Chapters 10-12 form a parenthetical trilogy. Thomas Hora's psychiatric-philosophical meditation on the self is contrasted with a personalist-religious meditation on the I-Thou relation as found in Buber. The first leads to self-acceptance; the second leads to the Absolute Center, God. In Chapter 12, an effort is made by W. Norris Clarke, S.J., to find common ground between such apparently contrasting approaches as typically found in Eastern and Western religious experience.

In Chapter 13, Charles De Celles offers a description of Pentecostalism, which we see as a social phenomenon of self-transcendence, community under the experience of the Spirit. Finally, in Chapter 14, H. Richard Neff considers the self transcendence investigated by parapsychology, particularly as found in the study of the phenomenon of survival beyond death.

Part II begins with a transitional chapter by Viktor Frankl on the question of meaning and self-transcendence. William James, in

Chapter 16, provides an existential-pragmatic approach to the Reality luring man beyond himself, God, but a "finite" God. In Chapter 17, we see Maurice Blondel's "logic of action" which leads to a conviction about the presence of God, both within and beyond man, as the condition of the possibility of all action or self-transcendence. In Chapter 18, Joseph Donceel, S.J., presents Karl Rahner's analysis of the dynamism of the Spirit in the world which leads to a conclusion similar to that of Blondel. In Chapter 19, Paul Tillich studies the mutual relationship between theology and psychoanalysis. This study implicitly relies on Tillich's symbol of God as the Ground of Being, which is the base of all self-transcendence. L. Charles Birch, in Chapter 20, presents a view of evolution, ongoing even before the human psyche existed, in which he utilizes process theology to ground all growth, both human and nonhuman, in the Divine Cosmic Lure.

The last chapters, therefore, present a Divine, Hyper-Personal, Cosmic Ground as the base which makes coherent the data of the experience of self-transcendence, and they suggest that, without such a Ground, the data of humanistic psychology are not adequately accounted for. These chapters offer sketches of a religious philosophy or fundamental theology which supports the Christian experience of transcendence. I have not included in these chapters excerpts from those philosophers who reject theism or a Personal Transcendent. Such a polar approach, I believe, is more relevant to works in the philosophy of religion, and many such books are readily available. The normative principle underlying this collection is that of a Judaeo-Christian fundamental theology in dialogue with humanistic psychology. Both traditions, it seems, are in a process of change through mutual influence.

The wider social psychology of religious movements and institutions has not been handled in any extensive way in these readings. The limitations of space have precluded such a consideration, but the reader should be aware of this dimension which is generally treated in works on the sociology of religion.

I wish to express my gratitude to my wife, Patricia, for her contribution on Buber, for much critical insight and encouragement; to Dr. Doris Donnelly and W. Norris Clarke, S.J., of Fordham University, and Rev. Francis Elmo, for helpful suggestions; to

Patricia Plovanich, O.S.F., for the summaries in the table of contents and for bibliographical assistance; to Marie Anne Mayeski, C.S.J. and Mrs. Rhonda Dunwoody of Paulist/Newman Press for invaluable help with typing and manuscript preparation; and finally, to Mr. Robert Heyer, editor of Paulist/Newman Press, for continued encouragement and support.

John J. Heaney
Fordham University

I

IMMANENCE AND SELF-TRANSCENDENCE

1 The Phenomenon of Religion

SIGMUND FREUD

Sigmund Freud (1856-1939) has been aptly called a "natural atheist," and yet throughout his productive life he was fascinated by the phenomenon of religion. The persistence of this interest is clearly seen if one glances at the chronology of Freud's works which are most pertinent to our present study: "Obsessive Actions and Religious Practices" (1907); *Totem and Taboo* (1913); *The Future of An Illusion* (1927); *Civilization and Its Discontents* (1930); *Moses and Monotheism* (1939).

The two following excerpts are from *The Future of An Illusion* * and *Civilization and Its Discontents.***
In the first, Freud says that man's sense of power-lessness before the universe brings about the projection of the father image into nature. The result of this is the idea of God as an all-powerful protector. The second excerpt concerns a common phenomenon of mystical experience, the "oceanic feeling," and what is said here will be of interest in relation to much of the rest of this book.

As Freud looked back at *The Future of An Illusion,* he wrote that he was there "much less concerned with the deepest sources of religious feeling than with what the common man understands by his religion . . ."

* From *The Future of An Illusion* by Sigmund Freud. By permission of Liveright, Publishers, New York. Pages 21-27, 47-50, 88-89, in the Anchor Books edition (Garden City, N.Y.: Doubleday & Company, Inc., 1964).
** Reprinted from *Civilization and Its Discontents* by Sigmund Freud. Translated from the German and edited by James Strachey. By permission of W. W. Norton & Company, Inc. Copyright 1961 by James Strachey, pp. 13-15.

(*Civilization and Its Discontents,* p. 21). Later in life, he even spoke somewhat disparagingly of the book. He seems to have preferred *Totem and Taboo* and *Moses and Monotheism,* where the origin of religion is connected with an early ancestral event, the slaying of the father of the primal horde. The reader should become acquainted with the ideas in those two books, especially with the notion of guilt and its repression, and the concept of yearning for the father. However, I have chosen to excerpt from *The Future of An Illusion* and *Civilization and Its Discontents* because the theory there presented is not so closely tied to an interpretation of anthropological data about which we know so little, and because the type of thinking found in these excerpts has had a much more lasting impact upon later writers in the area of psychology and religion.

It is worth noting that a number of authors, as for example Erich Fromm in *Sigmund Freud's Mission,* have presented solid evidence to support the idea that Freud identified with Moses, and they have suggested he believed that in psychoanalysis he would, as a new Moses, lead mankind to the Promised Land.

We know already how the individual reacts to the injuries which civilization and other men inflict on him: he develops a corresponding degree of resistance to the regulations of civilization and of hostility to it. But how does he defend himself against the superior powers of nature, of Fate, which threaten him as they threaten all the rest?

Civilization relieves him of this task; it performs it in the same way for all alike; and it is noteworthy that in this almost all civilizations act alike. Civilization does not call a halt in the task of defending man against nature, it merely pursues it by other means. The task is a manifold one. Man's self-regard, seriously menaced, calls for consolation; life and the universe must be robbed of their terrors; moreover his curiosity, moved, it is true, by the strongest practical interest, demands an answer.

A great deal is already gained with the first step: the humanization of nature. Impersonal forces and destinies cannot be approached; they remain eternally remote. But if the elements have passions that rage as they do in our own souls, if death itself is not something spontaneous but the violent act of an evil Will, if everywhere in nature there are Beings around us of a kind that we know in our own society, then we can breathe freely, can feel at home in the uncanny and can deal by psychical means with our senseless anxiety. We are still defenseless, perhaps, but we are no longer helplessly paralysed; we can at least react. Perhaps, indeed, we are not even defenceless. We can apply the same methods against these violent supermen outside that we employ in our own society; we can try to adjure them, to appease them, to bribe them, and, by so influencing them, we may rob them of a part of their power. A replacement like this of natural science by psychology not only provides immediate relief, but also points the way to a further mastering of the situation.

For this situation is nothing new. It has an infantile prototype, of which it is in fact only the continuation. For once before one has found oneself in a similar state of helplessness: as a small child, in relation to one's parents. One had reason to fear them, and especially one's father; and yet one was sure of his protection against the dangers one knew. Thus it was natural to assimilate the two situations. . . . A man makes the forces of nature not simply into persons with whom he can associate as he would with his equals—that would not do justice to the overpowering impression which those forces make on him—but he gives them the character of a father. He turns them into gods, following in this, as I have tried to show,[1] not only an infantile prototype but a phylogenetic one.

In the course of time the first observations were made of regularity and conformity to law in natural phenomena, and with this the forces of nature lost their human traits. But man's helplessness remains and along with it his longing for his father, and the gods. The gods retain their threefold task: they must exorcize the terrors of nature, they must reconcile men to the cruelty of Fate, particularly as it is shown in death, and they must compensate them for the sufferings and privations which a civilized life in common has imposed on them. . . .

And thus a store of ideas is created, born from man's need to make his helplessness tolerable and built up from the material of memories of the helplessness of his own childhood and the childhood of the human race. It can clearly be seen that the possession of these ideas protects him in two directions—against the dangers of nature and Fate, and against the injuries that threaten him from human society itself. Here is the gist of the matter. Life in this world serves a higher purpose; no doubt it is not easy to guess what that purpose is, but it certainly signifies a perfecting of man's nature. It is probably the spiritual part of man, the soul, which in the course of time has so slowly and unwillingly detached itself from the body, that is the object of this elevation and exaltation. Everything that happens in this world is an expression of the intentions of an intelligence superior to us, which in the end, though its ways and byways are difficult to follow, orders everything for the best—that is, to make it enjoyable for us. Over each one of us there watches a benevolent Providence which is only seemingly stern and which will not suffer us to become a plaything of the over-mighty and pitiless forces of nature. Death itself is not extinction, is not a return to inorganic lifelessness, but the beginning of a new kind of existence which lies on the path of development to something higher. And, looking in the other direction, this view announces that the same moral laws which our civilizations have set up govern the whole universe as well, except that they are maintained by a supreme court of justice with incomparably more power and consistency. In the end all good is rewarded and all evil punished, if not actually in this form of life then in the later existences that begin after death. In this way all the terrors, the sufferings and the hardships of life are destined to be obliterated. Life after death, which continues life on earth just as the invisible part of the spectrum joins on to the visible part, brings us all the perfection that we may perhaps have missed here. And the superior wisdom which directs this course of things, the infinite goodness that expresses itself in it, the justice that achieves its aim in it—these are the attributes of the divine beings who also created us and the world as a whole, or rather, of the one divine being into which, in our civilization, all the gods of antiquity have been condensed. The people which first succeeded in thus concentrating the divine attributes was not a little proud of the advance. It had laid open to view the father who had all along been hidden behind every divine figure as its nucleus. . . .

Thus the benevolent rule of a divine Providence allays our fear of the dangers of life; the establishment of a moral world-order ensures the fulfilment of the demands of justice, which have so often remained unfulfilled in human civilization; and the prolongation of earthly existence in a future life provides the local and temporal framework in which these wish-fulfilments shall take place. Answers to the riddles that tempt the curiosity of man, such as how the universe began or what the relation is between body and mind, are developed in conformity with the underlying assumptions of this system. It is an enormous relief to the individual psyche if the conflicts of its childhood arising from the father-complex—conflicts which it has never wholly overcome—are removed from it and brought to a solution which is universally accepted.

When I say that these things are all illusions, I must define the meaning of the word. An illusion is not the same thing as an error; nor is it necessarily an error. Aristotle's belief that vermin are developed out of dung (a belief to which ignorant people still cling) was an error; so was the belief of a former generation of doctors that *tabes dorsalis* is the result of sexual excess. It would be incorrect to call these errors illusions. On the other hand, it was an illusion of Columbus's that he had discovered a new sea-route to the Indies. The part played by his wish in this error is very clear. One may describe as an illusion the assertion made by certain nationalists that the Indo-Germanic race is the only one capable of civilization; or the belief, which was only destroyed by psycho-analysis, that children are creatures without sexuality. What is characteristic of illusions is that they are derived from human wishes. In this respect they come near to psychiatric delusions. But they differ from them, too, apart from the more complicated structure of delusions. In the case of delusions, we emphasize as essential their being in contradiction with reality. Illusions need not necessarily be false—that is to say, unrealizable or in contradiction to reality. . . .

Thus we call a belief an illusion when a wish-fulfilment is a prominent factor in its motivation, and in doing so we disregard its relations to reality, just as the illusion itself sets no store by verification.

Having thus taken our bearings, let us return once more to the question of religious doctrines. We can now repeat that all of them are illusions and insusceptible of proof. No one can be compelled to think them true, to believe in them. Some of them are so improbable, so incompatible with everything we have laboriously discovered about the reality of the world, that we may compare them—if we pay proper regard to the psychological differences— to delusions. Of the reality value of most of them we cannot judge; just as they cannot be proved, so they cannot be refuted. We still know too little to make a critical approach to them. . . .

The primacy of the intellect lies, it is true, in a distant, distant future, but probably not in an *infinitely* distant one. It will presumably set itself the same aims as those whose realization you expect from your God (of course within human limits—so far as external reality, 'Ανάγκη, allows it), namely the love of man and the decrease of suffering. This being so, we may tell ourselves that our antagonism is only a temporary one and not irreconcilable. We desire the same things, but you are more impatient, more exacting, and—why should I not say it?—more self-seeking than I and those on my side. You would have the state of bliss begin directly after death; you expect the impossible from it and you will not surrender the claims of the individual. Our God, Λόγος,[2] will fulfil whichever of these wishes nature outside us allows, but he will do it very gradually, only in the unforeseeable future, and for a new generation of men. He promises no compensation for us, who suffer grievously from life. On the way to this distant goal your religious doctrines will have to be discarded, no matter whether the first attempts fail, or whether the first substitutes prove to be untenable. You know why: in the long run nothing can withstand reason and experience, and the contradiction which religion offers to both is all too palpable. Even purified religious ideas cannot escape this fate, so long as they try to preserve anything of the consolation of religion. No doubt if they confine themselves to a belief in a higher spiritual being, whose qualities are indefinable and whose purposes cannot be discerned, they will be proof against the challenge of science; but then they will also lose their hold on human interest.

Editor's note: after the publication of *The Future of An Illusion,* Romain Rolland (1866-1914, a French dramatist, novelist and biographer) wrote to Freud to complain that he had omitted from the book any consideration of the true source of religious sentiments, "the oceanic feeling." The following excerpt contains part of Freud's analysis of the origin of the oceanic feeling. Freud concluded his discussion by admitting that there may be more to it than he has said, "but for the present it is wrapped in obscurity" (*Civilization and Its Discontents,* p. 19).

An infant at the breast does not as yet distinguish his ego from the external world as the source of the sensations flowing in upon him. He gradually learns to do so, in response to various promptings.[3] He must be very strongly impressed by the fact that some sources of excitation, which he will later recognize as his own bodily organs, can provide him with sensations at any moment, whereas other sources evade him from time to time—among them what he desires most of all, his mother's breast—and only reappear as a result of his screaming for help. In this way there is for the first time set over against the ego an 'object', in the form of something which exists 'outside' and which is only forced to appear by a special action.[4] A further incentive to a disengagement of the ego from the general mass of sensations—that is, to the recognition of an 'outside', an external world—is provided by the frequent, manifold and unavoidable sensations of pain and unpleasure the removal and avoidance of which is enjoined by the pleasure principle, in the exercise of its unrestricted domination. A tendency arises to separate from the ego everything that can become a source of such unpleasure, to throw it outside and to create a pure pleasure-ego which is confronted by a strange and threatening 'outside'. The boundaries of this primitive pleasure-ego cannot escape rectification through experience. Some of the things that one is unwilling to give up, because they give pleasure, are nevertheless not ego but object; and some sufferings that one seeks to expel turn out to be inseparable from the ego in virtue of their internal origin. One comes to learn a procedure by which, through a deliberate direction of one's sensory activities and through suitable muscular action, one can differentiate between what is in-

ternal—what belongs to the ego—and what is external—what emanates from the outer world. In this way one makes the first step
towards the introduction of the reality principle which is to dominate future development.[5] This differentiation, of course, serves the
practical purpose of enabling one to defend oneself against sensations of unpleasure which one actually feels or with which one is
threatened. In order to fend off certain unpleasurable excitations
arising from within, the ego can use no other methods than those
which it uses against unpleasure coming from without, and this is
the starting-point of important pathological disturbances.

In this way, then, the ego detaches itself from the external
world. Or, to put it more correctly, originally the ego includes
everything, later it separates off an external world from itself. Our
present ego-feeling is, therefore, only a shrunken residue of a much
more inclusive—indeed, an all-embracing—feeling which corresponded to a more intimate bond between the ego and the world
about it. If we may assume that there are many people in whose
mental life this primary ego-feeling has persisted to a greater or
less degree, it would exist in them side by side with the narrower
and more sharply demarcated ego-feeling of maturity, like a kind
of counterpart to it. In that case, the ideational contents appropriate to it would be precisely those of limitlessness and of a bond
with the universe—the same ideas with which my friend elucidated
the 'oceanic' feeling.

NOTES

1. See Section 6 of the fourth essay in *Totem and Taboo* (1912-13),
Standard Ed., 13, 146ff.
2. The twin gods Λόγος (*Logos:* Reason) and 'Ανάγκη (*Ananke:* Necessity) of the Dutch writer Multatuli. (Cf. an Editor's footnote to 'The Economic Problem of Masochism' (1924c), *Standard Ed.*, 19, 168.)
3. In this paragraph Freud was going over familiar ground. He had
discussed the matter not long before, in his paper on 'Negation' (1925h),
Standard Ed., 19, 236-8. But he had dealt with it on several earlier occasions.
See, for instance, 'Instincts and their Vicissitudes' (1915c), ibid., 14, 119
and 134-6, and *The Interpretation of Dreams* (1900a), ibid., 5, 565-6. Its

essence, indeed, is already to be found in the 'Project' of 1895, Sections 1, 2, 11 and 16 of Part I (Freud, 1950a).

4. The 'specific action' of the 'Project'.

5. Cf. 'Formulations on the Two Principles of Mental Functioning' (1911b), *Standard Ed.*, 12, 222-3.

SUGGESTED READINGS

For the beginner, the best introductions to Freud's religious thought are *The Future of An Illusion* (N.Y.: Doubleday, 1964, Anchor paperback), which is the simplest work, and *Civilization and Its Discontents* (N.Y.: W.W. Norton, 1961, paperback), which covers a wider spectrum of thought. In the latter, one might pay special attention to Freud's discussion of love, pp. 46-54, and to his description of the struggle between Eros and Thanatos. *Totem and Taboo* (N.Y.: Random House, Vintage paperback, 1939) and *Moses and Monotheism* (N.Y.: Random House, Vintage paperback, 1939) rely heavily on anthropological theory, some of which is now dated. This, however, is not to deny the importance of either work. Both have been called masterpieces. In *Totem and Taboo* Freud drew a parallel between three stages in the evolution of culture and three stages in the life of an individual. The animistic stage corresponded to the narcissism of infancy, the religious stage to childhood dependence on parents, the scientific stage to "the individual's state of maturity where, having renounced the pleasure principle and having adapted himself to reality, he seeks his object in the outside world" (Cf. Costigan *infra*, p. 187). While not acceptable as presented, the thought has been influential and is a useful point of departure for a discussion of the meaning of religion. In *Moses and Monotheism* one can find a great deal of provocative, religious insight which might tend to be obscured by the general thrust of the book. In this ingenious but somewhat fantastic work, Freud conjectured that Moses was an Egyptian who passed on monotheistic religion to the Hebrews, who later murdered him. At the death of Jesus, there occurred "the return of the repressed" memory of the original father slaying and of the killing of Moses. This return of repressed guilt then played a part in Paul's interpretation of Jesus' life. For a discussion of the theory, see W. W. Meissner, S.J., "Notes on Monotheism—The Argument," *Journal of Religion and Health,* Oct. 1967, pp. 269-279, and the continuation of this in the Jan. and Apr. 1968 issues, pp. 43-60, 151-163. "Obsessive Actions and Religious Practices," found in *The Standard Edition of the Complete Psychological Works of Sigmund Freud,* vol. IX, pp. 117-127 (London: Hogarth Press, 1959), is readily accessible in *Personality and Religion,* edited by William A. Sadler, Jr. (N.Y.: Harper & Row, 1970, paperback), pp. 47-56. *Psychoanalysis and Faith—The Letters of Sigmund Freud and Oscar Pfister* (N.Y.: Basic Books, 1963) contains an exchange of ideas on religion between Freud and his friend, a Swiss pastor.

The classic biography is by Freud's disciple, Ernest Jones, *The Life and Work of Sigmund Freud,* 3 vols. (N.Y.: Basic Books, 1953-1957). This has been edited and abridged into one volume by Lionel Trilling and Steven Marcus (Garden City, N.Y.: Doubleday, 1963, paperback). Erich Fromm's *Sigmund Freud's Mission* (N.Y.: Harper & Row, 1959, paperback) is illuminating and critical, but perhaps overly distanced from Freud himself. *Sigmund Freud—A Short Biography* by Giovanni Costigan (N.Y.: Macmillan, 1965) is a solid work which weaves an analysis of Freud's thought into his personal history.

Philip Rieff's *The Mind of the Moralist* (Garden City, N.Y.: Doubleday, 1961, paperback) includes thorough sections on Freud's religious thought. G. S. Spinks in *Psychology and Religion* (Boston: Beacon Press, 1963, paperback) presents a good, brief summary and critique of Freud's thought. Many chapters in *Psychoanalysis and History,* edited by Bruce Mazlish (Englewood Cliffs, N.J.: Prentice-Hall, 1963), are most helpful. On Freud's notion of love, see William Cole's *Sex in Christianity and Psychoanalysis* (N.Y.: Oxford University Press, 1966, paperback); Douglas Morgan's *Love: Plato, the Bible & Freud* (Englewood Cliffs, N.J.: Prentice-Hall, 1964); and Robert Hazo's *The Idea of Love* (N.Y.: Frederick A. Praeger, 1967). For further references, see Chapter 2.

(The reader will no doubt realize that the religious aspect of the thought of the authors mentioned in this book cannot be fully understood without some acquaintance with the overall psychological theory of the author. Helpful introductions are Calvin S. Hall and Gardner Lindzey's *Theories of Personality* (N.Y.: John Wiley & Sons, 1970, 2nd ed.); J. A. C. Brown's *Freud and the Post-Freudians* (Baltimore: Penguin Books, 1964); Patrick Mullahy's *Oedipus: Myth and Complex* (N.Y.: Grove Press, 1948, paperback).

2 Reaction to Freud

Paul Ricoeur (b. 1913) a professor of philosophy at the Sorbonne, has written extensively on the phenomenology of existence in such works as *The Symbolism of Evil* and *Fallible Man*. In particular, he is the author of a penetrating reinterpretation of Freud: *Freud and Philosophy—An Essay on Interpretation*. Ricoeur has described three relationships between man and his symbols: a stage of primitive naiveté in which man is immersed in his symbols; a second stage of critical distancing, of truth at a distance, in which questioning supplants commitment; a third stage, called the second naiveté, in which man returns to the immediacy of his symbols but without discarding the critical mode which becomes now, not reductive, but restorative. The last stage, which is a revivification of symbol, is reached only after critical distance is achieved in hermeneutical de-mythologization.

Ricoeur's analysis * suggests that Freud's thought stands as a purification of the religious sense. Passing through Freud's criticism prepares for the second naiveté, which is the conjunction of criticism and belief. Since psychoanalysis "does not speak about God but only about the god which man has made," the consolation from the Spirit fully emerges only after the deprivation of the prior infantile consolation.

One has only to read *The Future of an Illusion*,[1] *Civilization and Its Discontents*,[2] and *Moses and Monotheism*[3] to be convinced that Freud is one of the

* From "Is God Dead?" *Concilium,* Vol. 16, N.Y.: Paulist Press, 1966, pp. 59-72.

outstanding atheists of contemporary culture. It is more important to determine what kind of atheism is found in his thought and, above all, what is its actual connection with psychoanalysis properly so called.

As regards the kind of atheism, Freud's criticism of religion is not exactly of the positive school. For Freud religion is undoubtedly an illusion that must be replaced by science. However, Freud bears the positivist label in company with the large majority of the scientists of his day. It is far more interesting to connect his atheism with the critique of religion found in the philosophies of Feuerbach, Nietzsche and Marx. These thinkers treat religion as a cultural phenomenon. They trace it to a genesis or a genealogy, to use Nietzsche's phrase, which consists in discovering in the *hidden* movements of conscience the source of an "illusion" whose function is myth-making. Psychoanalysis of religion issues forth as a new type of this criticism. The illusion that it claims to unmask has nothing in common with error in the epistemological meaning of the word, nor is it like a conscious and deliberate lie in the moral sense. Rather, it is a production of the senses, the key to which eludes its possessor. In fact, a special deciphering or decoding technique is required. Such an *exegesis* of "false consciousness" demands a technique of interpretation closer to philology and textual criticism than to physics or biology. This is the reason why its attendant atheism does not have the same basis as scientific materialism or logical empirical positivism. It is, rather, a question of a reductionist heremeneutic applied to the "sensual effects" belonging to the culture. In this regard Freudian psychoanalysis of religion is much closer to the genealogy of morals in the Nietzschean sense or even to the Marxian theory of ideologies than it is to the theological and metaphysical critique of Aŭguste Comte.

The relationship to Feuerbach, Marx and Nietzsche goes even deeper. With all these thinkers the reduction of illusion is merely the reverse side of a positive undertaking of liberating, and, by the same token, of affirming man *as man*. In a different manner, and often by ways that on the surface seem opposed, these masters of suggestion set out to bring to light the power of man which had been displaced and lost in an alien transcendence. Whether it is a question of the Marxist leap from the realm of necessity into that of liberty by means of scientific understanding of the laws of history, or of the Nietzschean contemplation of destiny and eternal recurrence, or, in Freud's language, of the passage from the pleasure principle to the reality principle,[4] it is always the same undertaking: to reveal man to himself, in his power of affirmation and creation of meaning.

In connection with this undertaking, whether proximate or long-range, interpretation in its negative aspects is simply ascesis. It must pass through human desire before being restored to its own greatness. It is under this long-range aspect of the influence exercised by suggestion and interpretation that Freud has so profound an influence on modern man. He has not only, or even principally, introduced a new kind of therapy, but a global interpretation of the phenomena of culture and of religion as an aspect of culture. Our culture analyzes itself through him—a fact of extreme importance that must be understood and evaluated.

I
THE LEGITIMACY OF A
PSYCHOANALYSIS OF RELIGION

Just what is the relationship between this critique of religion and psychoanalysis properly so called? Perhaps one might be tempted to avoid this critique by denying the competence of psychoanalysis. Is it not primarily an explanation and a therapy useful only for dreams and neuroses, that is to say, for the lower life of man, for his lower nature and his darker side? What right has psychoanalysis to speak *also* of art, of morality and religion? In the face of this objection, it seems to me that three things must be asserted with equal emphasis. First of all, the competence of psychoanalysis extends to the total human reality; secondly, it also embraces religion as a manifestation of culture; thirdly, insofar as it is psychoanalysis, it is necessarily iconoclastic.

Psychoanalysis deals with human reality in its totality. It would be a grave mistake in regard to its significance to assign instinct as its domain and object. Instinct, in the Freudian sense, is always a relation antagonistic to other factors which place it first in a cultural setting. What else is the "censor" in the theory of dreams but a cultural factor playing the role of inhibitor of the "more basic instincts"? In this way the dream, in its dynamism, reveals the same elements which ethnology arrives at in the prohibition of incest.[5] In the depths of the individual psyche the Superego [6] represents the social function of inhibition and the model which makes possible the education of instinct. More exactly, the father,[7] the bearer of language and culture, is at the heart of the Oedipus drama, whose role is precisely the introduction of desire into the realm of culture. Thus there is sketched out a vast area which can be called the semantics of instinct; in fact, culture is seen to become in a certain sense a complex form of this semantics of instinct.

The right of psychoanalysis as psychoanalysis to speak about religion now becomes clear. It embraces religion as one of the dimensions of culture.[8] Indeed, culture, considered in economic terms—that is to say, from the point of view of emotional costs in pleasure and displeasure, in satisfaction and in privation—has a many-faceted relationship to human desire. It inhibits and consoles; it forbids incest, cannibalism and murder. In this sense it demands of the individual the sacrifice of instinct. However, at the same time, its true *raison d'être* is to protect us against nature. In this role, it sets out to lighten the burden of the sacrifice of instinct which is imposed on men, to reconcile individuals with those sacrifices which are inevitable, to offer them compensatory satisfactions for these sacrifices. It is in this meaning of the term that culture is a compensating factor. Considered in its cultural grandeur, religion is the supreme instrument of this ascesis and this reconciliation. In this dual role, it encounters desire and fear: the fear of punishment and the desire for consolation. Its truest aspect is its compensating function.

Religion is the supreme response which man finds in culture to the harshness of life: impotence in the face of the crushing forces of nature, in the face of sickness and death; impotence in controlling human relations which are geared to hatred and war; impotence of man to master the forces of instinct which threaten him from within, and to satisfy at the same time the implacable master who takes the part of the Superego. The consolation of religion is the response to the rigors of life.

However, if psychoanalysis encounters religion as a cultural factor, its attitude toward it is necessarily iconoclastic, independent of the faith or lack of faith of the psychoanalyst. Psychoanalysis does not speak about God, but only about the god which man has made. For psychoanalysis, religion is the illusion which belongs to the strategy of desire. Psychoanalysis is well-armed to approach cultural phenomena in general—and the religious phenomenon in particular—from the aspect of the semantics of instinct. It has at its command an initial model by which it looks for analogues on other levels of human existence. This model is the dream, or, to speak more exactly, the dream-symptom. It presents in the most elementary form the process known as "wish fulfillment" (*Wunscherfüllung*).[9] This process deals with all of the manifestations of culture insofar as these can be considered as analogous extensions of accomplishment disguised as repressed desires, after the manner of compensation.

II
THE GREAT THEMES OF THE FREUDIAN CRITIQUE OF RELIGION

Let us examine this critique in more detail in order to grasp its bearing on psychoanalytic practice and theory. Several points are latent in the interpretation. At the lowest level, the critique is based on a certain number of more or less close analogies to the phenomena relevant to clinical psychoanalysis. On the second level, the criticism relies on an origin, historico-cultural in nature, and on a reconstruction of the origins of man. On a third level—namely, that of the actual functioning of the religious phenomenon—an attempt is made to establish the economic balance sheet of the totality of these phenomena which have been examined in turn on the individual and on the collective plane.

Freud's first onslaught is contained in an essay written in 1907 entitled *Obsessive Acts and Religious Exercises*.[10] Here religious practice and, in particular, the observance of a ritual are compared point by point with neurotic ceremonial. Great care is taken to respect the detail of the ritual, and not to omit any part of it. There is even a tendency to complicate its arrangement and to suffer anguish of mind when some fragment or other has been omitted, to show a defensive and protective attitude toward the ceremonial on account of a threat of punishment coming from outside. This parallel is extremely important. We must not forget

that Freud is also the one who has discovered that obsessive ceremonial has a meaning. The comparison progresses from one level
of meaning to another. First of all, it signifies that man has
simultaneously a potential for religion and for neurosis, in such a
way that their analogy can constitute a true reciprocal imitation.
"In view of these similarities and these analyses," writes Freud,
"we might go so far as to consider obsessional neurosis as the
counterpart of religion and to describe this neurosis as a private
religious system, and religion as a universal form of obsessional
neurosis." [11] We can see that this formula has more than one
meaning: religion is what can be caricatured in neurotic ceremonial. "Obsessive neurosis presents the tragi-comic caricature of
a private religion." [12] It remains a question whether this caricature
realizes the profound purpose of religion or merely its degeneration
and regression when it begins to lose the sense of its own symbolism. On this point, however, psychoanalysis as such cannot
make the decision.

From the essay written in 1908 to *Moses and Monotheism* in
1939, the search for analogies is carried on in many directions.
For example, *Totem and Taboo* [13] conceives of the projection
of the omnipotence of desire into divine figures in terms of paranoia. "This archaic religion corresponds to the narcissistic age of
the libido; this problem of projection is central to the Freudian
theory of illusion." Actually, while it interiorizes the ideals imposed by parental authority and the others which succeed it, desire
projects into a transcendent region the source of inhibition and,
even more so, perhaps, the source of consolation. The whole thing
falls into a pattern around the father figure, around nostalgia for
the father. The god of men, the idol of our instinct, is the enlarged
father figure who threatens, who inhibits, who lays down the law,
who gives names, who establishes the order of things and the
order of cities, who rewards and consoles, who reconciles man to
the harshness of life.

However, the interpretation cannot remain on this level, first
of all because the analogy remains indeterminate and must, according to Freud, be taken for an identity, and medicine cannot prove
this. But, above all, there remains a difference between the private
character of the religion of the neurotic and the universal character of the "neurosis of the religious man". Thus it is the function of

phylogenesis not only to consolidate the analogy into an identity but also to render an account of this difference on the level of manifest repressions. This is the reason why Freud during his entire lifetime, from *Totem and Taboo* in 1912 to *Moses and Monotheism* in 1937-39, has recourse to an ethnological explanation whose task is to provide, in the dimension of the human species, the equivalent of the Oedipus complex, whose importance clinical medicine shows in the personal mythology of the patient. In this way Freud was led to recast what might be called a myth of beginnings, by basing his work, first of all, on the ethnology of his day and the classic works on totemism at the beginning of the century, and later on certain works dedicated to the origins of Jewish monotheism. Freud asked but one thing of these various works: the more or less probable confirmation of the fact that humanity was involved in an original struggle, more precisely in a criminal episode which constitutes the nucleus of humanity's Oedipus complex. At the beginning of history, a very cruel father would have been slain by his sons in compact against him. The institution of society, properly so called, would have stemmed from this fraternal pact. However, the father's murder would have left a deep wound necessitating a reconciliation with the image of the injured father. Post-factum obedience to the father's law would constitute one of the elements of this reconciliation. The other would consist in the commemoration of the act of repentance through the totemic meal, at which would take place a disguised version of the father's murder along with the reconciliation with his internalized and sublimated image.[14]

In *Moses and Monotheism,* Freud is investigating another murder, that of the prophet, which would be for monotheistic religions what the murder of the primitive father had been for totemism. Thus the Jewish prophets would have been the artisans of the resurgence of the Mosaic god: under the features of the ethical god, the traumatic event would have re-emerged. In this way the return to the Mosaic god would be at the same time the return of the repressed trauma. Thus there would coincide a resurgence on the representative level and a return of what had been repressed on the emotional level.

The slaying of Christ would be, in its turn, a further reinforcement of the memory of origins. At the same time Freud returns here to his former hypothesis of the sons' rebellion. The redeemer would have to be the chief guilty one, the head of a band of brothers, just like the rebel heroes of Greek tragedy. "With him we have the return of the primordial father of the primitive band, transfigured, it is true, and having, in his role of son, taken his father's place." [15]

With this concept of "return of the repressed", we arrive at the third level of Freudian interpretation: the economic level proper. In *The Future of an Illusion* and in *Civilization and Its Discontents*, Freud attempts to replace this genesis of an illusion, on the individual as well as on the historical level, within the development of culture, in the way in which we have previously described it. He tries to lessen the charge of the instinctual sacrifices imposed on men, to reconcile individuals with those renunciations which are inevitable, and to offer them compensations in satisfaction for these sacrifices. The father figure, as it is evoked by the mechanism of the return of the repressed, becomes the pivot around which "compensation" revolves. Man remains always a prey to nostalgia for the father because he is forever helpless as a child. And if all suffering is nostalgia for the father, every consolation is a return to the father. Faced with nature, the man-child creates gods in the father's image. Thus the genetic explanation is incorporated in an economic explanation. The analogy—built on the clinical level between the traumatic neurosis which the history of the development of the child reveals, and what Freud has termed the universal obsessive neurosis of humanity—is transposed to the plane of the economic balance sheet. Premature traumatism, inhibition, secrecy, outburst of neurosis, partial recurrence of the repressed: all these elements constitute the analogy which is not only descriptive and clinical, but also functional and economic. This is the specifically psychoanalytic interpretation of religion. Its hidden meaning is nostalgia for the father.[16]

III
VALUE AND LIMITATIONS OF A
PSYCHOANALYSIS OF RELIGION

In conclusion, I propose to sketch the main lines of a debate which could bring together psychoanalysts, philosophers and theologians. First there would be a preliminary debate concerning the limits in principle of a psychoanalysis of culture. However important it may be, this debate must not be used as a substitute for a mutual questioning about the very basis of things.

Let us begin with the first dispute over method. It must be made clear that the psychoanalytic interpretation cannot be taken as exclusive of other interpretations, less intent on reducing and destroying, than in understanding and restoring, in all their authenticity, the symbolic content of the mythico-poetical level. The limits of the Freudian interpretation are not to be sought in the object itself, for nothing is either inaccessible or forbidden to it. The limit lies rather in the point of view and the model. As to the point of view: every human reality, every sign, every meaning, is grasped by the analyst from the angle of the semantics of instinct, that is to say, of the economic balance sheet of pleasure and pain, of satisfaction and frustration. Here lies his initial decision; here, too, lies his competence. As to the model, it has been established from the outset: it is *Wunschurfüllung,* wish fulfillment. Its primary illustrations are the dream and the neurotic symptom. It was understood that the whole of human reality could be interpreted from a psychoanalytic point of view, insofar as it offers analogues of this primitive deed. Both the validity and the limits of validity of a critique of religion have their basis here.

If this criterion of validity is applied to the particular analyses which Freud dedicates to religion, we might make the following observations:

(1) On the actual clinical level, the analogy between the religious phenomenon and the pathological phenomenon should be recognized for what it is: a simple likeness whose final meaning remains ambiguous. Man is susceptible to neurosis in the same way in which he is susceptible to religion, and vice versa. But what does the analogy signify? Psychoanalysis, insofar as it is analysis, knows nothing of this. There is no way for it to decide if the faith is merely faith, if the rite is originally, in its primordial function, an obsessional ritual, if faith is merely compensation on the infantile model. Psychoanalysis can manifest to the religious man a caricature of himself, but it leaves him the duty of meditating on the possibility of not resembling this hideous double. The value of analogy, and, likewise, the limits of analogy, seem to me to be decided on this critical point: Is there, in the affective dynamism

of religious belief, the wherewithal to rise above its own archaism?

(2) On the plane of the genealogy of religion, through ethnology, there appears another focus of indecision. Is the fantasy of father slaying, which Freud discovers at the basis of the form of the gods, only the vestige of a traumatic memory, or is it a veritable "primitive episode", a symbol, capable of providing the first stratum of meaning to an imaginative presentation of origins, more and more detached from its function of infantile and quasi-neurotic repetition, and more and more suited to an investigation of the fundamental meanings of human destiny?

Freud has sometimes discovered this fancied non-vestigial bearer of a new meaning, not so much, it is true, when he is speaking of religion, but when he is speaking of art. He shows how an artist, like Leonardo da Vinci, is able to transfigure the vestiges of the past and, with a traumatic memory, to create a work in which his past is at once "disowned and surpassed" by the strength of art.[17] Why is it that the "transfiguration" of the primitive father figure does not involve the same ambiguity, the same ambivalence of oneiric resurgence and of cultural creation? Is it not possible for a single phantasm to have vectors which move in opposite directions: the regressive vector which ties it to the past and a progressive vector which makes it a detector of meaning? This is the way which must be explored. Can it not be said that what constitutes the force of a religious symbol is the taking of a phantasm of a primitive scene and converting it into an instrument of discovery and of exploration of origins? Through his symbolic representation, man states the establishment of his humanity. Through its vestigial function, the symbol shows at work an imagining of the origins which might be called "historical", *geschichtlich,* because it bespeaks an advent, a coming into being, but not historic, *historisch,* because it has no chronological significance.

(3) The properly economic interpretation of the religious phenomenon, insofar as it is a "return of the repressed", poses the final question: Is religion the monotonous repetition of its own origins, a sempiternal marking-time of its own archaism? For Freud there is no history of religion. Rather, his task is to show through what education of desire and of fear religion overcomes its own archaism. This mounting dialectic of affect must be meshed with a parallel dialectic of the phantasm. Then, however, we

would have to take into consideration the *texts* in and through which the religious man has "formed" and "educated" his faith. It is not possible to psychoanalyze belief without interpreting the "Scriptures" in which what is believed in is revealed. At least we have to say that *Moses and Monotheism* is by no means on the level of an exegesis of the Old Testament. That is why there is no chance that it will meet the creations of meaning through which religion outdistances its primitive model.

However, I would not like to conclude with these objections, lest the reader risk being protected from the *instruction* and the *harsh schooling* through which his faith must pass under the guidance of Freud and psychoanalysis. We are far from having incorporated the truth of Freud's teaching on religion. He has already reinforced the faith of unbelievers; he has scarcely begun to purify the faith of believers.

There are two points on which we still have something to *learn* from Freud. The first is concerned with the connection between religion and inhibition; the second, its relation to consolation. We will only regain the true biblical dimension of sin when we have destroyed in ourselves all that remains of the archaic, of the infantile, and of the neurotic in "guilt feelings". Guilt is a snare, an occasion of regression, of incursion into the pre-moral, of stagnation in archaism. There is no area in which it is more necessary to undergo "destruction" in order to recover the authentic sense of sin. But cannot the Freudian critique of the Superego bring us back to the Pauline critique of the law and good works? The result of this is that the central figure of religion which, according to psychoanalysis, proceeds from the prototype of the father would be unable to accomplish its own conversion in the direction of the true Father of Jesus Christ, except insofar as this central figure had himself gone through all the stages corresponding to the degrees of guilt, from the fear of taboo to the sin of injustice, in the sense in which the Jewish prophets use the term, and even to the sin of the just man, that is to say, to the evil of self-justification in the Pauline sense.

However, perhaps it is in the order of compensation that the lesson of psychoanalysis has not yet been perceived. There are actually two types of consolation inseparably bound up together: infantile consolation and idolatrous consolation, such as Job's comforters offered, and, on the other hand, consolation according to the spirit, which is free of all narcissism and self-seeking, which is in no way a protection against the calamities of existence or a refuge against the harshness of life. Such consolation is had only at the price of the most extreme obedience to reality. It emerges after the deprivation of the first consolation. The one who plumbs this movement to its depth will truly have taken on himself Freudian iconoclasm within the very movement of faith.

NOTES

1. S. Freud, *The Future of an Illusion* (Standard Edition, XXI), pp. 5-56.

2. *Idem, Civilization and Its Discontents* (S.E., XXI), pp. 60-145.

3. *Idem, Moses and Monotheism* (S.E., XXIII), pp. 7-137.

4. *Idem, Formulations on the Two Principles of Mental Functioning* (S.E., XII), pp. 218-26.

5. C. Levy-Straus, *Les Structures élémentaires de la parenté* (*The Basic Structures of Relation*) (Paris, P.U.F.), p. 949.

6. S. Freud, *The Ego and the Id* (S.E., XIX), pp. 12-66.

7. On the identification of the father, cf., besides the preceding essay, *Massenpsychologie und Ich-Analyse* (1921) (S.E., XIX), p. 30.

8. S. Freud, *The Future of an Illusion*. Chs. I and II.

9. *Idem, The Interpretation of Dreams* (S.E., V), pp. 536-49.

10. *Idem, Obsessive Actions and Religious Practices* (S.E., IX), pp. 117-27.

11. *Ibid.,* pp. 126-7.

12. *Ibid.,* p. 119.

13. S. Freud, *Totem and Taboo* (S.E., XIII).

14. *Ibid.,* Ch. IV.

15. S. Freud, *Moses and Monotheism* (S.E., XXIII), p. 90.

16. *Idem, The Future of an Illusion* (S.E., XXI), pp. 22-24.

17. *Idem, Leonardo da Vinci and a Memory of His Childhood* (S.E., XI).

SUGGESTED READINGS

Paul Ricoeur's *Freud and Philosophy—An Essay on Interpretation* (New Haven: Yale University Press, 1970) is a profound but extremely demanding re-reading of Freud which uncovers a rich and not often noted symbolism in the dialectics of Freud's thought. J. Bamberger, O.C.S.O., "Religion as Illusion? Freud's Challenge to Theology," *Is God Dead? Concilium,* Vol, 16, pp. 73-88 (N.Y.: Paulist Press, 1966) presents some helpful points of criticism. Similarly H. L. Philip's *Freud and Religious Belief* (N.Y.: Pitman, 1956) offers a book-by-book analysis and evaluation. Erich Fromm in *Psychoanalysis and Religion* (N.Y.: Yale University Press, 1950, paperback) includes an evaluation of Freud from the revisionistic perspective of psychological humanism. *Psychoanalysis and Religion* by Gregory Zilboorg (N.Y.: Farrar, Straus and Cudahy, 1962) is a gentle and wise book, both critical and sympathetic, which treats Freud's attitudes to God, guilt and love. Peter Homans' *Theology After Freud* (Indianapolis: Bobbs-Merrill, 1970) is a subtle but insightful study of the collapse of transcendence upon the removal of "the harsh superego" and of the possibilities for the recovery of transcendence. Unexpected mystical roots of Freud's thought are uncovered in *Sigmund Freud and the Jewish Mystical Tradition* by David Bakan (Princeton: D. Van Nostrand Co., 1958).

Peter Homans in "Toward a Psychology of Religion: By Way of Freud and Tillich," *The Dialogue Between Theology and Psychology,* edited by Peter Homans (Chicago: University of Chicago Press, 1968), pp. 53-81, is illuminating on the theological and psychological models. Philip Rieff in *The Triumph of the Therapeutic* (N.Y.: Harper and Row, 1959) includes discussion of Freud in developing the theme of the emergence of psychological man. The Eros-Thanatos theme has been re-assessed in Herbert Marcuse's *Eros and Civilization* (N.Y.: Random House, Vintage paperback, 1962) and Norman O. Brown's *Life Against Death* (Middleton, Conn.: Wesleyan University Press, 1959, paperback). Finally the reader will find valuable pastoral insight in "Coming to Terms with the Father: Prayer and Psychoanalysis," by Jean-Claude Sagne, *The Prayer Life,* in *Concilium,* edited by Christian Duquoc and Claude Geffre (N.Y.: Herder and Herder, 1972), pp. 15-25.

3 Conscience and Superego

John W. Glaser, S.J.

Some psychologists have equated the superego and conscience. Many others have carefully distinguished the two concepts, at times even in their interpretation of Freud. (Notice *Civilization and Its Discontents,* pp. 82-84, as an example of a treatment by Freud which is problematical.)

Theologians today, as a rule, make a clear distinction between conscience and the superego, though it is not unknown for a religious writer or speaker to yield to rhetorical temptation and make a universal identification of guilt feelings with "theological guilt." Because the superego has its origin in childhood, there is danger that it will continue to impose an infantile structure on the operation of the ego, unless a person becomes fully aware that it is not necessarily identical with conscience.

Such is the theme developed in the following essay.* The author, John W. Glaser, teaches theology at Detroit University and has published extensively in the area of moral and pastoral theology.

The superego first came to my attention when I did not know what to call it. The occasion was a relatively harmless instance: an Army officer and his wife,

* From "Conscience and Superego: A Key Distinction," by John W. Glaser, S.J., published in *Theological Studies,* Volume 32, Number 1, March 1971, pp. 30-47. Reprinted with permission of *Theological Studies* and the author.

who were by virtue of their military status dispensed from Friday
abstinence, told me how it had taken them almost a year to be able
to eat meat on Friday without feeling somewhat guilty about this—
in spite of their dispensation.

But another experience (which I shall take up later in this
article) bared the vicious set of incisors this source of pseudo-
moral guilt could have. I saw how this source of unconscious guilt
could actually cripple a person; it could keep the individual from
seeing the genuine values at stake—values which alone could
creatively call the person beyond his present fixation and the destructive circle of defeat, depression, "repentance," and further
failures.

In this article I want to (1) briefly describe moral conscience;
(2) then in some detail describe an entirely different but decep-
tively similar-looking reality: the superego; (3) finally reflect on a
number of areas where recognition of the radical difference between genuine conscience and superego is extremely important and
illuminating, where a failure to recognize this can do considerable
harm.

Before beginning the discussion itself, it might be pointed out
why the difference between conscience and superego has managed
to escape much notice outside the circle of psychologists.[1] In a
merely superficial consideration these two realities have functions
which appear strikingly similar: both have been described as primarily nonverbal, preconceptual; commanding, prohibiting; accus-
ing, approving; seeking reconciliation if norms are violated. This
describes some superficial similarities between conscience and superego; the radical differences should become clear from what
follows.

I
Moral Conscience

These drastically brief remarks concern conscience as it functions in the situation of grave moral decision—core freedom. Any
other use of the term conscience should be considered as analogous
to this primary meaning.[2]

If we can assume (1) that *the* moral action of man is love (the unity of the love of God and love of neighbor) and that this very action is, seen from the agent's point of view, the act of his own cocreation, his answering himself into abiding existence; and if we can assume (2) that this invitation to love occurs in ever deeper invitations, at not entirely predictable *kairoi* of God's loving initiative in each person's salvation history; and if we can assume (3) that this tridimensional "object" of man's freedom (God's self-offering; the created, personal other which mediates this divine initiative; the individual himself as offered possible abiding love) is primarily, though not necessarily exclusively, present to the agent's consciousness in a preconceptual manner of knowing (each dimension of this "object" in its own mode of preconceptual knowledge), then we can describe moral conscience as the preconceptual recognition of an absolute call to love and thereby to cocreate myself genuine future, or as the nonverbal insight into a radical invitation to love God in loving my neighbor and thereby become myself abiding love. This is a description of the positive, invitation aspect of *conscientia antecedens,* often described, less than ideally, as the command of conscience. The negative aspect, the prohibition of *conscientia antecedens,* can then be logically described as the preconceptually perceived ultimate futurelessness and absurdity of being invited to radically abiding growth in love and rejecting this invitation.

Conscientia consequens (a "good conscience"), in such a context, can be described as the preconceptually experienced harmony existing between the ultimate ground of reality, the created values, and that existence which I am, cocreated by my free act. A "bad conscience" can be described as the preconceptually experienced disharmony between the abiding futureless and futile existence that my freedom has caused in the very situation which invited me to cocreate myself abiding love.

In short, conscience is an insight into love; the call issued by the ultimate value and promise of love; the warning of the destructive power of indifference or hostility to this invitation; the peace (not self-satisfaction) that results from the creative yes to love: the disharmony and disintegration of existing as an abiding contradiction to this call of love which my whole being is made to answer affirmatively.

II
The Superego

The superego deals not in the currency of extroverted love but in the introversion of *being lovable*. The dynamic of the superego springs from a frantic compulsion to experience oneself as lovable, not from the call to commit oneself in abiding love.

To understand the superego, we have to begin there where every human being begins—as a child. The child is faced with a problem: he is a bundle of needs, desires, and impulses. They cannot all find satisfaction; very often the fulfilment of one excludes the satisfaction of another (e.g., if a child's desire to grab everything within reach is satisfied, he finds himself confronted with the displeasure and disapproval of his parents, i.e., with the frustration of another of his desires). These desires, needs, and impulses manifest a decided hierarchy of importance and power. Eicke indicates that opinions vary on *the* primary drive, but says that most psychologists seem to see the need to be loved, to enjoy approval and affection, as the strongest, most fundamental of these drives.[3] He goes on to say that the child experiences disapproval, temporary withdrawal of love, as a kind of annihilation. Therefore this fear of punishment is not so much an aversion to physical pain as it is panic at the withdrawal of love. Freud has remarked that being loved is equivalent to life itself for the ego.[4] In these terms the child experiences the disapproval of his parents as a mitigated withdrawal of life itself. In such a situation the child needs a means of so organizing and ordering his various desires that his main need, to be loved, does not get run over by the others. Since there is not yet enough mature psychic equipment at the child's disposal to handle this conflict, the problem is handled by a more primitive (i.e., less personal) mechanism. An instance of censorship forms on this prepersonal level; its function is to so regulate the conduct of the child that he does not lose the primary object of his desires: love, affection, and approval.[5]

One point should be made clear beyond all misunderstanding: the commands and prohibitions of the superego do not arise from any kind of perception of the intrinsic goodness or objectionableness of the action contemplated. *The* source of such commands and prohibitions can be described positively as the desire to be approved and loved or negatively as the fear of loss of such love and approval.[6]

Even this prepersonal instance of censorship manifests stages of development. It has been observed that during the first few years of a child's life the commands and prohibitions of parents are so identified with the parents themselves that the commands, as it were, leave the room with the parents. These norms are only really effective when the mother or father is actually present.[7]

But even during this time a process of internalization is taking place by which the orders of authority are assimilated in the child and eventually arise from within the child himself. This process involves the psychological mechanisms of introjection and identification.[8] Eicke sums this up thus:

Through identification a value emerges, a value which I am for myself; but this is also a value according to which I must conduct myself. If I fail to act according to this norm, I experience fears and feelings of guilt; more exactly, fear of not being loved, of being abandoned or persecuted; feelings of not having done the right thing, of not having made myself lovable. As Freud says: "Consciousness of guilt was originally fear of punishment by parents; more exactly, fear of losing their love." [9]

Several things characterize this process of introjection. It is a spontaneous mechanism whose commands speak with a remarkable power (which we will discuss shortly). It is also striking how graphically (almost "photographically" at times) the authority figure takes up a place within the child himself, so that not only the content but also the very voice and formulation of this external person arises from within the child. Zulliger recounts the comment of the nineteenth-century Swiss author Rodolphe Toepffer: "For a long time I was unable to distinguish the inner voice of my conscience from *that of my teacher.* When my conscience spoke to me, I thought I saw it before me in a black cape, with a teacher's frown and glasses sitting on its nose." [10]

Allport brings a delightful and illuminating example which illustrates this process of introjection and the controlling influence it exercises:

I am indebted for this example to my colleague, Henry A. Murray. A three-year-old boy awoke at six in the morning and started his noisy play. The father, sleepy-eyed, went to the boy's room and sternly commanded him, "Get back into bed and don't you dare get up until seven o'clock." The boy obeyed. For a few minutes all was quiet, but soon there were strange sounds that led the father again to look into the room. The boy was in bed as ordered; but putting an arm over the edge, he jerked it back in saying, "Get back in there." Next a leg protruded, only to be roughly retracted with the warning, "You heard what I told you." Finally the boy rolled to the very edge of the bed and then roughly rolled back, sternly warning himself, "Not until seven o'clock!" We could not wish for a clearer instance of interiorizing the father's role as a means to self-control and socialized becoming.[11]

The only exceptional thing about such an instance is that it happened to be observed by an adult, and by one who saw the psychological significance of the event. Zulliger offers numerous examples of the same phenomenon.[12]

The superego as discussed up to now could be characterized as having functions similar to those of what is traditionally known as *conscientia antecedens*: it commands and prohibits certain concrete possibilities in a given situation. The superego, however, also functions in a way similar to *conscientia consequens:* it accuses the offender, it condemns him when he fails to obey. The fury of the violated superego is described by Bergler: "The extent of the power yielded by the Frankenstein which is the superego is still largely unrealized. . . . Man's inhumanity to man is equaled only by man's inhumanity to himself." [13]

The reason for this violent reaction has already been touched upon. The superego must, on the psychological, subconscious level, provide for a person's being loved; it is the guardian of the individual's sense of value. We have already referred to Freud's statement that, for the ego, being loved is equivalent to life itself. Hence the violence of the offended superego arises from the panic of having lost one's right to be loved; on a primitive, psychological level he has "lost his life." [14] The fact that this plays itself out on a nonconceptual level of consciousness in terms of panic, fear, and guilt feelings makes it all the more difficult to cope with, if one is armed only with the weapons of reason and conceptual reflection.

Zulliger spells out the guilt feelings produced by the superego in terms of isolation. "When a child does something wrong, disobeys a command, etc., he experiences a feeling of isolation." [15] He feels that he is "bad" and isolated from those who are "good." Describing such guilt in terms of an experienced isolation helps us find a plausible and consistent explanation of several other phenomena closely connected with such guilt. There is no need here to recount the many examples offered by Zulliger, but by means of these examples several things are made clear: there is a powerful subconscious drive to re-create one's sense of belonging and being accepted by his community, of re-establishing the harmony and solidarity he has forfeited by his fault.

This drive to rejoin the "good" and thus regain one's sense of value, this drive to break out of the panic of isolation, can express itself in a variety of ways. Besides the direct approach of confessing to some authority figure and accepting punishment, there are various indirect ways of attempting to escape the tyranny of an offended superego. Zulliger enumerates three main indirect solutions. First, there is the unconscious betrayal of guilt. This drive to be found out (which is ultimately a drive to be reconciled), though conflicting with the conscious effort to escape detection, finds ways of exposing one's fault and in this way of indirectly confessing and ultimately being reconciled. Another substitute compensation takes the form of seeking punishment. [16] The original misdeed against the norms of the superego is not itself confessed and punished. Rather, the individual provokes punishment through further misdeeds and through this punishment for further and distinct failures attempts to quiet his need for punishment for the original unpunished misdeed. Through a further and distinct misdeed (whose real goal is the reconciliation to follow) he attempts to break out of the isolation created by the original misdeed. His subconscious goal is to have the second misdeed result in punishment-reconciliation and also take care of the original alienation. Finally, there is the indirect escape from isolation which takes the form of creating a new community where the individual wll be accepted. This implies provoking others to deeds similar to his own. Instead of re-establishing harmony with the "good," he tends to create a group which will accept him with his misdeeds and even esteem him precisely on their account. [17]

Zulliger's description of the power of the superego in terms of flight from a feeling of acute alienation—an alienation from that group represented by the authority figures in his life, who have communicated what is expected of him if he wants to "belong"— helps us see how much the formal structure of the superego differs from conscience. Conscience is precisely the call of genuine value which can well call one to an extremely isolated position. Motivating an individual's activity on the basis of "acceptance" serves well the socialization and normalization of individuals to prevailing norms; but as a basis of Christian morality (in the mature sense of this word), which should be characterized by a creative thrust into the future, i.e., into the not-yet-ready-to-be-thought, its dynamics are strikingly inadequate. The superego performs well in the process of socialization—training one to function well within a given set of limits; it works well and adequately in toilet-training an infant or housebreaking a pup (both useful results, without which life would be far less pleasant), but its legitimate function deals with the more primitive levels of psychic life. Görres points out that the relationship between superego and id is not so much that of spirit to instinct or rider to horse; rather, it concerns the relationship between instinct and training. "The superego, in Freud's sense, is primarily a function of organization of the primitive levels of psychic life. This is supported by the fact that higher animals are said to have a superego when they have been trained." [18]

The superego is basically a principle of prepersonal censorship and control. This does not mean that it has no meaningful function for man. On the contrary, the role of the superego in the life of an infant is quite meaningful and necessary. It is a primitive stage on the way to the development of genuine conscience and value perception.[19] Even in the life of a mature adult the superego is not superfluous. In certain sectors of life it provides for a conservation of psychic energy and ease of operation. Görres remarks: "When the superego is integrated into a mature conscience . . . it relieves an individual from having constantly to decide in all those situations which are already legitimately decided by custom, taste, and convention 'what one should do' and 'what one should not do.' " [20]

Psychologists are in agreement, however, that this organic development from the primitive and prepersonal censor of the infant to a mature and personal value perception does not automatically and infallibly take place. This means that the activity of superego in the average adult is not limited to the healthy and integrated function described above by Görres. In fact, Görres himself maintains that it is the task, not only of psychiatry but of education and pastoral practice as well, to reduce the influence of this childish censor more and more and thereby allow genuine value perception to grow.[21]

While it is true that the workings of the superego are generally discussed in the context of the child or the neurotic, Görres reminds us that the differences here between the neurotic and the "healthy" person are those of degree and not of kind.[22] According to Odier and Tournier, there are two moral worlds existing in the normal person: a genuine moral world and a world of false or pseudo morality and religiosity.[23] Both of these authors have written extensively on this subject precisely to call attention to the existence and influence of this all too often overlooked world of childish morality in the life of the average adult.[24] Felicitas Betz points out that the struggle to grow up in this regard does not cease at the end of childhood or adolescence but confronts us with a lifelong battle. "The maturing of one's conscience is a task that takes a lifetime; it is with us far beyond the end of adolescence. For one who has been the object more of conscience training than conscience education, this task of arriving at mature conscience will be particularly difficult, if not impossible." [25]

We might draw up some contrasting characteristics which exist between the superego and genuine conscience:

SUPEREGO	CONSCIENCE
commands that an act be performed for approval, in order to make oneself lovable, accepted; fear of love-withdrawal is the basis	invites to action, to love, and in this very act of other-directed commitment to cocreate self-value
introverted: the thematic center is a sense of one's own value	extroverted: the thematic center is the value which invites; self-value is concomitant and secondary to this
static: does not grow, does not learn; cannot function creatively in	dynamic: an awareness and sensitivity to value which develops and

a new situation; merely repeats a basic command	grows; a mind-set which can precisely function in a new situation
authority-figure-oriented: not a question of perceiving and responding to a value but of "obeying" authority's command "blindly"	value-oriented: the value or disvalue is perceived and responded to, regardless of whether authority has commanded or not
"atomized" units of activity are its object	individual acts are seen in their importance as a part of a larger process or pattern
past-oriented: primarily concerned with cleaning up the record with regard to past acts	future-oriented: creative; sees the past as having a future and helping to structure this future as a better future
urge to be punished and thereby earn reconciliation	sees the need to repair by structuring the future orientation toward the value in question (which includes making good past harms)
rapid transition from severe isolation, guilt feelings, etc., to a sense of self-value accomplished by confessing to an authority figure	a sense of the gradual process of growth which characterizes all dimensions of genuine personal development
possible great disproportion between guilt experienced and the value in question; extent of guilt depends more on weight of authority figure and "volume" with which he speaks rather than density of the value in question	experience of guilt proportionate to the importance of the value in question, even though authority may never have addressed this specific value

In light of this less than exhaustive list of contrasts, it should be clear that failing to distinguish these two realities will cause considerable confusion. This confusion is multiplied if one has taken superego data and allowed it to be the weightier element in understanding man as *free,* precisely because it arises from the prepersonal, prefree dimension of an individual. The pastoral and ascetic practice which flows from such a superego-weighted interpretation of guilt, etc., will be to a great extent in radical conflict with man's genuine freedom.

In the following section I want to reflect on some areas where it seems to me we have been mistaken in drawing theological conclusions or in projecting conduct (pastoral, ascetic, sacramental) from data of the superego. These remarks vary in their importance and are less systematically developed than might be desirable; they must stand as the fragmentary reflections that are prompted by my present situation. Hopefully they will stimulate further reflection and application, which will be, among other things, corrective of the following remarks.

III
Problem Areas Where
Superego Is Part of Problem

All the following reflections could be subsumed under one rubric: too much theory and practice in the Church arises from data whose source is the superego. Many problem areas which have emerged in the recent past can be traced to a failure to recognize the nature, presence, and power of the superego. This is not an accusation.[26] But given today's vantage point, this is a situation which can be overcome and should not be further tolerated.

Notion of God

Precisely because the voice of the superego is somehow cosmic, vast, and mysterious, arising as it does from the subconscious, it can easily be mistakenly called God's voice. This is true especially if our religious education trains us from childhood on to call this voice of the subconscious God's voice. This I see as the major danger of failing to distinguish conscience from superego. To associate the mystery of invitation, the absolute yes to man's future, the radical call to eternally abiding love—God—with the hot and cold, arbitrary tyrant of the superego is a matter of grave distortion. It reaches into the totality of a person's explicitly religious life and poisons every fresh spring of the Good News. Such a God deserves to die.

Gregory Baum's comments are much to the point on this question:

A second reason why the image of the God the punisher has flourished in the Christian and even post-Christian imagination is drawn from personal pathology. The idea of God as judge on a throne, meting out punishment, corresponds to a self-destructive trend of the human psyche. On a previous page we have mentioned man's primitive conscience or, as Freud called it, his superego. The person who is dominated by his superego—and no one is able to escape it altogether—has the accuser, judge, and tormentor all wrapt in one, built into his own psychic makeup. When such a person hears the Christian message with the accent on God the judge, he can project his superego on the divinity and then use religion as an instrument to subject himself to this court and, unknown to himself, to promote his own unconscious self-hatred. As we mentioned more than once in these pages, Jesus has come to save men from their superego. God is not punisher; God saves.[27]

Age of Reason and Transition between Grace and Sin

The theological literature on the fundamental option has drastically revised the common Catholic ideas concerning the "age of reason" and the frequency with which the transition between grace-sin-grace-sin can occur.[28] The speculation of theologians like Rahner, Schüller, Metz, and Mondin has so radically changed the atmosphere in which speculation on core freedom takes place that one is puzzled how thoughts on the "age of reason" (emergence of core freedom) and the frequency of core decisions—which were common fare in moral theology until the recent past—were ever possible. How could we have really thought that ten-year-olds could sin seriously? Or what ever possessed us to think that we could move through serious sin and grace with the frequency that we change shirts?

One major reason why such thoughts were thinkable is surely because theology failed to recognize various kinds of guilt experience and release from this guilt. Theology simply accepted all guilt experience and its release as theological data, as data arising from man's freedom. The nature of superego guilt and its radical difference from genuine moral guilt went unrecognized.

A striking example of this appears in Maritain's *Range of Reason*.[29] Maritain uses an excellent analysis of preconceptual knowledge of God to make a far from excellent explanation of why a child can engage his core freedom. At one point in his discussion of this question Maritain seems to reveal, at least in part, the source of his conviction that children can make core-freedom decisions. In what he seems to consider a phenomenological justification for his position he says:

Yet in some rare cases, the first act of freedom will never be forgotten, especially if the choice—however insignificant its object—through which the soul was introduced into moral life occurred rather late. In other cases there is a remembrance of some childish remorse, whose occasion was unimportant but whose intensity, out of proportion with its object, upset the soul and awakened its moral sense.[30]

To one aware of the dimensions of an act of core freedom on the one hand, and familiar with the nature of the superego on the other, the data described by Maritain is clearly relegated to the area of the superego, not genuine freedom. This acceptance of all guilt data as genuine theological data—which Maritain reveals in the quoted passage—remained for moral theology a silent but functioning presupposition in its consideration of the "age of reason." This error, coupled with an exaggerated conceptualistic model of conscience, helps explain in large part the now incredible conviction with which most of us grew up: children can commit serious sin.

The idea that an individual could sin seriously, repent only to sin seriously again, repent again—and this within a matter of days —also finds at least a partial explanation in the fact that superego guilt and its remission by an authority figure was mistaken for genuine moral guilt and its remission. A very common phenomenon, familiar to anyone who has done pastoral work with Catholic adolescents, certainly *seems* to support the theory that the transition between grace and serious sin can occur relatively frequently. We might describe this datum as the "storm and sunshine phenomenon." It occurs especially in questions of sexual morality. The individual experiences severe guilt feelings after a failing against the sixth commandment: the storm phase. Upon confessing, he experiences a wonderful release from his guilt: the sunshine phase. Such a moving between storm and sunshine might well occur on a weekly basis. The guilt feelings involved represent very often the most severe experience of guilt the individual has ever known; the freeing from this guilt through confession is often the most intense experience of liberation.

Such an undeniable phenomenon seems to offer more than

enough concrete evidence that an individual can fluctuate frequently between grace and serious sin. It can do this, however, only if we are ignorant of the nature of the superego; only if we overlook the fact that the area of sexuality is notoriously susceptible to the tyranny of the superego; and only if we fail to realize the vast dimensions of the transition between sin and grace. Because these very facts were not operative in reflection on core freedom (mortal sin), it is easy to understand why traditional moral theology and confessional practice took their theoretical and pastoral-practical categories from the superego-dominated data and found in such data unquestioned support for the conviction that the transition between grace and sin could occur with almost assembly-line frequency.

Diminishing Confessions

From the foregoing it is clear that at least some essential dimensions of confessional practice are based on the nature and laws of the superego and not of genuine freedom. It seems to me that these are not merely two exceptional, isolated instances, but two areas which are better seen as examples where confession's debt to the superego is more blatantly obvious. They are pocket-sized editions of what is true of confessional practice as a whole: it is, as traditionally realized, predominantly, though not exclusively, a service of the superego needs of individuals.

In traditional confession practice, therefore, we have an institution based on heavily-weighted nonfree (superego) data which purports to be an institutionalization but actually is a contradiction of genuine freedom. Now this genuine freedom and its categories of being, growing, etc., are not simply nonconscious, beyond all awareness; they are somehow present to man's awareness because of the essential relationship between freedom and knowledge. Hence we have an awareness, a consciousness "divided" against itself, contradicting itself on various levels. On the preconceptual level we have an awareness of the true nature and structure of freedom—its laws of growth, the "units" of core freedom, their duration and possible frequency, etc. On the conceptual level we have categories which attempt to represent this freedom but are actually derived to a great extent from the superego.

Since the categories drawn from the superego are far shallower, a much "thinner brew" (see the characteristics mentioned earlier), the person in question experiences present confessional practice as a trivialization of his genuine freedom. He experiences himself as dealing with the reality of his freedom—experienced preconceptually in its real depth, richness, laws of growth and engagement, etc.—in institutionalized categories derived from a far cheaper reality; hence the institutionalized categories are too cheap and too trivial for the reality to which they supposedly correspond and from which they supposedly derive.

The experience of this "misfit" is recognized, not necessarily in a reflexively formulated way, but in the depth of consciousness. It is, then, no wonder that a person reacts in a corresponding way; a person simply finds himself, in an unplanned and unarticulated way, distancing himself from the practice of confession.

This means that the phenomenon of diminishing confessions is, at least in part, a healthy recognition of the misfit existing between genuine freedom and a system of categories—institutionalized in the traditional practice of confession—derived to a great extent from the superego. Therefore this phenomenon, far from being regrettable, is a sign of health and insight. It cannot be reversed by mere rhetoric; the very nature of genuine freedom does not prompt us to attempt to reverse it. The more nuanced understanding of man's freedom does, however, prompt us to find more adequate forms for the sacrament of penance. Finding these new forms—be they communal and/or "private"—does demand that we recognize the reality of the superego for what it is and thereby avoid merely creating forms of serving the infantile needs of the superego in a new way.

Superego Can Blind to Genuine Value

In discussing some of the pastoral implication of the foregoing pages, I have often heard the comment: "Maybe an individual needs the dynamics of the superego to help himself avoid doing what he really wants to avoid, but cannot—e.g., masturbation. If we take this away, we may be robbing him of a real help."

Several observations on such a comment. First, there is the question of what such "support" is doing to his whole conception of God and his life of partnership with God. Second, the superego is far more infallible as a tormentor of failure than as a source of effective motivation. Hence the question: What is such support doing to his own self-concept? More often than not the superego will be ineffective in overcoming the urge to masturbate; but it will, with inexorable certainty, provide a self-devouring gloom following such an act. The disproportionate guilt will set up the very situation which immerses the individual in even deeper depressions, sense of failure and frustration, fixation on this matter, etc.; in short, the very situation which is most conducive to further masturbation.

Finally, the superego orientation can quite effectively block off the ultimate values at stake. The superego handles individual acts; it demands that these past actions be "confessed" to an authority figure and thereby erased. Such a frame of reference keeps the individual from seeing the larger and more important *process,* which is always the nature of genuine human growth. Instead of experiencing the individual acts precisely as part of a future-oriented growth process, concerned with values that of their inherent power call to growth, the center of attention is focused on righting past wrongs, seen as atomized units.

A counselor told me of a case in which a happily married man with several children had been plagued by masturbation for fifteen years. During these fifteen years he had dutifully gone the route of weekly confession, Communion, etc. The counselor told him to stop thinking of this in terms of serious sin, to go to Communion every Sunday and to confession every six weeks. He tried to help him see his introversion in terms of his own sexual maturity, in terms of his relationship to his wife and children. Within several months this fifteen-year-old "plague" simply vanished from his life. By refusing to follow a pattern of pastoral practice based on the dynamics of the superego, this counselor was able to unlock a logjam of fifteen years; by refusing to deal with the superego as if it were conscience, he freed the genuine values at stake; he allowed them to speak and call the person beyond his present lesser stage of sexual integration. We can pay rent to the superego but the house never becomes our own possession.

The same is true especially in questions of premarital sex. Fostering the mortal sin-grace horizon and plugging it into the confession-Communion-sin network can keep the person from doing the most important thing of all: honestly looking at the delicate, nuanced, process-structured values which are involved; and it is only by becoming increasingly sensitive to these values that one can be helped, through good and bad experience, to continue to grow. Allowing the superego to dominate this pattern of conduct, to atomize the acts, to deal with their guilt and its release in terms of past serious offenses against God which are set right by some authority figure can be the very manner of dealing with the problem which keeps the operative values from ever emerging and calling creatively to further growth.

Departures from Active Ministry and Religious Life

Understanding the superego also sheds some light on the phenomenon of increasing departures from the active ministry and religious life—a phenomenon badly in need of illumination from whatever source we can find. Understanding the superego helps us see a very positive side of this phenomenon—which does not mean that it is solely a positive reality or that such a consideration provides the only or primary horizon for understanding this extremely complex reality.[31] But I am convinced that the superego and its dynamics are involved to a considerable extent in this complex process.

First, I want to consider a striking example which Zulliger provides and which at first blush might seem to have little to do with departures from ministry and religious life. He recounts an incident that happened when he was a counselor at a boys' camp.[32] He was in charge of a small group of boys camping out together. One of the boys reported to Zulliger that money had been taken from his tent. Since a campfire and games had been planned for that same evening, Zulliger decided to include the Indian "swallow ordeal," never suspecting how well it would work. He explained to the boys gathered in the circle of light around the campfire that money had been taken and that the American Indians had a way of uncovering a thief in such a situation. They passed a cup of water around; each one had to take a big swallow of the water; the man who could not swallow the water was the thief. Then Zulliger proceeded with the "game," expecting no results. The cup moved smoothly, the whole group watching as each boy took the cup, filled his mouth, and swallowed. At one point a boy filled his mouth and struggled to swallow, only to choke on the water and spit it out. Zulliger made nothing of this at the time. After the games, when the boys were getting ready to bed down for the night, the boy who had almost strangled came to Zulliger, produced the stolen money, admitted he had stolen it, and asked to be forgiven and punished.

What does this example "prove"? First, it has its full weight only in the context of the many other examples Zulliger offers. Seen by itself, it could strike the reader as a fantastic coincidence; seen in the fuller context, it is a striking example of several characteristics of the superego: (1) its surprising power over an individual, touching even his ability to swallow; (2) the ratio that exists between this power to control an individual and the isolation of the social "accepting" group from a larger context.

In this example the power of the superego touches the delicate process of swallowing normally. As we have seen, the force of the superego can also affect the delicate process of seeing, perceiving, knowing.[33] Hence it can demand conduct, punish for disobedience by inducing guilt feelings, and at the same time suppress the very insight which could and should contradict and correct such tyranny.

Further, the power to influence the individual is in direct proportion to how much the immediate context of acceptance represents "all of reality." The more a person is cut off and isolated from a larger context, the more powerful will be the influence of the small and limited world which acts as the point of reference for guilt and isolation to produce such guilt experiences.

Apply this to the question of departures from ministry and religious life. When we reflect on the "world" in which those presently departing grew up (seminaries, novitiates, houses of study), we realize that these houses constituted "all of reality," an island of the "really-real" for those living there. Isolated from a larger context in principle and practice, they were institutionalized models of the campfire far from home on a dark night. So they had the power of hydraulically multiplied force to introject values; they could produce intense guilt over trivialities; they could control conduct with the subtleties of a raised eyebrow or a slightly chilled greeting.

As long as this "campfire isolation" can be maintained, the degree to which the superego operates can go unchallenged by the larger context of reality and can go unnoticed by those under its influence. But once this narrowly circumscribed context opens to a larger horizon, the misfit between superego demands-punishments and the genuine values at stake emerges in one's consciousness. As we saw in the case of confession, this misfit need not be conceptually articulated; it can remain a nonverbal but deeply intellectual experience of disproportion, discomfort, etc.

Using this frame of reference to understand departures from ministry and religious life, I would say that many, not all, are simply freeing themselves from a superego-dominated way of life. They are growing in genuine value perception and find that they never really embraced the values in question and cannot bring it off now. They find themselves in the situation of others who left the religious way of life at earlier stages, or of those who never entered such a way of life because they recognized that this particular incarnation of Christian values was not what God wanted of them. So they depart. In so far as this is the heart of many departures, we as Christians can only rejoice in the event. It must be affirmed, encouraged, and fostered, just as any other discovery of God's will is the object of our benevolence and beneficence.

Some other priests and religious grow beyond this superego-dominated conduct and in this very process encounter the real values in question and embrace them freely. This particular variation of liberation from the superego is likewise the flowering of genuine Christian freedom; it must also be affirmed, encouraged, and fostered. It should not be mistakenly assumed, however, that the difference between the prior group (those who leave) and the latter group (those who grow to freely accept this particular concrete form of Christian life) is a question of good will. The difference is simply that the prior group are freed from the superego to find their true Christian vocation "in the world"; the latter group are freed from the superego to find their specific Christian vocation, now freely embraced, in their *de facto* state.

The two poles considered here were presented as chemically pure alternatives. It should be clear that they never exist in such undiluted form; the concrete cases will always be a mixture of these various elements. But if this is kept in mind, the foregoing should provide help in understanding some aspects of the question considered. And it should reveal one frame of reference as clearly inadequate: that which would analyze the problem solely in terms of good or bad will, fidelity or infidelity. Understanding the superego shows such a limited set of categories to be a vast oversimplification which can serve neither truth nor Christian freedom. It also helps us realize how much we have to avoid any educational structures which produce conduct by superego rather than decisions of freedom.

Several points discussed in the third and final section of this article have been one-sided; they left many complexities of each question untouched. My goal was to call attention to a dimension of man whose roots can appear to be man's freedom but whose actual source is a compulsion to be accepted and lovable. To make this point with emphasis, many qualifications were deliberately omitted.

This article is meant to be a service to freedom, a service which does not relieve a man of all burdens, but hopes to locate the pain where it should be and where it can function creatively: in the context of love—the goal, reward, and best name of all freedom.

NOTES

1. There is certainly a growing number of theologians who recognize the distinction between the superego and genuine conscience, and the pastoral-practical implications of this distinction. My attention was first called to this distinction in a series of lectures on morality by Bruno Schüller in 1961. It should be noted in this context that not only theologians can be blind to certain dimensions of reality because of their specific and limited concerns. Some psychologists and psychiatrists fail to recognize that besides the superego there is also a genuine preconceptual recognition of moral values—conscience.

2. Some further amplification of these remarks on conscience can be found in the following articles: K. Rahner, "Reflections on the Unity of the Love of Neighbor and the Love of God," *Theological Investigations* 6 (Baltimore, 1969) 231-49; J. Glaser, "Transition between Grace and Sin," THEOLOGICAL STUDIES 29 (1968) 260-74; "Authority, Connatural Knowledge, and the Spontaneous Judgment of the Faithful," *ibid.* 29 (1968) 742-51; "Man's Existence: Supernatural Partnership," *ibid.* 30 (1969) 473-88; "The Problem of Theoretical and Practical Moral Knowledge," *American Ecclesiastical Review* 161 (1969) 410-17.

3. Dieter Eicke, "Das Gewissen und das Über-Ich," in *Das Gewissen als Problem* (Darmstadt, 1966) p. 72; cf. also Albert Görres, *Methode und Erfahrung der Psychoanalyse* (Munich, 1965) pp. 166-72.

4. S. Freud, *Gesammelte Werke* 13 (London, 1940ff.) 288.

5. Eicke, *op. cit.*, pp. 97ff.; cf. also Görres, *op. cit.*

6. Hans Zulliger, *Umgang mit dem kindlichen Gewissen* (Stuttgart, 1955) p. 30: "The primitive conscience is built on the basis of fear of punishment and a desire to earn love." Eicke, *op. cit.*, p. 79: "The superego has its source in the naked fear of retribution or withdrawal of love; its organizing function serves to protect the ego from the outside world." Melanie Klein, *Das Seelenleben des Kleinkindes und andere Beiträge zur Psychoanalyse* (Stuttgart, 1962) p. 140: "Experience of guilt is inextricably bound up with fear (more exactly, with a specific form of fear, namely, depressive fear); it drives one to reconciliation and reparation; it emerges in the first few months of an infant's life together with the early stages of the superego." Cf. also Görres, *op. cit.*, p. 170.

7. Felicitas Betz, "Entwicklungsstufen des kindlichen Gewissens," in *Beichte im Zwielicht* (Munich, 1966) p. 33.

8. Cf. Görres, *op. cit.*, p. 166; Eicke, *op. cit.*, pp. 77-80; Zulliger, *op. cit.*, pp. 63ff.; Bertha Sommer, "Über neurotische Angst und Schuldgefühle," in Wilhelm Bitter, ed., *Angst und Schuld* (Stuttgart, 1959) p. 44.

9. Eicke, *op. cit.*, p. 80.

10. Zulliger, *op. cit.*, p. 38.

11. Gordon W. Allport, *Becoming* (New Haven, 1966) p. 70.

12. Zulliger, *op. cit.*, pp. 11-45; Betz, *op. cit.*, pp. 29-39.

13. Edmund Bergler, *The Superego* (New York, 1952) p. x. A few pages earlier he says: "To get an approximate idea of the 'benevolence' of inner conscience, one has only to imagine the terms of the relationship between a dictator—any dictator—and an inmate of one of his concentration and extermination camps" (p. viii). Bergler is not given to understatement; but perhaps exaggeration in this question can serve as a needed corrective to emphasize something we have too long overlooked.

14. Klein, *op. cit.*, p. 135.

15. Zulliger, *op. cit.*, pp. 103f., 108f.

16. Besides numerous examples offered by Zulliger, cf. also T. Reik, *Geständniszwang und Strafbedürfnis* (Vienna, 1925); P. Tournier, *Echtes und falsches Schuldgefühl* (Freiburg, 1967).

17. Zulliger, *op. cit.*, pp. 108-24.

18. Görres, *op. cit.*, p. 170.

19. Cf. Tournier, *op. cit.*, p. 57.

20. Görres, *op. cit.*, p. 169. Odier also points out, besides the functions mentioned by Görres, that the superego acts as a censor in dreams, thereby preventing every dream from becoming a nightmare. This is no small service. Cf. Charles Odier, *Les deux sources consciente et inconsciente de la vie morale* (Neuchâtel, 1943) p. 28.

21. A. Görres, "Über-Ich," *Lexikon für Theologie und Kirche* 10 (2nd ed.; Freiburg, 1966) 437.

22. Görres, *Methode und Erfahrung*, p. 171.

23. The very titles of their books indicate and emphasize this conviction; cf. notes 16 and 20 above.

24. Melanie Klein, speaking of guilt as naked fear of rejection, says:

"...with a small child this is always the case; but even with many adults the only factor that changes is that the larger human society takes the place of the father or both parents" (*op. cit.*, p. 135, n. 22). Cf. also Eicke, *op. cit.*, p. 89.

25. Betz, "Entwicklungsstufen," p. 39. Cf. also Marc Oraison, *Was ist Sünde?* (Frankfurt/M., 1968) pp. 28, 63f.; Odier, *op. cit.*, p. 60; Tournier, *op. cit.*, p. 56.

26. I am *not* interested in assigning blame or assessing negligence; I *am* interested in the lesson we should learn from this: theology should be the first discipline to have its mind blown by new discoveries in other fields; it dare not be a slow-learning and suspicious discipline, threatened by whatever findings other sciences discover because this new data reshuffles the traditional deck.

27. Gregory Baum, *Man Becoming* (New York, 1970) pp. 223f.

28. Cf. the two articles mentioned in n. 2: "Transition" and "Man's Existence."

29. J. Maritain, *Range of Reason* (New York, 1952) pp. 66ff. For two other recent authors who share this basic viewpoint and for similar reasons, see Joseph Sikora, "Faith and the First Moral Choice," *Sciences ecclésiastiques,* May-September, 1965, pp. 327-37; Herman Reiners, *Grundintention und sittliches Tun* (Freiburg, 1966) esp. p. 26.

30. Maritain, *op. cit.,* p. 68.

31. I have attempted to explore another thin slice of this question from another point of view in the article "Anonymous Priesthood," *Commonweal* 93, no. 11 (Dec. 11, 1970) 271-74.

32. Zulliger, *op. cit.,* pp. 76ff.

33. *Ibid.,* pp. 138f.

SUGGESTED READINGS

Many valuable articles on conscience are found in *Conscience: Theological and Psychological Perspectives* by C. Ellis Nelson, editor (Paramus, N.J.: Newman Press, 1973). Of value also is *Conscience: Its Freedom and Limitations,* edited by William J. Bier, S.J. (N.Y.: Fordham University Press, 1971). See, in particular, "Superego and Conscience," by Robert Campbell, pp. 82-91, and "The Mature Conscience as Seen by a Psychiatrist," by John Cavanagh, pp. 379-387. E. Blum studies the general movement of Freud's thought in "Freud and Conscience," from *Conscience,* edited by the Curatorium of the C. G. Jung Institute (Evanston: Northwestern University Press, 1970), pp. 159-178. Similarly, see Gregory Zilboorg's *Psychoanalysis and Religion,* previously cited, pp. 169-188, and the chapter by David H. Jones on Freud and conscience in *Conscience,* John Donnelly and Leonard Lyons, eds. (N.Y.: Alba House, 1973, paperback).

For more general approaches, see Erich Fromm's *Man for Himself* (Greenwich, Conn.: Fawcett Publications, 1947, paperback), pp. 145-175, where he contrasts "authoritarian conscience" with "humanistic conscience." Rollo May treats of "creative conscience" in *Man's Search for Himself* (N.Y.: New American Library, 1967), especially pp. 150-190.

"Theology and Self-Understanding: The Christian Model of Man as Sinner," by Fred Berthold, Jr., *The Dialogue Between Theology and Psychology* (Chicago: University of Chicago Press, 1968), pp. 11-32, is an important theological and psychological discussion of the fact that at the heart of the Gospel is conviction that God loves us, and suggests that the root of sin is not so much willful self-assertion as it is a desperate response to a feeling of unworthiness, a point which leads to an attempt at self-justification when over-emphasized. Paul Pruyser points out the psychological importance of the theological model employed, in "Anxiety, Guilt, and Shame in the Atonement," *Theology Today* vol. 21, 1964, pp. 15-33, and abridged in *Theology Digest,* Autumn 1966, pp. 183-187. Also useful are E. Stein's *Beyond Guilt* (Philadelphia: Fortress Press, 1972, paperback); Arnold Uleyn's *Is It I, Lord? —Pastoral Psychology and the Recognition of Guilt* (N.Y.: Meredith Corporation, 1969). A good, brief presentation of the positions of the major psychologists on guilt is found in *Man in Triumph —An Integration of Psychology and Biblical Faith* by Harold W. Darling (Grand Rapids: Zondervan Publishing House, 1969) pp. 30-61.

On the question of conscience, guilt and aggression, one might relate the controversial *Human Aggression* by Anthony Storr (N.Y.: Bantam Books, 1970, paperback) to "Toward a Theology of Human Aggression" by W. Meissner, S.J., in the *Journal of Religion and Health,* October 1971, pp. 324-333, and in the same journal, G. Jackson's "The Problem of Hostility Psychologically and Theologically Considered," January 1972, pp. 73-93. Lastly, the jolt which comes from reading O. Hobart Mowrer's *The Crisis in Psychiatry and Religion* (Princeton: D. Van Nostrand, 1961, paperback) might be a valuable corrective to any one-sidedness in the discussion of guilt. Mowrer believes that much of the psychopathology of guilt is *real* guilt and that what has been repressed is often conscience.

4 C. G. Jung and Religion

REGINA BECHTLE, S.C.

The thought of C. G. Jung (1875-1961) resembles a dense jungle with much overgrowth, and apart from his popular works he writes in a circling style, much less structured than Freud's. Excerpts representative of his religious thought are therefore more difficult to find.

The author of the following essay, Regina Bechtle, S.C., has undertaken the difficult task of presenting an overview of Jung's religious thought in a brief space. She has published in *Thought* and is currently completing doctoral work in theology at Fordham University on the mysticism of Evelyn Underhill. The chapter ends with an excerpt from Jung's *Psychology and Alchemy.*

Freud looked at the religious psyche from the perspective of purification, both as to its past origins and with regard to its hopes for the future. Jung looked at the same psyche to probe the positive depths and richness of the unconscious.

Freud once said that "the only happiness is the satisfaction of a childhood wish" (E. Jones, p. 217). He also saw man as the bearer of a "longing for the father" (*Moses and Monotheism,* p. 140). Yet his main thrust was that the construction of a wish usually introduces delusion into reality (*Civilization and Its Discontents,* p. 28). Jung sees it differently: "Truth to tell, I have a very high opinion of fantasy. To me it is actually the maternally creative side of the masculine spirit. . . . All the works of man have

57

their origin in creative fantasy" (*Modern Man in Search of a Soul,* p. 66).

In Jung, one must distinguish between archetype and symbol. The archetype is a power or potency which is cross cultural. It is not an innate idea but an *a priori* power of representation. The specific symbol is generally culturally determined and appears in the form of religious stories, myths, fairy tales and dreams (*Man and His Symbols,* pp. 56-57). One of its chief patterns is "the drama of repentance, sacrifice and redemption."

Born in 1875 in Switzerland, the son of a minister of the Swiss Reformed Church, Carl Gustave Jung studied medicine at the University of Basel and spent his first ten years as a doctor in a hospital in Burghölzli near Zürich, while also serving as professor in charge of the course in psychiatry at the university there. His experiments in "idea-association" led to collaboration with Sigmund Freud from 1907 to 1913, and Jung's writings during this time evidence how profound was Freud's influence upon him. Initially he accepted Freud's theory of sexuality as the basic motivation behind man's conscious acts, but he soon discovered that a more comprehensive concept was needed, as well as a more dynamic theory which pointed ahead to a developmental process of self-realization rather than merely behind to the hidden and deeply-rooted causes of psychic disturbance. The publication in 1911-12 of Jung's *Wandlungen und Symbole der Libido* (translated as *The Psychology of the Unconscious*) marked his definitive break with the Freudian school.

In his second period, Jung left his teaching and medical positions to immerse himself in psychotherapy. He collected vast amounts of data from the dreams of his patients as well as from first-hand research into primitive cultures in Central Africa and North America. To trace similar patterns more thoroughly, he studied the religious and philosophical thought of the East, ancient Gnostic writings and medieval alchemical treatises. His 1937 Terry lectures at Yale entitled "Psychology and Religion" reflected his growing interest in religion and signaled the beginning of a new phase of work.

His post-war writings centered mainly on the nature and expressions of symbolism, especially in its religious manifestations, and specifically on the psychological meaning of Catholic doctrines such as the Mass, the Trinity, Christ and the Assumption of Mary.[1]

Our investigation of the work of Jung in relation to religion and revelation must begin with a brief exposition of his psychology —method, object and basic concepts. We will then be in a position to examine the origins, purpose and progress of his dialogue with religion. In particular, we will touch on his explanation of symbol in connection with the nature of religious experience and the function of dogma and myth. Finally, the charge of psychologism leveled against Jung will be evaluated, and his contribution to theology assessed.

I
Jung's Psychology

A. *Use of Empirical Method*

Influenced by the methodology of the natural sciences, as was almost inevitable for a man of his times, Jung was a thoroughgoing empiricist. This fact is important for understanding both his strictly psychological research and his observations of religious phenomena. He realized that absolute and unbiased objectivity was impossible to attain, especially when dealing with the complexities of the human psyche; the very act of determining an experimental procedure limited the phenomena to be observed and conditioned the results expected. Yet within these limitations, Jung tried to be as unprejudiced as possible as he formulated hypotheses based on the correlations between observed facts. Each patient he treated was a unique case, to be sure, yet over the years of his psychoanalytic practice, he perceived strikingly similar patterns of response, from which he could draw tentative conclusions as to the presence of some objective psychic reality. With admirable scientific detachment, he viewed a hypothesis as a mere tool to aid further research—thus his readiness to abandon one and to adopt another, perhaps contradictory to the first, if it offered a simpler and more complete explanation of the data. This factor adds to the unsystematic character of his work and has often been interpreted by philosophically-minded critics as symptomatic of confusion and lack of logic, whereas in reality it is but the natural outgrowth of his scientific procedure.[2]

The overriding characteristic of Jung's psychological methodology, then, is his commitment to empirical observation of data and to their interpretation in broad hypotheses which are always subject to modification and improvement.

B. *Object: Psychic Reality*

Jung's investigations cover all of psychic reality, a realm which he sees as qualitatively different from, and not to be reduced to, the physical, though its exact essence cannot be defined precisely.

In his earlier writing, Jung handled the problem of the spiritual and material aspects of reality in a somewhat simplistic fashion, but one which nevertheless indicates the importance which he attached to the category of "psychic reality." He wrote:

The conflict of nature and mind is itself a reflection of the paradox contained in the psychic being of man. This reveals a material and a spiritual aspect which appear a contradiction as long as we fail to understand the nature of psychic life.[3]

He proceeded to assert that only the psychic constitutes the realm of immediate experience. Even sense-impressions can be modulated or intensified by the psyche, and it is only these psychic images which form the immediate objects of consciousness. "We are in all truth so enclosed by psychic images that we cannot penetrate to the essence of things external to ourselves." [4]

If expressed in mutually exclusive terms—"Which principle alone explains reality: matter or spirit?"—the problematic admits of only unsatisfactory solutions. Jung preferred to view the physical and the mental as two distinct points of contact initiating the psychic process.

If I change my concept of reality in such a way as to admit that all psychic happenings are real—and no other use of the concept is valid—this puts an end to the conflict of matter and mind as contradictory explanatory principles. Each becomes a mere designation for the particular source of the psychic contents that crowd into my field of consciousness.[5]

So reality in the psychological sense is affirmed of anything which exerts a psychic influence on a subject. Thus an "imaginary" voice which haunts a disturbed patient is psychically real and must be treated as such. So too the tremendous power and attraction of the idea of God throughout man's history points to the psychic reality of God. When indignant believers reacted against this as a reduction of God to the psychological, Jung took pains to assure them that the affirmation of the psychic existence of God was not a denial of his ontological reality but merely the only conclusion he could legitimately draw from his empirical observations; metaphysical proofs were not within his area of competence.[6]

After these somewhat abstract considerations, it might be well to make a few brief remarks on the nature of human knowing as an introduction to some of the fundamental concepts which Jung uses in his work. Contrary to the prophets of the Enlightenment and to modern rationalists, man's movement to comprehend reality is not exhausted by the intellectual activity of his consciousness.

Do we ever understand what we think? We only understand that thinking which is a mere equation, and from which nothing comes out but what we have put in. That is the working of the intellect. But beyond that there is a thinking in primordial images—in symbols which are older than historical man; . . . It is only possible to live the fullest life when we are in harmony with these symbols; wisdom is a return to them. It is neither a question of belief nor of knowledge, but of the agreement of our thinking with the primordial images of the unconscious.[7]

Neglect of this area of the unconscious has resulted in a psychologically unbalanced culture. Rational man, who should be master of his own fate, finds himself prey to irrational and destructive powers, which all his technological expertise cannot control; should modern man be tempted to consider himself the crown of the centuries, he need only recall the barbarism with which he still wages war on his fellows. Now that he has experienced the evil within himself, he can no longer trust in his own capabilities to realize any of the rosy visions of progress which earlier reformers dreamed, and neither can he project the cause of this failure onto the external world.

Through his skepticism the modern man is thrown back upon himself; his energies flow towards their source and wash to the surface those psychic contents which are at all times there, but lie hidden in the silt as long as the stream flows smoothly in its course.[8]

The myths and metaphysical systems in which earlier times objectified and thus dealt with their deepest human hopes, fears, longings and anxieties have disappeared; the hopes and fears have returned to the darkness within the self, and it is to this unknown territory that modern man is drawn.

C. Basic Concepts

1. *The Unconscious.* Jung's central thrust, as he expressed it, was "to penetrate into the secret of the personality." [9] That thrust took him below the surface of consciousness to the depths of the *unconscious,* the realm of psychic reality which influences consciousness yet is not identical with it, and which assumes an autonomous existence over against it. Jung's notion of the unconscious is unavoidably vague; it functions as a "boundary concept" (*Grenzbegriff*) to describe that non-conscious area whose boundaries are unspecified but which yet acts as though conscious, e.g., through all the manifestations attributed in other cultures to gods, demons, spirits and supernatural powers.[10]

In tracing the causes of psychological illness back to some aberration in sexual development, repressed into the unconscious, Freud linked the entire theory and practice of his psychotherapy to sexuality. Jung, though an early follower of Freud, was led to postulate a concept of psychic energy, or *libido,* broader than the merely sexual; for Jung, libido refers to the undifferentiated and uncontrolled psychic impulses and tendencies at the root of all human action. When its normal course is blocked, this energy is forced to backtrack, so to speak, and returns to regressive patterns of behavior. But this movement backwards has a positive side: it is an attempt, however unsatisfactory, to find some solution which will remove the inner obstacle.[11]

Phenomena such as dreams, fantasies, hallucinations, etc. witness to the presence of unexplored, non-conceptualized and repressed aspects of our lives in the *personal unconscious.* Beyond this, however, Jung's psychoanalytic research and his comparative studies in primitive religion and alchemy led him to the conclusion that predispositions toward forming certain symbol-patterns are found trans-culturally and trans-temporally. No generation can consider itself psychologically severed from previous ages.

Our modern attitude looks back proudly upon the mists of superstition and of medieval or primitive credulity and entirely forgets that it carries the whole living past in the lower stories of the skyscraper of rational consciousness. Without the lower stories our mind is suspended in mid-air. . . . The true history of the mind is not preserved in learned volumes but in the living mental organism of everyone.[12]

Thus he postulated the *collective unconscious* as the sum total of man's inherited psychic experience, shared by all men as a transindividual psychological substratum of life.[13]

Among the contents of the unconscious are; the *shadow,* or the dark and undeveloped side of one's personality, which must be confronted if self-integration is to occur; the *anima (animus),* or personification of feminine qualities in the male (masculine in the female), complementing the conscious tendencies of the person toward one sexual orientation rather than another. These and other psychic realities can be subsumed under the heading of *archetypes.*

2. *Archetypes of the Collective Unconscious.* The identity and continuity of man's psychic structures is expressed in his innate predispositions toward the formation of certain common images.

In the mythology and folklore of different peoples, certain motives repeat themselves in almost identical form. I have called those motives archetypes and by them I understand forms or images of a collective nature which occur practically all over the earth as constituents of myths and at the same time as autochthonous, individual products of unconscious origin.[14]

Examples of these primordial archetypal figures and patterns include the passage from darkness to light, or from death to rebirth;

the Mother; the wise old man who mediates meaning; the dying god; the eternal child; the hidden treasure. As "organs of the pre-rational psyche," the archetypes are not encountered directly but only through the medium of *symbols*.

3. *Symbol.* In contradistinction to signs, symbols in Jung's terminology are not just convenient ways of expressing concisely something which is already known, much as a striped pole outside a shop stands for the presence of a barber within. Rather they are mediators of an unknown reality, polyvalent in meaning, capable of arousing many different thoughts and feelings because they arise spontaneously from the soil not only of past and forgotten consciousness but of the as-yet-unrealized unconscious.[15] Etymologically, symbol (from the Greek *sym-ballo*) connotes a process of totalizing or unifying, and herein lies its therapeutic power:

As a uniter of opposites, the symbol is a totality which can never be addressed only to one faculty in a man—his reason or intellect, for example—but always concerns our wholeness, touches and produces a resonance in all four of our functions at once. The symbol as 'image' has the character of a summons and stimulates a man's whole being to a total reaction; his thought and feeling, his senses and his intuition participate in this reaction and it is not, as some mistakenly suppose, a single one of his functions that is actualized.[16]

We have attempted in this section to clarify several concepts basic to Jung's psychology—libido, unconscious, archetype, symbol—without defining them exhaustively. We will now study the application of these terms to the rhythm of human development.

D. *The Process of Individuation*

Jung believed that the psyche was oriented toward a state of dynamic self-fulfillment, toward a unified psychic totality which would integrate all the disparate components of the personality, both conscious and unconscious. This process of individuation has been described as "the systematic confrontation, step by step, between the ego and the contents of the unconscious," [17] and more fully, as "the open conflict and open collaboration between the conscious and the unconscious by means of which the individual is forged into an indestructible whole." [18] Although this growth does occur naturally in some, many others shun the effort and discipline required, and so the individuation process must often be assisted by external means, such as psychoanalysis, in which the consciousness is summoned to intervene in the spontaneous movement of the psyche in order knowingly to accept and integrate its contents.[19] The dialectic between conscious and unconscious is bridged by symbols, and it is in symbolic terms that the conflicting claims of the various elements of the psyche are acted out.

The symbols that rise up out of the unconscious in dreams point rather to a confrontation of opposites, and the images of the goal represent their successful reconciliation. Something empirically demonstrable comes to our aid from the depths of our unconscious nature. It is the task of the conscious mind to understand these hints.[20]

Whether in the first half of life, which could be described as a period of initiation into external reality, or in the second, a time of reduction to the essential, inner reality, an underlying dynamic toward wholeness is operative. "The goal of psychic development is the self. There is no linear evolution; there is only a circumambulation of the self." [21] The archetype of the Self, embodying this "ultimately unknowable, transcendent 'centre' of the personality," usually appears in dreams, legends, myths, fairy tales and fantasies under the guise of a *mandala* or symmetrical arrangement of elements in relation to a center. When the tension between conscious and unconscious is experienced as confusing, threatening or destructive, the emergence of such a symbol serves to reconcile the opposites and to restore psychic order, balance and security to the person.[22]

We might summarize this brief outline of the individuation process and set the stage for Jung's specific application of his psychological framework to the spiritual situation of modern man in the following words of Hostie:

As long as the totality of the self remains hidden from the eyes of that inveterate rationalist, Western man, he goes on basking in the illusion that he can be a complete autocrat. Only the emergence into consciousness of this totality can bring him out of this dream state. If he does not allow it to emerge, the neglected psychic components go on tyrannizing over him as projections; a clear acceptance of it, however, leads to submission to the self and this in turn leads to a harmonious integration of all the psychic potentialities. And then, individuation, or the confrontation of consciousness and the unconscious, reaches its culmination.[23]

II
PSYCHOLOGY AND RELIGION

A. *The Spiritual Situation of Modern Man*

As long as man's conscious patterns of action and systems of thought harmonize with the archetypal structures of his unconscious, he can live in relative inner peace and security, guaranteed meaning by an objective world order which satisfies the projections of his psychic needs. In our day, however, the darkness of the unconscious is effectively ignored in the technology-centered day-to-day living of one-dimensional man; his ideals of wealth and progress seem to admit of no realization; his systems of belief and metaphysical certainties no longer adequately express his experience.[24] The creative tension between the conscious and the unconscious, and the resolution of that tension through meaningful symbols, has yielded to a destructive polarization and fragmentation of self.

As soon as [man] has outgrown whatever local form of religion he was born to—as soon as this religion can no longer embrace his life in all its fulness—then the psyche becomes something in its own right.[25]

This 'psychological' interest of the present time shows that man expects something from psychic life which he has not received from the outer world: something which our religions, doubtless, ought to contain, but no longer do contain—at least for the modern man. The various forms of religion no longer appear to the modern man to come from within—to be expressions of his own psychic life; for him they are to be classed with the things of the outer world.[26]

Jung sees the current renewal of interest in the psychic realm as a positive factor; it signals a rejection both of materialism and of pseudo-intellectualism, and a humble embracing of the totality of life—spirit and instinct—which he describes as profoundly "religious." [27]

B. *Meaning and Function of Religion*

Religion has indeed failed the man of today, in Jung's opinion —but why should religion play any part at all in the life of enlightened man? Departing from the Freudian school, Jung repeatedly emphasized not only the psychological importance of religion but also the irreducible religious orientation of man. Even in his early writings, while refusing to grant any objective reality to the concept of God, he nevertheless is forced to admit the benefits which religion brings to mankind.

The religious myth meets us here as one of the greatest and most significant human institutions which, despite misleading symbols, nevertheless gives man assurance and strength, so that he may not be overwhelmed by the monsters of the universe. The symbol, considered from the standpoint of actual truth, is misleading, indeed, but it is *psychologically true,* because it was and is the bridge to all the greatest achievements of humanity.[28]

In a later development of his thought, Jung described religion as "the attitude peculiar to a consciousness which has been altered by the experience of the numinosum," [29] that is, by a dynamic factor outside the voluntary control of the subject. And in a short work published in 1958, Jung further refined his concept of religion in terms of its counterbalancing effect against a totalitarian State:

Religion means dependence on and submission to the irrational facts of experience. . . . Its evident purpose is to maintain the psychic balance, for the natural man has an equally natural 'knowledge' of the fact that his conscious functions may at any time be thwarted by uncontrollable happenings coming from inside as well as from outside.[30]

In essence, then, true religion participates in the numinous, the irrational, the experiential. Before we discuss the objectification of religion in dogma, we must examine the Jungian concept of God.

C. *The Idea of God*

Perhaps no position of Jung's has been so misunderstood as

his concept of God. True to his empirical and phenomenological methodology, he has repeatedly asserted that the *objective existence* of God remains outside the scope of his investigation; all that he can study is the psychological effect of subjective experience.

The idea of God is an absolutely necessary psychological function of an irrational nature, which has nothing whatever to do with the question of God's existence. The human intellect can never answer this question, still less give any proof of God. Moreover such proof is superfluous, for the idea of an all-powerful divine Being is present everywhere, unconsciously if not consciously, because it is an archetype.[31]

This archetypal character of the God-image is revealed most clearly in Christ. Christ lived a concrete historical existence which assumed earth-shaking significance because he participated so deeply in the archetypal life of mankind. In the life of Christ is reflected man's experience, his striving for self-integration and wholeness through the process of individuation.

Looked at from the psychological standpoint, Christ, as the Original Man . . . represents a totality which surpasses and includes the ordinary man, and which corresponds to the total personality that transcends consciousness. We have called this personality the 'self'.[32]

The Self is the transcendent center of the personality, which organizes and guides all the psychic functions, the unknown yet beneficent power to whom the person must submit himself in order to achieve wholeness.[33] Christ then becomes for man a symbol of the Self, his incarnation a paradigm of self-realization, and his passion a prototype of the suffering involved in the task of individuation: the submission of the ego to the wider dimension of the Self. In summary,

the drama of the archetypal life of Christ describes in symbolic images the events in the conscious life—as well as in the life that transcends consciousness—of a man who has been transformed by his higher destiny.[34]

In a passage reminiscent of Tillich, Jung wrote: "Psychologically the God-concept includes every idea of the ultimate, of the first or last, or the highest or lowest. The name makes no difference." [35] No matter what its ultimate reference or meaning, the fact of man's innate orientation towards "God," as a primordial

psychic structure, cannot be arbitrarily ignored. From his observations of patients during a 30-year span of time, Jung concluded:

Among all my patients in the second half of life . . . there has not been
one whose problem in the last resort was not that of finding a religious
outlook on life. It is safe to say that every one of them fell ill because he
had lost that which the living religions of every age had given to their
followers, and none of them has really been healed who did not regain
his religious outlook.[36]

What function did these "living religions" perform for man?
Why does modern man reject the systems of belief which his prede-
cessors found adequate? Is his "religious outlook" to be regained
apart from, or even in opposition to, the structures of the established religions? An answer to these questions demands an examination of the roles of religious experience and of dogmatic
formulation in Jung.

D. *Religious Experience and Objectification*

It comes as no surprise to find that for Jung, the experience of
the numinous comprised the essence of religion, as well as its
starting-point. In this connection Jung likened our times to the
first and second centuries A.D., when Gnostic thought attained its
peak. Distrust of reason, expectation of a heavenly revelation, exaltation of inner awareness and participation in the arcane mys-
teries characterized the Gnostic reaction to the over-rational atmosphere of late Greek culture. So too modern man only accepts
common formulations of belief when they correspond to his own
psychic experience.[37]

Creeds and dogmas merely codify and systematize the original religious experience. Even revelation, for Jung, is not primarily a transmission of knowledge about God, but a discovery of what
lies within the person.

Revelation is an unveiling of the depths of the human soul first and foremost, a 'laying bare,' hence it is an essentially psychological event, though
this does not of course tell us what else it could be.[38]

In some instances, Jung criticizes the established religions for
preserving systems "no longer based on their own inner experience

but on *unreflecting belief.* . . . Belief is no adequate substitute for inner experience. . . . People call faith the true religious experience, but they do not stop to think that actually it is a secondary phenomenon arising from the fact that something happened to us in the first place which instilled πίστις into us—that is, trust and loyalty." [39]

On the other hand, dogma exercises a positive function in that it 'shields' the believer from the unknown dangers of an immediate experience of the divine or else serves as a criterion by which his experience can be judged as coming from God or the devil. Dogma protects because it reflects the workings of the unconscious (here Jung is referring to archetypal patterns which Christianity expresses in such doctrines as the Incarnation of the God-Man, the Virgin Birth, the Trinity, the Redemption, etc.); once a ritual has been formulated, whether in words or in actions, the dark and lurking powers of the unconscious can be dealt with harmlessly.[40] "The whole life of the collective unconscious has been absorbed without remainder, so to speak, in the dogmatic archetypes, and flows like a well-controlled stream in the symbolism of ritual and of the church calendar." [41]

Yet the indictment remains: the religious bodies of today have ceased to incarnate meaning for man.

Since they are compromises with mundane reality, the creeds have accordingly seen themselves obliged to undertake a progressive codification of their views, doctrines and customs and in so doing have externalized themselves to such an extent that the authentic religious element in them —the living relationship to and direct confrontation with their extra-mundane point of reference—has been thrust into the background.[42]

Since dogmas no longer act as "reconciling symbols" between the conscious and the unconscious, the psyche must retrace its steps inward, back to the primal experience which alone can make it whole.

No matter what the world thinks about religious experience, the one who has it possesses the great treasure of a thing that has provided him with a source of life, meaning and beauty. . . . Where is the criterium by which you could say that such a life is not legitimate, that such experience is not valid and that such pistis is mere illusion? Is there, as a matter of fact, any better truth about ultimate things than the one that helps you to live? [43]

E. *The Role of Christianity* [44]

Lest we begin to think of Jung as a cynical anti-institutionalist, we must recall the high regard in which he held Christianity both from the historical and the psychotherapeutic perspectives. The inadequacy of the Christian symbol in expressing the deepest needs of modern man does not signal irreversible defeat.

It is not Christianity, but our conception and interpretation of it, that has become antiquated in face of the present world situation. The Christian symbol is a living thing that carries in itself the seeds of further development. It can go on developing; it depends only on us, whether we can make up our minds to meditate again, and more thoroughly, on the Christian premises.[45]

One of these "Christian premises" is at the same time a contribution and a burden to mankind: centered on Jesus, the Word made flesh, Christianity has become the "religion of the word," and has specified our civilization by the supremacy and autonomy which it accords to the word, and the consequent rupture it promotes between faith and knowledge.[46]

F. *Religion in East and West*

It is understandable that those to whom Christian symbols no longer speak meaningfully should, in their journey back along the paths of the psyche, discover the attraction of the East. According to the psychological law of *enantiodromia* (the tendency against a one-sided orientation of the psyche because of which its opposite emerges) an overemphasis on the materialistic and rational provokes a reaction favoring the otherworldly and intuitive—and this is precisely the experience of many today.[47] Yet Jung wonders whether modern man can with impunity abandon the tradition of his own symbols in favor of those of the East. Neither matter nor spirit suffices in itself to embrace the totality of reality, just as neither the conscious nor the unconscious can be allowed to tip the balance of the person if wholeness is to be won.

When the primitive world disintegrated into spirit and nature, the West rescued nature for itself. It was prone to a belief in nature, and only became the more entangled in it with every painful effort to make itself spiritual. The East, on the contrary, took mind for its own, and by explaining away matter as mere illusion *(maya)*, continued to dream in Asiatic filth and misery. But since there is only *one* earth and *one* mankind, East and West cannot rend humanity into two different halves.[48]

Perhaps the East—in the sense of contemplative reflection, detachment and stability—is within our very selves.[49]

In the first part of this essay, we have attempted to sketch the basic points of Jung's analytical psychology, noting his empirical-phenomenological method, his investigation of psychic rather than ontological reality, his conceptual framework and his key developmental category of "individuation." Next we addressed ourselves to his religious concerns, rooted in the spiritual crisis of modern man, and viewed religion, God, dogma and religious experience from his perspective. We now propose to discuss the main criticism brought against Jung's approach—that of "psychologism."

III
CRITICISMS

It was inevitable that Jung's treatment of religious themes from a psychological point of view should leave him open to the charge of "psychologism." According to his own understanding of the term as any theory in which religion is merely the projection or transformation of an instinct, Jung is exonerated from this charge, since he maintains that religion is irreducible and non-derivative.[50]

Hostie feels that, while Jung, especially in his later period, rejected the idea that God was nothing more than a psychic reality, his sketchy knowledge of, and his aversion to, metaphysics and theology prevented him from grappling more satisfactorily with the problem. Jung's own attitude is revealed in a remark he made to Hostie: "It is quite clear that God exists but why are people always asking me to prove this psychologically?" [51]

In this connection, the question of methodological consistency has been raised by Hostie, who takes issue with Jung's assertion that his empiricism does not allow him to make any statements whatsoever about the existence of the non-observable, specifically, God. In actual fact, Hostie feels, Jung overstepped the limits he set for himself for he repeatedly shifts his argumentation, especially in his earlier works, from: "It is impossible *for me* to know or prove *scientifically* that God exists," to: "It is impossible to know or prove that God exists," a statement which completely discounts the validity of philosophical or theological knowledge.[52] On this basis, we would concur with Hostie in Goldbrunner's evaluation of Jung as an "agnostic positivist" up until 1940.

Jung's later work in religious symbolism does give evidence of a growing recognition of the validity of "the religious point of view," but for him this classifies metaphysics, faith and theology alike under the one rubric: acceptance of something as true on the basis of a subjective conviction.[53] Jung wrote in 1944: "The religious-minded man is free to accept whatever metaphysical explanations he pleases . . . ; not so the intellect, which must keep strictly to the principles of scientific interpretation." [54]

We feel that Jung does at times seem to over-generalize his assertion that he can say nothing at all about ontological reality. This lack of methodological precision must be acknowledged. He grappled constantly with what he perceived as the conflicting paths of faith and knowledge:

I do not fiddle with dogma. In my eyes it has the highest authority, but I try to *understand* it, since unfortunately I cannot believe anything I do not understand, and in this I am like many other people today. If it were otherwise, I should only be believing in empty words, and this surely cannot be the meaning of belief . . .[55]

It is strange that Jung who always upheld the primacy of subjective experience disliked the word "faith." Faith, for him, seems to have connoted an externally imposed belief bereft of the inner experience. Perhaps his usage merely reflects his own personal struggle to reconcile scientific method and religious experience. Be that as it may, we feel that on no account can the later Jung, at least, be accused of agnosticism in the usual sense of the word. As he wrote in his autobiography, "The decisive question for man is: Are you related to something infinite or not?" [56]

IV
JUNG'S CONTRIBUTIONS

This essay has barely skimmed the surface of the Jungian

corpus of writings. We have not treated such topics as his concept of evil within God, or his analysis of the Trinity. These conclusions, therefore, are based not on specific points but on a general overview of Jung's attempt to achieve a *rapprochement* between psychology and religion.

A. *Synthesis of Opposites*

Valuable as a model for Christian revelation is Jung's synthetic approach. Beginning with the fundamental duality of conscious and unconscious in the personality, and the need to integrate them under the guidance of the Self-archetype in order to achieve wholeness, Jung showed himself deeply aware of the principle that truth is many-sided and that a narrow insistence on either end of a mutually exclusive polarity could only result in an impoverishment of the truth; thus the creative tension between causality and finality, psychic structure and external images, personal and collective unconscious.[57]

In its applications to religion, the method of synthesis offers a hermeneutic for understanding modern culture with its emphasis on the body:

If we are still caught by the old idea of an antithesis between mind and matter, the present state of affairs means an unbearable contradiction; it may even divide us against ourselves. But if we can reconcile ourselves with the mysterious truth that spirit is the living body seen from within, and the body the outer manifestation of the living spirit—the two being really one—then we can understand why it is that the attempt to transcend the present level of consciousness must give its due to the body.[58]

Frei comments:

On his way towards the 'self' man must not restrict himself by being solely a creature of instinct nor solely a disembodied mind, but seek to be a complete human being, combining both spirit and matter. He must accept the tension between mind and flesh as his cross, and must endeavour through this Golgotha to attain to the Easter resurrection. . . . The shell of our small 'I' must be broken and an existential link forged with God and the cosmos, in a union which emanates both from within and from without.[59]

Jung's own words with regard to the culmination of the individuation process reiterate the profound significance of synthesis: "The self then functions as a union of opposites and thus constitutes the most immediate experience of the Divine which it is psychologically possible to imagine." [60]

B. *Respect for the Irrational*

The concept of the unconscious, autonomous in its own sphere over against the ego, has provided a counterbalance to the tyranny of the intellect. Jung has shown that, severed from its instinctual roots, consciousness becomes sterile and thinks itself sufficient. Recognition of the independence of the unconscious, both personal and collective, leads to an attitude of humility before reality that allows us to relinquish our desperate hold on life and to stand before it in awe and wonder, as did primitive man, knowing that the ultimate decisions lie outside our control. Such a stance is similar to the believer's, who "is accustomed to the thought of not being sole master in his own house." [61]

With all of his emphasis on the non-rational, however, Jung cannot be accused of being anti-rational. For him, the distinguishing characteristic of man is his consciousness, and with all the infinite complexity of the archetypal and symbolic depths of man,

it is the task of the conscious mind, as the ordering and understanding principle in man, to help one or the other of these aspects to become operative, and to add its sense- and form-giving energy to the indifferent sway of our primordial psychic nature, in order that neither instinct nor intellect, but a spirit that surveys them both, may keep the psychic balance.[62]

V

CONCLUSION

To ask whether Jung has succeeded or failed in his attempt to illuminate religion in the light of psychology is, we think, to pose the wrong question. Inevitably there are points at which his theories cast doubt on and even contradict traditional interpretations of Christian dogma. Yet does not the revelation of man to himself play a role in preparing him for the revelation of God? The incarnational principle of Christianity affirms that God communicates himself through the structures of man's consciousness and history, and it is this belief which must ultimately condition our acceptance of the valid findings of every human science.

With regard to revelation, Jung's contribution is to be found primarily in his elucidation of the human pole of the divine-human dialogue. For him, as for Karl Rahner, man is a being open to the transcendent, but not only because of the thrust of human knowing. Jung saw the traces of the divine imprinted on the hiddenmost layers of the psyche as its origin, and as the symbol of wholeness towards which it strives.

EDITOR'S NOTE: The following passages from Jung's writings * provide a fitting conclusion to this chapter.

Yet when I point out that the soul possesses by nature a religious function and when I stipulate that it is the prime task of all education (of adults) to convey the archetype of the God-image, or its emanations and effects, to the conscious mind, then it is precisely the theologian who seizes me by the arm and accuses me of "psychologism." But were it not a fact of experience that supreme values reside in the soul (quite apart from the αντιμιμον πνευμα [rival spirit] who is also there), psychology would not interest me in the least, for the soul would then be nothing but a miserable vapour. I know, however, from hundredfold experience that it is nothing of the sort, but on the contrary contains the equivalents of everything that has been formulated in dogma and a good deal more, which is just what enables it to be an eye destined to behold the light. This requires limitless range and unfathomable depth of vision. I have been accused of "deifying the soul." Not I but God himself has deified it! I did not attribute a religious function to the soul; I merely produced the facts which prove that the soul is *naturaliter religiosa,* i.e., possesses a religious function. . . .

* From *The Collected Works of C. G. Jung,* ed. by G. Adler, M. Fordham, and H. Read, trans. by R. F. C. Hull, Bollingen Series XX, volume 12, *Psychology and Alchemy,* pp. 12 and 17 (copyright © 1953 and 1968 by Bollingen Foundation), reprinted by permission of Princeton University Press.

The archetypes of the unconscious can be shown empirically to be the equivalents of religious dogmas. In the hermeneutic language of the Fathers the Church possesses a rich store of analogies with the individual and spontaneous products to be found in psychology. What the unconscious expresses is far from being merely arbitrary or opinionated; it is something that just happens to be what it is, as is the case with every other natural being. It stands to reason that the expressions of the unconscious are natural and not formulated dogmatically; they are just like the patristic allegories which draw the whole of nature into the orbit of their amplifications. If these present us with some astonishing *allegoriae Christi*, we find much the same sort of thing in the psychology of the unconscious. The only difference is that the patristic allegory *ad Christum spectat*—refers to Christ—whereas the psychic archetype is simply itself and can therefore be interpreted according to time, place, and milieu. In the West the archetype is charged with the dogmatic figure of Christ; in the East, with Purusha, the Atman, Hiranyagarbha, Buddha, and so on. The religious point of view, understandably enough, puts the accent on the imprinter, whereas scientific psychology emphasizes the typos, the imprint— the only thing it can understand. The religious point of view understands the imprint as the working of an imprinter; the scientific point of view understands it as the symbol of an unknown and incomprehensible content. Since the typos is less definite and more variegated than any of the figures postulated by religion, psychology is compelled by its empirical material to express the typos by means of a terminology not bound by time, place, or milieu. If, for example, the typos agreed in every detail with the dogmatic figure of Christ, and if it contained no determinant that went beyond that figure, we would be bound to regard the typos as at least a faithful copy of the dogmatic figure, and to name it accordingly. The typos would then coincide with Christ. But as experience shows, this is not the case, seeing that the unconscious, like the allegories employed by the Church Fathers, produces countless other determinants that are not explicitly contained in the dogmatic formula; that is to say, non-Christian figures such as those mentioned above are included in the typos. But neither do these figures comply with the indeterminate nature of the archetype. It is altogether inconceivable that there could be any definite figure capable of expressing archetypal indefiniteness. For this reason I have found myself obliged to give the corresponding archetype the psychological name of the "self"—a term on the one hand definite enough to convey the sum of human wholeness and on the other hand indefinite enough to express the indescribable and indeterminable nature of this wholeness. The paradoxical qualities of the term are in keeping with the fact that wholeness consists partly of the conscious man and partly of the unconscious man. But we cannot define the latter or indicate his boundaries. Hence in its scientific usage the term "self" refers neither to Christ nor to Buddha but to the totality of the figures that are its equivalent, and each of these figures is a symbol of the self. This mode of expression is an intellectual necessity in scientific psychology and in no sense denotes a transcendental prejudice.

NOTES

1. Raymond Hostie, *Religion and the Psychology of C. G. Jung* (New York: Sheed and Ward, 1957), pp. 1-2, 111. Jung's autobiography is found in *Memories, Dreams, Reflections,* ed. by Aniela Jaffé, trans. by Richard and Clara Winston (New York: Pantheon Books, 1963).

2. For a fuller discussion of Jung's use of empirical method, see Hostie, pp. 7-14, upon which the above analysis has drawn.

3. C. G. Jung, *Modern Man in Search of a Soul,* trans. by W. S. Dell and Cary F. Baynes (London: Kegan Paul, Trench, Trubner & Co., 1933), p. 219.

4. *Ibid.,* p. 220.

5. *Ibid.*

6. Hostie, pp. 14-17. Cf. especially *Psyche & Symbol.* Ed. by Violet de Laszlo. N.Y.: Doubleday, 1958, pp. 344, 349-350.

7. Jung, *Modern Man,* pp. 129-130.

8. *Ibid.,* p. 235.

9. Jung, *Memories, Dreams, Reflections,* p. 206.

10. Victor White, O.P., *God and the Unconscious* (Chicago: Henry Regnery, 1953), p. 37.

11. Hostie, p. 33.

12. C. G. Jung, *Psychology and Religion* (New Haven: Yale University Press, 1938), p. 41.

13. Gebhard Frei, "Appendix—On Analytical Psychology: the Method and Teaching of C. G. Jung" in White, *God and the Unconscious,* p. 238. The following outline of Jungian concepts owes much to Frei's clear exposition.

14. Jung, *Psychology and Religion*, p. 63.

15. Cf. C. G. Jung, *Psychological Types*, trans. by H. G. Baynes (London: Kegan Paul, 1923): "The symbol is alive only so long as it is pregnant with meaning." (p. 602); also White, p. 221; Hostie, pp. 41-43.

16. Jolande Jacobi, *Complex-Archetype-Symbol in the Psychology of C. G. Jung*, trans. by Ralph Manheim, Bollingen Series LVII (New York: Pantheon Books, 1959), p. 88. Cf. also Hostie's remark: "The symbol . . . understands both conscious and unconscious, past and future, unifying them in an actualized present. . . . It likewise totalizes the rational and the irrational in man." (p. 42)

17. Jolande Jacobi, *The Way of Individuation*, trans. by R. F. C. Hull (New York: Harcourt, Brace & World, 1967), p. 34. This section on Jung's theory of individuation depends to a great extent on Jacobi's perceptive analysis, both in this work and in *Complex-Archetype-Symbol*, cited above.

18. Frieda Fordham, *An Introduction to Jung's Psychology* (Penguin Books, 1966), p. 77.

19. Jacobi, *Individuation*, pp. 12-20.

20. C. G. Jung, *Answer to Job*, trans. by R. F. C. Hull (London: Routledge and Kegan Paul, 1954), p. 460.

21. Jung, *Memories, Dreams, Reflections*, pp. 196-7. Jacobi comments: "In this sense one can regard the individuation process as a growing of the ego out of the Self and as a re-rooting in it." (*Individuation*, p. 42).

22. Jacobi, *Individuation*, pp. 57-8.

23. Hostie, p. 83.

24. June K. Singer, "Religion and the Collective Unconscious: Common Ground of Psychology and Religion," *Zygon* 4 (1969), 329: "In his mad dash toward the materialistic goals of our time, man has destroyed the symmetry between his intrinsic nature and his striving after personal growth."

25. Jung, *Modern Man*, p. 233.

26. *Ibid.*, p. 237.

27. Jacobi, *Individuation*, pp. 107-8.

28. C. G. Jung, *The Psychology of the Unconscious*, trans. by B. M. Hinkle (London: Kegan, Trench, Trubner and Co., 1919), p. 39.

29. Jung, *Psychology and Religion*, p. 6.

30. C. G. Jung, *The Undiscovered Self*, trans. by R. F. C. Hull (Boston: Little, Brown and Company, 1958), pp. 19, 26.

31. C. G. Jung, *Two Essays in Analytical Psychology*, trans. by H. G. Baynes (London: Baillière, 1928), p. 70.

32. C. G. Jung, *Psychology and Religion: West and East*, Bollingen Series XI (New York: Pantheon Books, 1958), p. 273. Cf. also p. 88.

33. Hostie feels that Jung was forced by his scientific method to postulate the Self as the totality *within the psyche* (though at the same time beyond it) because this was the only way Jung could reconcile the observable effects of the attraction of the numinous upon man (the "religious attitude") with his empiricism which prohibited him from asserting anything about an unobservable in a realm beyond the subject. (Hostie, p. 145) For a different view, cf. Jacobi, *Individuation*, pp. 51-7, 108-9.

34. Jung, *Psychology and Religion: West and East*, p. 157.

35. *Ibid.*, p. 455. Hanna comments: "For Jung the experience of God was the impact of totality upon the soul." [*The Face of the Deep: The Re-*

ligious Ideas of C. G. Jung (Philadelphia: Westminster Press, 1967), p. 37.]
Cf. also Jung, *Psychology and Religion*, p. 75; Jacobi, *Individuation*, p. 56.

36. Jung, *Memories, Dreams, Reflections*, p. 69.

37. Jung, *Modern Man*, pp. 238-9; White, pp. 192-5.

38. Jung, *Psychology and Religion: West and East*, p. 74.

39. Jung, *The Undiscovered Self*, pp. 36-7.

40. Jung, *Psychology and Religion*, pp. 52-8.

41. C. G. Jung, *The Integration of the Personality*, trans. by S. Dell
(New York: Farrar and Rinehart, 1939), p. 60.

42. Jung, *The Undiscovered Self*, p. 21.

43. Jung, *Psychology and Religion*, pp. 113-14.

44. Rather than discuss the parallels which Jung finds between Christian
symbols and archetypal myth patterns, I prefer to present here some general
remarks of Jung on Christianity as a symbol system.

45. Jung, *The Undiscovered Self*, pp. 62-3.

46. *Ibid.*, pp. 73-77.

47. Jung, *Modern Man*, pp. 241-2.

48. *Ibid.*, p. 221.

49. *Ibid.*, p. 250.

50. Hostie, p. 160.

51. *Ibid.*

52. Hostie, pp. 131-5. Cf. a typical example of Jung's position at this
time: "The human intellect can never answer this question [of God's exis-
tence], and still less can it give any proof of God. . . . Our intellect has long
known that one cannot think god, much less conceive in what fashion he
really exists, if indeed at all." (*Two Essays*, p. 73)

53. Hostie, pp. 156-9.

54. C. G. Jung, *Psychology and Alchemy*, trans. by R. F. C. Hull,
Bollingen Series XII (New York: Pantheon Books, 1953), p. 14.

55. Letter dated 13 January 1948, cited in White, p. 261.

56. Jung, *Memories, Dreams, Reflections*, p. 325.

57. Hostie, pp. 86-7.

58. Jung, *Modern Man*, pp. 253-4.

59. White, pp. 248-9.

60. Jung, *West and East*, p. 261.

61. Jung, *The Undiscovered Self*, p. 86.

62. Jacobi, *Complex-Archetype-Symbol*, p. 124. Cf. also Jung, *Psyche
and Symbol*, p. 314.

SUGGESTED READINGS

Two excellent introductions to Jung's thought are: Frieda
Fordham's *An Introduction to Jung's Psychology* (Baltimore: Penguin Books, 1966, 3rd ed.), and Jolande Jacobi's *The Psychology
of C. G. Jung* (New Haven: Yale University Press, 1968, 7th ed.).

Both contain a short biography of Jung and a preface by him. The first is simpler; the second is more probing. The beginner might profit most from *Man and His Symbols,* edited and with an introduction by Jung (N.Y.: Dell, 1968, paperback), *Psychology and Religion* (New Haven: Yale University Press, 1938, paperback) and *The Undiscovered Self* (Boston: Little, Brown and Co., 1958, paperback). *Psyche and Symbol* (Garden City, N.Y.: Doubleday, 1958, paperback) is for the more advanced reader. *Answer to Job* (N.Y.: Meridian Books, 1954, paperback) reflects Jung's struggle with the Job experience, presented in the form of the psychological history of the God image.

Jung's autobiography is entitled *Memories, Dreams, Reflections* (N.Y.: Random House, 1961, paperback), recorded and edited by his secretary Aniela Jaffé. Whoever finds the autobiography too long should try Jaffé's *From the Life and Work of C. G. Jung* (N.Y.: Harper & Row, 1971, paperback), which is an absorbing discussion of Jung's interest in parapsychology, alchemy, synchronistic phenomena, and the personality traits of his last years. Jaffé's *The Myth of Meaning in the Work of C. G. Jung* (London: Hodder & Stoughton, 1970), besides giving a general treatment, adds to our knowledge of Jung's personal beliefs. He discusses with Erich Neumann, not whether there is a God, but whether God evolves. A most pleasant way to see Jung's use of the principle of synchronicity (a deep connection between psychical and physical phenomena is to read *Flying Saucers* (N.Y.: New American Library, 1959, paperback), although I doubt that this is the best way to study UFO sightings. Jung contrasts his work with Freud's in a chapter in *Modern Man in Search of a Soul* (N.Y.: Harcourt, Brace & World, 1933, paperback).

The Portable Jung (N.Y.: Viking Press, 1971, paperback), edited by Joseph Campbell, is a useful collection, and Jolande Jacobi's *C. G. Jung—Psychological Reflections* (N.Y.: Princeton University Press, 1972, 2nd ed., paperback) is an anthology edited according to themal headings. "Aggression and Religion: The Psychology and Theology of the Primitive Element in Man," by Morton T. Kelsey, *Religious Education,* May-June 1973, pp. 366-386, is a study of some major psychologists on the question, with an option for a Jungian solution. For further references, cf. chapter 5.

5 Reaction to Jung

MARTIN BUBER

Jung's thought has evoked much enthusiasm and much criticism. Some critics have felt that Jung's symbolical approach to religion is more dangerous to Christianity than Freud's negative stance. (Cf. e.g., E. Glover's *Freud or Jung?* N.Y.: Meridian Books, 1956). On the other hand, V. White, O.P., an early Catholic disciple of Jung, endeavored to show the positive contribution of Jung to Christian experience. (*God and the Unconscious.* Chicago: Regnery, 1953).

The selection below is from Martin Buber's *Eclipse of God* (1952).* Buber (1878-1965) insisted that in Jung's thought there is no relation of an I to a Thou. "This is, however, the way in which the unmistakably religious of all ages have understood their religion even if they longed most intensely to let their I be mystically absorbed into that Thou." Buber challenged Jung's methodology, and spoke prophetically for the absolute Thou (cf. his *I and Thou*) as well as for the social aspect of religion which he found missing in Jung.

In contrast to Heidegger and Sartre, Jung, the leading psychologist of our day, has made religion in its historical and biographical forms the subject of comprehensive observations. He is not to be blamed for including among these observations an abundance of phenomena which I must characterize as pseudo-religious. I characterize them so because they do not bear witness to an essential personal relation to One who is experienced or believed in as being absolutely over

* From pp. 104-106, 111-114, 116-120 in *Eclipse of God* (hardbound edition) by Martin Buber. Copyright, 1952 by Harper & Row, Publishers, Inc. Reprinted by permission of the publishers.

83

against one. Jung properly explains he does not wish to overstep the self-drawn boundaries of psychology. This psychology offers no criterion for a qualitative distinction between the two realms, the religious and the pseudo-religious, even as little as, say, sociology as Max Weber understood it enabled him to make a distinction in kind between the charisma of Moses and that of Hitler. What Jung is to be criticized for instead is that he oversteps with sovereign license the boundaries of psychology in its most essential point. For the most part, however, he does not note it and still less account for it.

There is certainly no lack in Jung of exact psychological statements concerning religious subjects. Many times these are even accompanied by explicit emphasis on the limited validity of the statement. An example is when [1] revelation, as "the disclosure of the depths of the human soul," is termed "to begin with a psychological mode . . . from which, of course, nothing is to be concluded about what it may otherwise be." Occasionally, moreover, he declares [2] on principle that "any statement about the transcendent" shall "be avoided," for such a statement is "always only a ridiculous presumption of the human mind which is unconscious of its boundaries." If God is called a state of the soul, that is "only a statement about the knowable and not about the unknowable, about which [here the formula which has just been cited is repeated word for word] simply nothing is to be concluded." Such sentences express the legitimate position of psychology, which is authorized, like every science, to make objectively based assertions so long as in doing so it takes care not to overstep its boundaries.

They have already been overstepped if it is said [3] of religion that it is "a living relation to psychical events which do not depend upon consciousness but instead take place on the other side of it in the darkness of the psychical hinterland." This definition of religion is stated without qualification. Nor will it tolerate any. For if religion is a relation to psychic events, which cannot mean anything other than to events of one's own soul, then it is implied by this that it is not a relation to a Being or Reality which, no matter how fully it may from time to time descend to the human soul, always remains transcendent to it. More precisely, it is not the relation of an I to a Thou. This is, however, the way in which the unmistakably religious of all ages have understood their religion even if they longed most intensely to let their I be mystically absorbed into that Thou. . . .

"Modern consciousness, in contrast to the nineteenth century, turns with its most intimate and intense expectations to the soul." "Modern consciousness abhors faith and also as a result the religions that are founded on it." Despite his early protest that one can find in his teaching no "barbs . . . against faith or trust in higher powers," [4] it is evident to any careful reader [5] that Jung identifies himself with the modern consciousness that "abhors" faith. According to Jung, this modern consciousness now turns itself with its "most intimate and intense expectations" to the soul. This cannot mean anything other than that it will have nothing more to do with the God believed in by religions, who is to be sure present to the soul, who reveals Himself to it, communicates with it, but remains transcendent to it in His being. Modern consciousness turns instead toward the soul as the only sphere which man can expect to harbour a divine. In short, although the new psychology protests [6] that it is "no world-view but a science," it no longer contents itself with the rôle of an interpreter of religion. It proclaims the new religion, the only one which can still be true, the religion of pure psychic immanence.

Jung speaks once,[7] and with right, of Freud's inability to understand religious experience. He himself concludes his wanderings through the grounds and abysses of religious experience, in which he has accomplished astounding feats, far outstripping all previous psychology, with the discovery that that which experiences the religious, the soul, experiences simply itself. Mystics of all ages, upon whom in fact Jung also rests his position, have proclaimed something similar; yet there are two distinctions which must be kept in mind. First, they meant by the soul which has this experience only that soul which has detached itself from all earthly bustle, from the contradictoriness of creaturely existence, and is therefore capable of apprehending the divine which is above contradictions and of letting the divine work in it. Second, they understood the experience as the oneness and becoming one of the soul with the self-contained God who, in order to enter into the reality of the world, "is born ever again in the soul.

In the place of that detachment of the whole man from the bustle of life, Jung sets the process of "individuation," determined by a detachment of the *consciousness*. In the place of that becoming one with the Self-contained, he sets the "Self," which is also, as is well known, an originally mystical concept. In Jung, however, it is no longer a genuinely mystical concept but is transformed instead into a Gnostic one. Jung himself expresses this turning toward the Gnostic. The statement quoted above that modern consciousness turns itself to the soul is followed by the explication, "and this . . . in the Gnostic sense." We have here, if only in the form of a mere allusion, the mature expression of a tendency characteristic of Jung from the beginning of his intellectual life. In a very early writing, which was printed but was not sold to the public, it appears in direct religious language as the profession of an eminent Gnostic god, in whom good and evil are bound together and, so to speak, balance each other. This union of opposites in an all-embracing total form runs since then throughout Jung's thought. It is also of essential significance for our consideration of his teaching of individuation and the self.

Jung has given a most precise expression to that which is in question here in one of his mandala-analyses. Mandalas, as Jung has found them, not only in different religious cultures, especially those of the Orient and of the early Christian Middle Ages, but also in the drawings of neurotics and the mentally disturbed, are circular symbolic images. He understands them as representations, arising in the collective unconscious, of a wholeness and completeness which is as such a unification of opposites. They are supposed to be "unifying symbols" which include the feminine as well as the masculine, evil as well as good in their self-contained unity. Their centre, the seat of the Godhead according to Jung's interpretation, is in general, he says, especially accentuated.

There are supposed to exist, however, a few ancient mandalas and many modern ones in whose centre "no trace of divinity is to be found." [8] The symbol which takes its place in the modern images is understood by the creators of these mandalas, according to Jung, as "a centre within themselves." "The place of the deity," Jung explains, "appears to be taken by the wholeness of man." This central wholeness, which symbolizes the divine, Jung, in agreement with ancient Indian teaching, calls the self. This does not mean, says Jung, that the self takes the place of the Godhead in these images in which the unconscious of modern man expresses itself. One would grasp Jung's idea better if one said that from now on the Godhead no longer takes the place of the human self as it did in mankind up till now. Man now draws back the projection of his self on a God outside of him without thereby wishing to deify himself (as Jung here emphasizes, in contrast to another passage, in which, as we shall see, deification is clearly stated as a goal). Man does not deny a transcendent God; he simply dispenses with Him. He no longer knows the Unrecognizable; he no longer needs to pretend to know Him. In His place he knows the soul or rather the self. It is indeed not a god that "modern consciousness" abhors, but faith. Whatever may be the case concerning God, the important thing for the man of modern consciousness is to stand in no further relation of faith to Him. . . .

But now, once again, what does it mean to set the soul in the place of the direction-giving and direction-preserving, the litigating and judging conscience? In the context of Jung's thought it cannot be understood in any other way than "in the Gnostic sense." The soul which is integrated in the Self as the unification in an all-encompassing wholeness of the opposites, especially of the opposites good and evil, dispenses with the conscience as the court which distinguishes and decides between the right and the wrong. It itself arbitrates an adjustment between the principles or effects the preservation of accord between them or their balancing out or whatever one may call it. This "way," which Jung certainly correctly qualifies as "narrow as a knife-edge," has not been described and obviously is not suitable to description. The question about it leads to the question about the positive function of evil.

Jung speaks somewhat more clearly in another place [9] of the condition necessary for "the birth of the 'pneumatic man.'" It is "liberation from those desires, ambitions and passions, which imprison us in the visible world," through "intelligent fulfillment of instinctive demands"; for "he who lives his instincts can also separate himself from them." The Taoist book that Jung interprets in this way does not contain this teaching; it is well known to us from certain Gnostic circles. [10]

The "process of development proper to the psyche" which Jung calls individuation leads through the integration in the consciousness of the personal and above all the collective, or archetypal, contents of the unconscious to the realization of a "new complete form" which, as has been said, he calls the self. Here a pause for clarification is necessary. Jung wishes [11] to see the self understood as "both that or those others and the I" and individuation as a process which "does not exclude, but rather includes the world." It is necessary to grasp exactly in what sense this holds good and in what it does not. In the personality structure which arises out of the "relatively rare occurrence" [12] of the development discussed by Jung, "the others" are indeed included. However, they are included only as contents of the individual soul that shall, just as an individual soul, attain its perfection through individuation.

The actual other who meets me meets me in such a way that my soul comes in contact with his as with something that it is not and that it cannot become. My soul does not and cannot include the other, and yet can nonetheless approach the other in this most real contact. This other, what is more, is and remains over against the self, no matter what completeness the self may attain, as the other. So the self, even if it has integrated all of its unconscious elements, remains this single self, confined within itself. All beings existing over against me who become "included" in my self are possessed by it in this inclusion as an It. Only then when, having become aware of the unincludable otherness of a being, I renounce all claim to incorporating it in any way within me or making it a part of my soul, does it truly become Thou for me. This holds good for God as for man.

This is certainly not a way which leads to the goal which Jung calls the self; but it is just as little a way to the removal of self. It simply leads to a genuine contact with the existing being who meets me, to full and direct reciprocity with him. It leads from the soul which places reality in itself to the soul which enters reality.

Jung thinks that his concept of the self is also found in Meister Eckhart. This is an error. Eckhart's teaching about the soul is based on the certainty of his belief that the soul is, to be sure, like God in freedom, but that it is created while He is uncreated.[13] This essential distinction underlies all that Eckhart has to say of the relationship and nearness between God and the soul.

Jung conceives of the self which is the goal of the process of individuation as the "bridal unification of opposite halves" [14] in the soul. This means above all, as has been said, the "integration of evil," [15] without which there can be no wholeness in the sense of this teaching. Individuation thereby realizes the complete archetype of the self, in contrast to which it is divided in the Christian symbolic into Christ and the Antichrist, representing its light and its dark aspects. In the self the two aspects are united. The self is thus a pure totality and as such "indistinguishable from a divine image"; self-realization is indeed to be described as "the incarnation of God." This god who unites good and evil in himself, whose opposites-nature also expresses itself in his male-femaleness,[16] is a Gnostic figure, which probably is to be traced back ultimately to the ancient Iranian divinity Zurvan (not mentioned, so far as I know, among Jung's numerous references to the history of religions) as that out of which the light god and his dark counterpart arose.

From the standpoint of this basic Gnostic view Jung recasts the Jewish and Christian conception of God. In the Old Testament the Satan, the "Hinderer," is only a serving element of God. God allows Himself to be represented by Satan, particularly for the purpose of "temptation," that is, in order to actualize man's uttermost power of decision through affliction and despair. Out of this God of the Old Testament Jung makes a demiurge who is himself half-Satanic.

NOTES

1. *Psychologie und Religion* (1942), 133. This passage is not in the English edition.
2. Wilhelm-Jung, *Das Geheimnis der goldenen Blüte* (1929), 73. Cf. Wilhelm-Jung, *The Secret of the Golden Flower,* translated by Cary F. Baynes (1935), p. 135.
3. Jung-Kerényi, *Einführung in das Wesen der Mythologie* (1941), 109. Cf. C. G. Jung and K. Kerényi, *Essays on a Science of Mythology* (1949), 102.
4. *Geheimnis,* 73. Cf. *The Secret of the Golden Flower,* 135.
5. Cf. especially the second part of the sentence cited above from "Seelenprobleme" 417: "Modern consciousness . . . wishes to *know,* i.e., to have primal experience" with the sentence contained in the same book (p. 83): "We moderns are directed to experience again the spirit, i.e., to make primal experience." Cf. *Modern Man,* 140.

6. *Ibid.*, 327. Cf. *Modern Man*, 217ff.
7. *Ibid.*, 77. Cf. *Modern Man*, 135.
8. *Religion*, 145ff. Cf. *Psychology and Religion*, 97ff.
9. *Geheimnis*, 61. Cf. *The Secret*, 80.
10. Cf. *Religion*, 139ff; *Psychology and Religion*, 94ff.
11. "Der Geist der Psychologie," 477.
12. *Ibid.*, 474.
13. "Since God alone is free and uncreated, he is like the soul in being free—but not in uncreatedness, for the soul is created." Sermon 13, Raymond Blakney, *Meister Eckhart, A Modern Translation* (1941), 159. For original cf. *Predigten*, ed. Quint, 13ff.
14. "Über das Selbst" (*Eranos-Jahrbuch*, 1948), 315. Cf. *Psychologie und Alchemie*, 61.
15. *Symbolik des Geistes* (1948), 385.
16. *Ibid.*, 410.

SUGGESTED READINGS

Buber's critique of Jung is found in *Eclipse of God* (N.Y.: Harper and Row, 1957 paperback edition) pp. 78-92 and 133-137. Maurice Friedman, a Buber scholar, has an incisive critique in *To Deny Our Nothingness* (N.Y.: Delta, 1967, paperback) pp. 146-167. On the positive side, see Frank Bockus, "The Archetypal Self: Theological Values in Jung's Psychology," in *The Dialogue Between Theology and Psychology,* edited by P. Homans (Chicago: University of Chicago Press, 1968) pp. 221-247; P. Homans' "Psychology and Hermeneutics: Jung's Contribution" and J. Singer's "Religion and the Collective Unconscious: Common Ground of Psychology and Religion," both in the journal *Zygon,* Dec. 1969, pp. 333-355, 315-332. Two valuable studies, both critical and sympathetic, are C. B. Hanna's *The Face of the Deep: The Religious Ideas of C. G. Jung* (Philadelphia: Westminster Press, 1967), and *Religion and the Psychology of C. G. Jung* by R. Hostie, S.J., (N.Y.: Sheed and Ward, 1957). On the question of "otherness" in Jung's thought, see the perceptive article by Ann B. Ulanov, "The Self as Other," *Journal of Religion and Health,* April 1973, pp. 140-168.

6 Humanistic Religion

ERICH FROMM

Erich Fromm (b. 1900) saw Freud as the one who opposed religion in the name of ethics, and Jung as the one who reduced religion to a psychological phenomenon and elevated the unconscious to a religious phenomenon (*Psychoanalysis and Religion,* p. 20). He felt that it is unfair to Freud to say he was "against" religion unless we define what aspects of religion he was critical of. Fromm works from a remark of Freud in which he criticizes people who think that someone is "deeply religious" merely for having a sense of man's insignificance or impotence in the face of the universe and not taking action to combat this powerlessness. Fromm believed that there is "no one without a religious need," but that there are lower and neurotic forms of religion, and man can free himself from the lower forms "only if he is capable of adopting a higher form of religion." Fromm reinterpreted Freud's Oedipus Complex in interpersonal rather than in sexual terms. The "incestuous craving" is not sexual but the much more profound desire to remain a child, to return to the womb. He defines religion as "any system of thought and action shared by a group which gives the individual a frame of orientation and an object of devotion." Fromm proposed an intra-worldly humanistic religion as opposed to authoritarian religion. Fromm's thought, here as well as elsewhere, closely resembles Ludwig Feuerbach's development of the notion of God as man's highest self.*

* Reprinted by permission of Yale University Press from *Psychoanalysis and Religion,* by Erich Fromm, pp. 34-38. Copyright © 1950 by Erich Fromm.

Can we trust religion to be the representative of religious needs or must we not separate these needs from organized, traditional religion in order to prevent the collapse of our moral structure?

In considering an answer to this question we must remember that no intelligent discussion of the problem is possible as long as we deal with religion in general instead of differentiating between various types of religion and religious experience. It would far transcend the scope of this chapter to attempt a review of all types of religion. Even to discuss only those types which are relevant from the psychological standpoint cannot be undertaken here. I shall therefore deal with only one distinction, but one which in my opinion is the most important, and which cuts across nontheistic and theistic religions: that between *authoritarian* and *humanistic* religions.

What is the principle of authoritarian religion? The definition of religion given in the *Oxford Dictionary,* while attempting to define religion as such, is a rather accurate definition of authoritarian religion. It reads: "[Religion is] recognition on the part of man of some higher unseen power as having control of his destiny, and as being entitled to obedience, reverence, and worship."

Here the emphasis is on the recognition that man is controlled by a higher power outside of himself. But this alone does not constitute authoritarian religion. What makes it so is the idea that this power, because of the control it exercises, is *entitled* to "obedience, reverence and worship." I italicize the word "entitled" because it shows that the reason for worship, obedience, and reverence lies not in the moral qualities of the deity, not in love or justice, but in the fact that it has control, that is, has power over man. Furthermore it shows that the higher power has a right to force man to worship him and that lack of reverence and obedience constitutes sin.

The essential element in authoritarian religion and in the authoritarian religious experience is the surrender to a power transcending man. The main virtue of this type of religion is obedience, its cardinal sin is disobedience. Just as the deity is conceived as omnipotent or omniscient, man is conceived as being powerless and insignificant. Only as he can gain grace or help from the deity by complete surrender can he feel strength. Submission to a powerful authority is one of the avenues by which man escapes from his feeling of aloneness and limitation. In the act of surrender he loses his independence and integrity as an individual but he gains the feeling of being protected by an awe-inspiring power of which, as it were, he becomes a part.

In Calvin's theology we find a vivid picture of authoritarian, theistic thinking. "For I do not call it humility," says Calvin, "if you suppose that we have anything left. . . . We cannot think of ourselves as we ought to think without utterly despising everything that may be supposed an excellence in us. This humility is unfeigned submission of a mind overwhelmed with a weighty sense of its own misery and poverty; for such is the uniform description of it in the word of God." [1]

The experience which Calvin describes here, that of despising everything in oneself, of the submission of the mind overwhelmed by its own poverty, is the very essence of all authoritarian religions whether they are couched in secular or in theological language.[2] In authoritarian religion God is a symbol of power and force, He is supreme because He has supreme power, and man in juxtaposition is utterly powerless.

Authoritarian secular religion follows the same principle. Here the Führer or the beloved "Father of His People" or the State or the Race or the Socialist Fatherland becomes the object of worship; the life of the individual becomes insignificant and man's worth consists in the very denial of his worth and strength. Frequently authoritarian religion postulates an ideal which is so abstract and so distant that it has hardly any connection with the real life of real people. To such ideals as "life after death" or "the future of mankind" the life and happiness of persons living here and now may be sacrificed; the alleged ends justify every means and become symbols in the names of which religious or secular "elites" control the lives of their fellow men.

Humanistic religion, on the contrary, is centered around man and his strength. Man must develop his power of reason in order to understand himself, his relationship to his fellow men and his position in the universe. He must recognize the truth, both with regard to his limitations and his potentialities. He must develop his powers of love for others as well as for himself and experience the solidarity of all living beings. He must have principles and norms to guide him in this aim. Religious experience in this kind of religion is the experience of oneness with the All, based on one's relatedness to the world as it is grasped with thought and with love. Man's aim in humanistic religion is to achieve the greatest strength, not the greatest powerlessness; virtue is self-realization, not obedience. Faith is certainty of conviction based on one's experience of thought and feeling, not assent to propositions on credit of the proposer. The prevailing mood is that of joy, while the prevailing mood in authoritarian religion is that of sorrow and of guilt.

Inasmuch as humanistic religions are theistic, God is a symbol of *man's own powers* which he tries to realize in his life, and is not a symbol of force and domination, having *power over man.*

Illustrations of humanistic religions are early Buddhism, Taoism, the teachings of Isaiah, Jesus, Socrates, Spinoza, certain trends in the Jewish and Christian religions (particularly mysticism), the religion of Reason of the French Revolution. It is evident from these that the distinction between authoritarian and humanistic religion cuts across the distinction between theistic and nontheistic, and between religions in the narrow sense of the word and philosophical systems of religious character. What matters in all such systems is not the thought system as such but the human attitude underlying their doctrines.

NOTES

1. Johannes Calvin, *Institutes of the Christian Religion* (Presbyterian Board of Christian Education, 1928), p. 681.
2. See Erich Fromm, *Escape from Freedom* (Farrar & Rinehart, 1941), pp. 141ff. This attitude toward authority is described there in detail.

SUGGESTED READINGS

The best introduction is Fromm's *Psychoanalysis and Religion* (New Haven: Yale University Press, 1950, paperback). Much interesting material which might be related to the previously mentioned "oceanic experience" is found in *Zen Buddhism and Psychoanalysis*, by D. T. Suzuki, E. Fromm and R. De Martino (N.Y.: Harper and Row, 1960, paperback). A helpful contrast with some of Freud's ideas on love, as for example in *Civilization and Its Discontents* (pp. 56ff, 90ff), is found in Fromm's *The Art of Loving* (N.Y.: Bantam Books, 1963, paperback).

A Christian theological critique of Fromm is found in J. Stanley Glenn's *Erich Fromm: A Protestant Critique* (Philadelphia: Westminster Press, 1966). Glenn is particularly helpful in his critique of Fromm's use of "the Feuerbachian formula" and of Calvin's thought. John H. Schaar's *Escape From Authority—The Perspectives of Erich Fromm* (N.Y.: Harper and Row, 1961, paperback) is a more general criticism of Fromm. Some other works of Fromm which pertain to the area of psychology and religion are: *The Dogma of Christ—And Other Essays on Religion, Psychology, and Culture* (Garden City, N.Y.: Doubleday, 1966, paperback); *Man for Himself—An Inquiry into the Psychology of Ethics* (Greenwich, Conn.: Fawcett Publications, 1947, paperback); *The Heart of Man* (N.Y.: Harper and Row, 1964, paperback) which studies man's destructiveness and narcissism; *You Shall Be as Gods—A Radical Interpretation of the Old Testament and Its Tradition* (N.Y.: Holt, Rinehart and Winston, 1966, paperback). A comparison of the thought of Fromm and Paul Tillich is found in Guyton Hammond, *Man in Estrangement* (Nashville: Vanderbilt University Press, 1965). *Erich Fromm* by Don Hausdorff (N.Y.: Twayne Publishers, 1972) contains a useful annotated bibliography of works on Fromm as well as a good synthesis of his thought.

7 Religion and Peak Experience

ABRAHAM MASLOW

Abraham Maslow (1908-1970) believed that psychological theory had centered to such a degree on neurotic experience that it had missed the insights to be gained from studying "healthy" people. The most intense of these experiences he called peak experiences and he found them similar to what has been called religious experience. These experiences are described in the following excerpt.* Maslow held that the higher experiences and values like love were "instinctoid," that is, they are real needs of the human organism. He said that "neurosis seemed to be in its essence a deficiency disease of the same sort that the nutritionists were discovering" with regard to vitamin B_{12} (*The Psychology of Science,* Chicago: Regnery, 1966, p. 124). He uses the letter B as shorthand for Being, e.g., B—values, and the letter D, for Deficiency, e.g., D—love which is "deficiency-love" or selfish love.

It has been discovered that this same kind of subjective experiential response (which has been thought to be triggered only in religious or mystical contexts, and which has, therefore, been considered to be only religious or mystical) is also triggered by many other stimuli or situations, e.g., experiences of the aesthetic, of the creative, of love, of sex, of insight, etc. If we insist on calling the peak-experience a religious experience, then we must say that religious experiences can be pro-

* From *"Religions, Values, and Peak Experiences"* by Abraham H. Maslow, The Kappa Delta Pi Lecture Series, pp. xi-xiv, 59-68. Copyright 1964 by Kappa Delta Pi. Reprinted with permission of Kappa Delta Pi, an Honor Society in Education.

duced by sexual love, or by philosophical insight, or by athletic success, or by watching a dance performance, or by bearing a child. This inevitably means, as James and Dewey both saw, that we must take the word "religious" out of its narrow context of the supernatural, churches, rituals, dogmas, professional clergymen, etc., and distribute it in principle throughout the whole of life. Religion becomes then not one social institution among others, not one department of life distinct from others, but rather a state of mind achievable in almost any activity of life, if this activity is raised to a suitable level of perfection.

Peak-experiences, as I have defined them for this analysis, are secularized religious or mystical or transcendent experiences; or, more precisely, peak-experiences are the raw materials out of which not only religions can be built but also philosophies of any kind: educational, political, aesthetic, etc. Not only are these experiences not dependent on churches or specific religions, as James and Dewey saw, they do not necessarily imply any supernatural concepts. They are well within the realm of nature, and can be investigated and discussed in an entirely naturalistic way. . . .

This thesis that religious experiences are natural experiences could be seen by churchmen with dismay, as simply and only a further instance of science carving another chunk out of the side of organized religion—which, of course, it is. But it is also possible for a more perceptively religious man to greet this development with enthusiasm, when he realizes that what the mystics have said to be essential to the *individual's* religion is now receiving empirical support and no longer needs rest only on tradition, blind faith, temporal power, exhortation, etc. If this development is a secularizing of all religion, it is also a religionizing of all that is secular. This lecture is a critique, not only of traditional, conventional religion, but also of traditional and conventional atheism. As a matter of fact, I am addressing myself much more to the latter than to the former. Religion is easy to criticize but difficult to explain. It begins to be clear to me that in throwing out *all* of religion and everything to do with it, the atheists have thrown out too much. Also, religion has been "reduced" too much, e.g., by Freud, by Feuerbach, etc. Undoubtedly correct to a large extent, yet they went too far in their generalizations and, in any case, were, I think, attacking organized religions more than private, transcendent experiences. (See also Allport on "growth-religion" vs "safety-religion.") [1] Also, it is clear that they didn't realize, as we do today, how deep and possibly even "instinctoid" is the need for a framework of values (Fromm), for meaning (Frankl), for understanding (Maslow). Nor did they anticipate that a psychology of ends (an ontopsychology, a psychology of Being) could become possible, offering us in the distance not too far ahead the possibility of a "scientific" or objective value system. (In a fuller treatment I would also bring up the possibility of a "need for transcendence" beyond the need for understanding, as Fromm has.) . . .

RELIGIOUS ASPECTS OF PEAK-EXPERIENCES

Practically everything that happens in the peak-experiences, naturalistic though they are, could be listed under the headings of religious happenings, or indeed have been in the past considered to be only religious experiences.

1. For instance, it is quite characteristic in peak-experiences that the whole universe is perceived as an integrated and unified whole. This is not as simple a happening as one might imagine from the bare words themselves. To have a clear perception (rather than a purely abstract and verbal philosophical acceptance) that the universe is all of a piece and that one has his place in it—one is a part of it, one belongs in it—can be so profound and shaking an experience that it can change the person's character and his Weltanschauung forever after. In my own experience I have two subjects who, because of such an experience, were totally, immediately, and permanently cured of (in one case) chronic anxiety neurosis and, in the other case, of strong obsessional thoughts of suicide.

This, of course, is a basic meaning of religious faith for many people. People who might otherwise lose their "faith" will hang onto it because it gives a meaningfulness to the universe, a unity, a single philosophical explanation which makes it all hang together. Many orthodoxly religious people would be so frightened by giving up the notion that the universe has integration, unity, and, therefore, meaningfulness (which is given to it by the fact that it was all created by God or ruled by God or *is* God) that the only alternative for them would be to see the universe as a totally unintegrated chaos.

2. In the cognition that comes in peak-experiences, characteristically the percept is exclusively and fully attended to. That is, there is tremendous concentration of a kind which does not normally occur. There is the truest and most total kind of visual perceiving or listening or feeling. Part of what this involves is a peculiar change which can best be described as non-evaluating, non-comparing, or non-judging cognition. That is to say, figure and ground are less sharply differentiated. Important and unimportant are also less sharply differentiated, i.e., there is a tendency for things to become equally important rather than to be ranged in a hierarchy from very important to quite unimportant. For instance, the mother examining in loving ecstasy her new-born infant may be enthralled by every single part of him, one part as much as another one, one little toenail as much as another little toenail, and be struck into a kind of religious awe in this way. This same kind of total, non-comparing acceptance of everything, as if everything were equally important, holds also for the perception of people. Thus it comes about that in peak-experience cognition a person is most easily seen per se, in himself, by himself, uniquely and idiosyncratically as if he were the sole member of his class. Of course, this is a very common aspect not only of religious experience but of most theologies as well, i.e., the person is unique, the person is sacred, one person in principle is worth as much as any other person, everyone is a child of God, etc.

3. The cognition of being (B-cognition) that occurs in peak-experiences tends to perceive external objects, the world, and individual people as more detached from human concerns. Normally we perceive everything as relevant to human concerns and more particularly to our own private selfish concerns. In the peak-experiences, we become more detached, more objective, and are more able to perceive the world as if it were independent not only of the perceiver but even of human beings in general. The perceiver can more readily look upon nature as if it were there in itself and for itself, not simply as if it were a human playground put there for human purposes. He can more easily refrain from projecting human purposes upon it. In a word, he can see it in its own Being (as an end in itself) rather than as something to be used or something to be

afraid of or something to wish for or to be reacted to in some other personal, human, self-centered way. That is to say, B-cognition, because it makes human irrelevance more possible, enables us thereby to see more truly the nature of the object in itself. This is a little like talking about god-like perception, superhuman perception. The peak-experience seems to lift us to greater than normal heights so that we can see and perceive in a higher than usual way. We become larger, greater, stronger, bigger, taller people and tend to perceive accordingly.

4. To say this in a different way, perception in the peak-experiences can be relatively ego-transcending, self-forgetful, ego-less, unselfish. It can come closer to being unmotivated, impersonal, desireless, detached, not needing or wishing. Which is to say, that it becomes more object-centered than ego-centered. The perceptual experience can be more organized around the object itself as a centering point rather than being based upon the selfish ego. This means in turn that objects and people are more readily perceived as having independent reality of their own.

5. The peak-experience is felt as a self-validating, self-justifying moment which carries its own intrinsic value with it. It is felt to be a highly valuable—even uniquely valuable—experience, so great an experience sometimes that even to attempt to justify it takes away from its dignity and worth. As a matter of fact, so many people find this so great and high an experience that it justifies not only itself but even living itself. Peak-experiences can make life worthwhile by their occasional occurrence. They give meaning to life itself. They prove it to be worthwhile. To say this in a negative way, I would guess that peak-experiences help to prevent suicide.

6. Recognizing these experiences as end-experiences rather than as means-experiences makes another point. For one thing, it proves to the experiencer that there are ends in the world, that there are things or objects or experiences to yearn for which are worthwhile in themselves. This in itself is a refutation of the proposition that life and living is meaningless. In other words, peak-experiences are one part of the operational definition of the statement that "life is worthwhile" or "life is meaningful."

7. In the peak-experience there is a very characteristic disorientation in time and space, or even the lack of consciousness of

time and space. Phrased, positively, this is like experiencing universality and eternity. Certainly we have here, in a very operational sense, a real and scientific meaning of "under the aspect of eternity." This kind of timelessness and spacelessness contrasts very sharply with normal experience. The person in the peak-experiences may feel a day passing as if it were minutes or also a minute so intensely lived that it might feel like a day or a year or an eternity even. He may also lose his consciousness of being located in a particular place.

8. The world seen in the peak-experiences is seen only as beautiful, good, desirable, worthwhile, etc. and is never experienced as evil or undesirable. The world is accepted. People will say that then they understand it. Most important of all for comparison with religious thinking is that somehow they become reconciled to evil. Evil itself is accepted and understood and seen in its proper place in the whole, as belonging there, as unavoidable, as necessary, and, therefore, as proper. Of course, the way in which I (and Laski also) gathered peak-experiences was by asking for reports of ecstasies and raptures, of the most blissful and perfect moments of life. Then, of course, life *would* look beautiful. And then all the foregoing might seem like discovering something that had been put in a priori. But observe that what I am talking about is the perception of evil, of pain, of disease, of death. In the peak-experiences, not only is the world seen as acceptable and beautiful, but, and this is what I am stressing, the bad things about life are accepted more totally than they are at other times. It is as if the peak-experience reconciled people to the presence of evil in the world.

9. Of course, this is another way of becoming "god-like." The gods who can contemplate and encompass the whole of being and who, therefore, understand it must see it as good, just, inevitable, and must see "evil" as a product of limited or selfish vision and understanding. If we could be god-like in this sense, then we, too, out of universal understanding would never blame or condemn or be disappointed or shocked. Our only possible emotions would be pity, charity, kindliness, perhaps sadness or amusement. But this is precisely the way in which self-actualizing people do at times react to the world, and in which all of us react in our peak-experiences.

10. Perhaps my most important finding was the discovery of

what I am calling B-values or the intrinsic values of Being. (See Appendix G.) When I asked the question, "How does the world look different in peak-experiences?", the hundreds of answers that I got could be boiled down to a quintessential list of characteristics which, though they overlap very much with one another can still be considered as separate for the sake of research. What is important for us in this context is that this list of the described characteristics of the world as it is perceived in our most perspicuous moments is about the same as what people through the ages have called eternal verities, or the spiritual values, or the highest values, or the religious values. What this says is that facts and values are not totally different from each other; under certain circumstances, they fuse. Most religions have either explicitly or by implication affirmed some relationship or even an overlapping or fusion between facts and values. For instance, people not only existed but they were also sacred. The world was not only merely existent but it was also sacred.

11. B-cognition in the peak-experience is much more passive and receptive, much more humble, than normal perception is. It is much more ready to listen and much more able to hear.

12. In the peak-experience, such emotions as wonder, awe, reverence, humility, surrender, and even worship before the greatness of the experience are often reported. This may go so far as to involve thoughts of death in a peculiar way. Peak-experiences can be so wonderful that they can parallel the experience of dying, that is of an eager and happy dying. It is a kind of reconciliation and acceptance of death. Scientists have never considered as a scientific problem the question of the "good death"; but here in these experiences, we discover a parallel to what has been considered to be the religious attitude toward death, i.e., humility or dignity before it, willingness to accept it, possibly even a happiness with it.

13. In peak-experiences, the dichotomies, polarities, and conflicts of life tend to be transcended or resolved. That is to say, there tends to be a moving toward the perception of unity and integration in the world. The person himself tends to move toward fusion, integration, and unity and away from splitting, conflicts, and oppositions.

14. In the peak-experiences, there tends to be a loss, even though transient, of fear, anxiety, inhibition, of defense and con-

trol, of perplexity, confusion, conflict, of delay and restraint. The profound fear of disintegration, of insanity, of death, all tend to disappear for the moment. Perhaps this amounts to saying that fear disappears.

15. Peak-experiences sometimes have immediate effects or aftereffects upon the person. Sometimes their aftereffects are so profound and so great as to remind us of the profound religious conversions which forever after changed the person. Lesser effects could be called therapeutic. These can range from very great to minimal or even to no effects at all. This is an easy concept for religious people to accept, accustomed as they are to thinking in terms of conversions, of great illuminations, of great moments of insight, etc.

16. I have likened the peak-experience in a metaphor to a visit to a personally defined heaven from which the person then returns to earth. This is like giving a naturalistic meaning to the concept of heaven. Of course, it is quite different from the conception of heaven as a place somewhere into which one physically steps after life on this earth is over. The conception of heaven that emerges from the peak-experiences is one which exists all the time all around us, always available to step into for a little while at least.

17. In peak-experiences, there is a tendency to move more closely to a perfect identity, or uniqueness, or to the idiosyncracy of the person or to his real self, to have become more a real person.

18. The person feels himself more than at other times to be responsible, active, the creative center of his own activities and of his own perceptions, more self-determined, more a free agent, with more "free will" than at other times.

19. But it has also been discovered that precisely those persons who have the clearest and strongest identity are exactly the ones who are most able to transcend the ego or the self and to become selfless, who are at least relatively selfless and relatively egoless.

20. The peak-experiencer becomes more loving and more accepting, and so he becomes more spontaneous and honest and innocent.

21. He becomes less an object, less a thing, less a thing of the world living under the laws of the physical world, and he becomes more a psyche, more a person, more subject to the psychological

laws, especially the laws of what people have called the "higher life."

22. Because he becomes more unmotivated, that is to say, closer to non-striving, non-needing, non-wishing, he asks less for himself in such moments. He is less selfish. (We must remember that the gods have been considered generally to have no needs or wants, no deficiencies, no lacks, and to be gratified in all things. In this sense, the unmotivated human being becomes more god-like.)

23. People during and after peak-experiences characteristically feel lucky, fortunate, graced. A common reaction is "I don't deserve this." A common consequence is a feeling of gratitude, in religious persons, to their God, in others, to fate or to nature or to just good fortune. It is interesting in the present context that this can go over into worship, giving thanks, adoring, giving praise, oblation, and other reactions which fit very easily into orthodox religious frameworks. In that context we are accustomed to this sort of thing—that is, to the feeling of gratitude or all-embracing love for everybody and for everything, leading to an impulse to do something good for the world, an eagerness to repay, even a sense of obligation and dedication.

24. The dichotomy or polarity between humility and pride tends to be resolved in the peak-experiences and also in self-actualizing persons. Such people resolve the dichotomy between pride and humility by fusing them into a single complex superordinate unity, that is by being proud (in a certain sense) and also humble (in a certain sense). Pride (fused with humility) is not hubris nor is it paranoia; humility (fused with pride) is not masochism.

25. What has been called the "unitive consciousness" is often given in peak-experiences, i.e., a sense of the sacred glimpsed *in* and *through* the particular instance of the momentary, the secular, the worldly.

NOTE

1. Gordon Alport, *The Individual and His Religion* (N.Y.: Macmillan Co., 1950, paperback).

SUGGESTED READINGS

Religions, Values, and Peak Experiences (N.Y.: The Viking Press, 1970, 2nd ed., paperback) is the simplest introduction, although it by no means gives a full view of Maslow's thought. The second edition has an important preface. In this, Maslow added some correctives to a possible overemphasis on peak experiences. Seeking peak experiences, he wrote, may cause one to turn from the world, to use others as triggers for peak experiences, to become selfish, anti-rational, anti-empirical, anti-verbal. Consistently seeking peak experiences might bring about the need to escalate triggers, through drugs for example. It might cause one to rely too heavily on inner voice experiences, to lose sight of the sacred in the ordinary, to become individualistic and lose sight of the value of organizations and communities. Lastly, Maslow said he also would see more value now in nadir experiences and "plateau" experiences. The latter are more cognitive and more casual, arising perhaps out of a personal philosophy.

The same ideas appear in an appendix in *The Farther Reaches of Human Nature* (N.Y.: The Viking Press, 1972, paperback), a posthumous collection of essays. In this work he also discusses the many varied forms of transcendence, e.g., to transcend being a child by becoming father and mother to oneself, to transcend one's own will, to transcend to cosmic consciousness in which one feels part of the world family, with a sense of belonging rather than of being a world orphan. He also contrasts active, healthy people whom he calls "self-transcending actualizers" with peaking transcenders. *Toward a Psychology of Being* (N.Y.: D. Van Nostrand, 1968, 2nd ed., paperback) presents Maslow's basic theory, together with *Motivation and Personality* (N.Y.: Harper and Row, 1970, 2nd ed.). The reader might be particularly interested in chapter 8 of the latter book, which has interesting material on higher and lower needs. *The Psychology of Science* (Chicago: Regnery, 1969, paperback) has many pertinent chapters, especially chapter 14 on the resacralization of science.

Frank Goble's *The Third Force* (N.Y.: Pocket Books, 1971, paperback) is a good synthetic survey which also links Maslow with other "third force" movements, that is those which are neither exclusively Freudian nor "experimentalistic-positivistic-behavioristic." Colin Wilson's *New Pathways in Psychology* (N.Y.: Taplinger Publishing Co., 1972, paperback) links Maslow's thought to the history of psychology and contains interesting biographical material.

At one time, Viktor Frankl was critical of "self-actualization" for making what is a by-product into an end. (Cf. *Psychotherapy and Existentialism,* N.Y.: Simon and Schuster, 1967, paperback.) There is an interesting exchange between Frankl and Maslow in *Readings in Humanistic Psychology* (N.Y.: The Free Press, 1969), edited by A. Sutich and M. Vich, chapters 5 and 6. Finally, one might spend a most pleasant hour listening to Maslow's voice on tape, "The Psychology of Religious Awareness," Big Sur Recordings, San Rafael, Calif.

8 Religion and Mind-Expanding Drugs

WALTER N. PAHNKE, WILLIAM A. RICHARDS
AND HUSTON SMITH

Peak experience or self-transcending consciousness is a value, whether viewed religiously or psychologically. Therefore, it is of interest that many researchers now claim to have achieved, in some specially prepared subjects, a kind of self-transcending consciousness through the use of psychedelic or mind-expanding drugs. Compare, for example, the similarities between Maslow's peak experiences and the qualities listed below by Walter N. Pahnke and William A. Richards in their essay, "Implications of LSD and Experimental Mysticism." * The second excerpt is from the conclusion of an article by Huston Smith, "Do Drugs Have Religious Import?" ** Dr. Smith here makes some distinctions which are helpful in evaluating the relationship between religion and the effects of mind-expanding drugs.

Walter N. Pahnke, M.D. (1930-1971), was the Director of Clinical Sciences Research at the Maryland State Psychiatric Research Center in Baltimore. William A. Richards, S.T.M., received his B.D. degree in teaching and research in religion from Yale Divinity School in 1965, and spent a year in Göttingen, Germany, working on the relationship be-

* From "Implications of LSD and Experimental Mysticism," by Walter N. Pahnke and William A. Richards. Reprinted with permission of the editors of *Theology Digest*, from Vol. XVI, No. 1, Spring 1968, pp. 54-58 (originally published in full in *Journal of Religion and Health* 5, 1966, pp. 175-208, with extensive bibliography).

** From "Do Drugs Have Religious Import?," *The Journal of Philosophy*, Vol. LXI, No. 18, October 1, 1964, pp. 517-530, excerpt from pp. 529-530; reprinted with the permission of the editors and of the author.

tween theology, psychedelics and psychiatry. Dr. Huston Smith, Professor of Philosophy at Massachusetts Institute of Technology, is a specialist in comparative religions. He has published extensively in this area and is perhaps best known for his work, *The Religions of Man.*

In a culture already saturated with drug usage, it is worth noting that there are dangers involved in drug experimentation, in some cases possibly even danger of genetic damage. However, the following presentations center on the results of controlled experimentation and their potentiality for deepening our understanding of religion.

Mirrored in the sensationalistic array of recent articles focusing upon the uses of drugs like LSD is a blurred spectrum of attitudes, ranging from an indignant desire to destroy a terrifying plague of drug-induced psychoses, to a naive belief that the keys to Utopia have finally been placed into the hands of man. In the light of this controversy, the need soberly to consider the potential dangers and values inherent in this field of research from theological, psychiatric, and societal perspectives has become crucial. The special class of drugs in question, including lysergic acid diethylamide (LSD), psilocybin, and mescaline, to name the major examples, are often termed *psycholytic* (mind-releasing) in Europe and *psychedelic* (mind-opening) in the United States. These drugs are not narcotics, sedatives, or energizers, but have the unique effect on the human psyche of bringing into awareness forms of consciousness that are usually hidden or unconscious.

At the outset it must be stated that the statistics of the first major attempts at controlled experimentation in this field are still being compiled; none of the proposed uses of these drugs can at present be supported by conclusive empirical data. The hopes that constructive uses of these drugs may be validated empirically, however, are reflected in the formation of such groups as the International Association for Psychodelytic Therapy.

Mystical Consciousness

The form of psychedelic experience here called *mystical consciousness,* for want of a better term, can best be described as a dimension of experience that, when expressed on paper by an experimental subject and subsequently content-analyzed, corresponds to nine interrelated categories. These categories were derived from a historical survey of the literature of spontaneous mysticism, including the commentaries of scholars such as William James and W. T. Stace. As Stace has emphasized, such categories attempt to describe the core of a universal psychological experience. The ontological status of such descriptions may be debated.

1. *Unity.* Experience of an undifferentiated unity, we suggest, is the hallmark of mystical consciousness. Such unity may be either *internal* or *external.* Both forms of unity are known to occur within the same person, even in the same psychedelic session.

Internal unity reportedly occurs in the following manner: Awareness of all normal sense impressions (visual, auditory, cutaneous, olfactory, gustatory, and kinesthetic) ceases, and the empirical ego (i.e. the usual sense of individuality) seems to fade away, while pure consciousness of what is being experienced paradoxically remains and seems to expand as a vast inner world is encountered. Internal unity occurs when consciousness merges with a "ground of being," beyond all empirical distinctions.

In contrast, external unity generally seems to occur as follows: Awareness of one or more particular sense impressions grows in intensity until suddenly the object of perception and the empirical ego simultaneously seem to cease to exist as separate entities, while consciousness seems to transcend subject and object and become impregnated by a profound sense of unity, accompanied by the insight that is ultimately "all is One."

2. *Objectivity and Reality.* Intrinsic to this second category are two interrelated elements: (1) insightful knowledge about being in general that is felt at an intuitive, nonrational level and gained by direct experience, and (2) the authoritativeness or the certainty for the experiencer that such knowledge is ultimately real, in contrast to the feeling that the experience is a subjective delusion.

3. *Transcendence of Space and Time.* This category refers on one hand to the loss of a person's orientation as to where he is during the experience, and on the other hand to a radical change in perspective in which he suddenly feels as though he is outside of time. However, one may feel that he can look back upon the totality of history from this transcendent perspective.

4. *Sense of Sacredness.* Sacredness is here defined as a non-rational, intuitive response in the presence of inspiring realities. An acute awareness of finitude is reported, as though one had stood before the Infinite in profound humility.

5. *Deeply-Felt Positive Mood.* This category focuses upon the feelings of joy, love, blessedness, and peace inherent in mystical consciousness. Joy may be exuberant or quiet. Love may vary in intensity, though it is generally dissociated from any excitation of the sexual organs. Peace entails a conviction that ultimately there is no ground for anxiety.

6. *Paradoxicality.* This category reflects the manner in which significant aspects of mystical consciousness are felt by the experiencer to be true in spite of the fact that they violate the laws of Aristotelian logic. For example, he may claim to have experienced an empty unity that at the same time contains all reality.

7. *Alleged Ineffability.* When a subject attempts to communicate mystical consciousness verbally to another person, he usually claims that the available linguistic symbols—if not the structure of language itself—are inadequate to contain or even accurately reflect such experience.

8. *Transiency.* This refers to the temporary duration of mystical consciousness in contrast to the relative permanence of the level of usual experience. This characteristic marks one of the important differences between it and psychosis.

9. *Positive Changes in Attitude and/or Behavior.* Persons who have experienced the contents of the eight categories discussed above are also known to report concomitant changes in

attitudes (1) toward themselves, (2) toward others, (3) toward life, and (4) toward mystical consciousness itself. The duration and permanence of such changes and the extent to which they are manifested in everyday existence are topics in need of research.

Nonmystical States Seen

Many experimental subjects, who have only seen visionary imagery and felt powerful emotions, may be understood to have had nonmystical experiences of an aesthetic, cognitive, psychodynamic, or psychotic nature. In these forms, the empirical ego generally exists as the subject viewing objects of a visionary nature, or pondering objects of a cognitive nature; only in mystical consciousness and some psychotic reactions is the subject-object dichotomy transcended and the empirical ego extinguished.

Aesthetic Phenomena. One of the first effects noted by many subjects is a change in spatial perception. As other changes in the nervous system occur, a person is likely to become increasingly sensitive to color and to form. Also, one frequently sees geometric patterns of multi-colored abstract lines that are visionary in nature. If music is being played, synesthesia often develops. The pattern thus seems to flow with the music, even changing color at appropriate places.

If the experience progresses beyond this level, one may seem to *go through* the pattern towards mystical consciousness, experience more definite psychoanalytic imagery and feelings, or enter states of more profound aesthetic imagery.

Psychodynamic Phenomena. One of the clearest forms of psychoanalytic experience is actual regression to infancy or early childhood. Another type of experience that may be strongly therapeutic involves the unexpected confrontation of guilt. Without competent psychiatric supervision, such experiences may, at best, remain frightening memories and, at worst, cause a person to decompensate under the stress.

Psychotic Phenomena. Here we reserve the term "psychotic" for experiences of paranoia, of panic, or of extreme disorientation and confusion. If nonpsychotic experiences are desired, subjects must be prepared, must feel secure in a friendly environment, and above all must be willing and able to trust reality greater than themselves.

Cognitive Phenomena. There is a form of psychedelic experience when one feels capable of thinking unusually sharply, quickly, and clearly. One often feels acutely sensitive to the meaning of words and to very fine differentiations between similar words. Chain reactions of associations and inferences may occur.

Other Phenomena Noted

Miscellaneous Phenomena. Photic phenomena are often reported by persons who experience mystical consciousness, usually in the sense of seeing a brilliant white light. *Electrical phenomena* occur fairly frequently as subjects seem to become aware of the flow of electrical energy in their bodies. *Psychosomatic phenomena* such as nausea, rapid heartbeat, clammy coldness, or contractions of the stomach occasionally occur. Some *parapsychological phenomena* of a telepathic, clairvoyant, or precognitive nature have been reported, but none have been conclusively validated at this stage of research. *Phenomena of somatic change* occur as people experience changes in kinesthetic and cutaneous reception. There are experiences of *altered perceptions of time* that do not entail the mystical transcendence of time. Finally, unusually acute consciousness of bodily processes may occur.

Religious Implications

The claim that spontaneous mystical experiences are similar to, if not identical with, psychedelic experiences of drug-facilitated mystical consciousness has caused considerable apprehension and dismay among some religious professionals, and the possible therapeutic potential of experiences of mystical consciousness has been somewhat embarrassing to those therapists who pride themselves on their scientific objectivity and lack of religious involvement. Whether or not the mystical experience is "religious" is naturally dependent upon one's definition of "religion," and to raise this point only confuses the issue, although such experiences may well have religious implications.

Pahnke in 1962 designed and executed a controlled, double-blind experiment to investigate the relationship between the experiences recorded in the literature of spontaneous mysticism and those reportedly associated with the ingestion of psychedelic drugs. Twenty subjects were chosen for the experiment, all graduate-student volunteers with middle class Protestant backgrounds from one denominational seminary, none of whom had ever taken any of the psychedelic drugs prior to the experiment. No mention was made of the characteristics of the typology of mystical consciousness.

Ninety minutes before a Good Friday service, capsules identical in appearance were administered, half containing thirty milligrams of psilocybin and half containing two hundred milligrams of nicotinic acid, a vitamin that causes feelings of warmth and tingling of the skin but has no effect upon the mind. Because double-blind technique was employed, neither the experimenter nor any of the participants knew the contents of any given capsule.

When the data from (1) a post-drug questionnaire, (2) a six-month followup questionnaire, and (3) the content-analysis of the written accounts were analyzed, the conclusion was drawn that, under the conditions of this experiment, those subjects who received psilocybin experienced phenomena that were apparently indistinguishable from, if not identical with, certain categories defined by the typology of mystical consciousness.

On the basis of the research findings discussed above, it now appears possible to select almost any normal, healthy person and, combining a sufficient dose of a psychedelic substance with a supportive set and setting, enable that person to experience various forms of consciousness.

Mysticism Studied

The mystical experience seems the most difficult to facilitate, perhaps because of the yet undetermined roles of personality variables; but nonetheless, these phenomena are now sufficiently reproducible to allow mysticism to be studied under laboratory conditions.

The medieval monk in his darkened cell and the hermit in the recesses of his cave, for example, used not psychedelic substances, but the tools of sensory deprivation, sleep deprivation, meditative disciplines, and fasting to elicit biochemical changes and unlock the door to unconscious levels of the mind. The Hindu yoga uses similar methods in addition to autohypnosis and breath control. It would appear logical to suggest that whenever altered forms of consciousness occur, whether they are anticipated or come as a complete surprise, underlying biochemical activity may be involved.

By no means is positive mystical experience with the psychedelic drugs automatic. It would seem that this specific "drug effect" is a delicate combination of psychological set and setting in which the drug itself is only the trigger or facilitating agent.

Need for Theological Study

In a paper of this scope, it is impossible to deal adequately with any of the theological questions raised by this field of research. Suffice it to say that there is an increasing need for contemporary theologians to include mystical consciousness in their rational reflections. Tillich has perceptively noted that "The alliance of psychoanalysis and Zen Buddhism in some members of the upper classes of Western society (those within the Protestant tradition) is a symptom of dissatisfaction with a Protestantism in which the mystical element is lost." In general, mysticism and *inner* experience have been stressed much more by Eastern than by Western religions. Perhaps Western culture is as far off balance in the opposite direction with its manipulation of the *external* world as exemplified by the emphasis on material wealth, control of nature, and admiration of science.

It is also possible that psychedelic drug experiences carefully employed in a religious setting could illumine our understanding of the dynamics and significance of worship. Such consideration raises the question of the place of emotion as opposed to cognition in religious worship. An even more basic question inquires into the validity of mystical consciousness in terms of religious truth.

The ethical implications relevant to this field of inquiry also merit careful examination. Any research that uses human volunteers must examine its motives and methods to make certain that human beings are not being manipulated like objects for purposes that they neither understand nor share. Potential abuses are indeed possible.

Implications for Psychiatry. If the claims of help from psycholytic and psychedelic therapy are substantiated in the controlled, clinical trials now being conducted, the need for, and relevance of, interdisciplinary discussion in this area between psychiatry and religion is accentuated.

When LSD was compared with narcotics as a pain-relieving agent for terminal cancer patients, a marked analgesic effect was noted; but perhaps of greater significance, it appears possible that psychedelic therapy can provide an opportunity for the dying patient to view his life and death in a new perspective. The obvious religious implications highlight the intersection of psychiatry and religion.

Even if the therapeutic effectiveness of psychedelic therapy is eventually demonstrated empirically, a further problem still remains. As yet there is no adequate theory to explain why the experience of mystical consciousness should facilitate this therapy.

Implications for Society. As is unfortunately true with many potentially beneficial but powerful discoveries, such as atomic energy, misuse and abuse are possible if the discoveries are improperly handled. The psychedelic drugs are no exception, as the growing black market ominously testifies. Such practices will inevitably lead to psychiatric casualties. The current increase in dangerous after-effects is almost entirely caused by the indiscriminate use of LSD among untrained persons. These very real dangers must not be allowed to obscure the potentials of a powerful therapeutic tool.

It is unfortunate that, at present, public opinion concerning these drugs is being molded primarily on the basis of the response of the beatnik dimension of society, a dimension that contains many persons already in poor states of mental health. There are relatively few experimental studies that provide information concerning the possible continuing benefits of psychedelic drug experiences in mentally healthy persons who have already established a responsible and creative position in society.

Religion has long been accused by sociologists of being a prime illustration of the phenomenon of the "cultural lag." Bruno was burned at the stake for his adherence to the Copernican view of the universe.

For the same heretical belief, Galileo was condemned and forced to recant. Similarly, Darwin was condemned for his heretical theory of evolution. Yet, in retrospect, Christian theology, including biblical interpretation, has been greatly enriched by the convictions of these men. New glimpses into the nature of reality always seem first to evoke defensive reactions of fear and, only later, reactions of wonder and praise.

With these drugs, science stands on an awesome threshold. Some religious leaders would undoubtedly consider it improper for man to tread upon the holy ground of the unconscious. But man's apparent destiny to seek an ever greater comprehension of the nature of reality cannot be thwarted or suppressed. The importance of research proceeding in harmony with the highest known ethical principles, however, is clear. Those who undertake such research carry a heavy responsibility.

EDITOR'S NOTE: The following excerpt contains only the last two pages of a lengthy and important essay by Huston Smith, "Do Drugs Have Religious Import?" already cited in the introductory material. Confer also the Suggested Readings at the conclusion of this chapter.

Suppose that drugs can induce experiences indistinguishable from religious experiences and that we can respect their reports. Do they shed any light, not (as we now ask) on life, but on the nature of the religious life?

One thing they may do is throw religious experience itself into perspective by clarifying its relation to the religious life as a whole. Drugs appear able to induce religious experiences; it is less evident that they can produce religious lives. It follows that religion is more than religious experiences. This is hardly news, but it may be a useful reminder, especially to those who incline toward "the religion of religious experience"; which is to say toward lives bent on the acquisition of desired states of experience irrespective of their relation to life's other demands and components.

Despite the dangers of a faulty psychology, it remains useful to regard man as having a mind, a will, and feelings. One of the lessons of religious history is that, to be adequate, a faith must rouse and involve all three components of man's nature. Religions of experience have their comparable pitfalls, as evidenced by Taoism's struggle (not always successful) to keep from degenerating into quietism, and the vehemence with which Zen Buddhism has insisted that once students have attained *satori,* they must be driven out of it, back into the world. The case of Zen is especially pertinent here, for it pivots on an enlightenment experience— *satori,* or *kensho*—which some (but not all) Zennists say resembles LSD. Alike or different, the point is that Zen recognizes that unless the experience is joined to discipline, it will come to naught:

Even the Buddha . . . had to sit. . . . Without *joriki,* the particular power developed through *zazen* [seated meditation], the vision of oneness attained in enlightenment . . . in time becomes clouded and eventually fades into a pleasant memory instead of remaining an omnipresent reality shaping our daily life. . . . To be able to live in accordance with what the Mind's eye has revealed through *satori* requires, like the purification of character and the development of personality, a ripening period of *zazen.*[1]

If the religion of religious experience is a snare and a delusion, it follows that no religion that fixes its faith primarily in substances that induce religious experiences can be expected to come to a good end. What promised to be a short cut will prove to be a short circuit; what began as a religion will end as a religion surrogate. Whether chemical substances can be helpful *adjuncts* to faith is another question. The peyote-using Native American Church seems to indicate that they can be; anthropologists give this church a good report, noting among other things that members resist alcohol and alcoholism better than do nonmembers.[2] The conclusion to which evidence currently points would seem to be that chemicals *can* aid the religious life, but only where set within a context of faith (meaning by this the conviction that what they disclose is true) and discipline (meaning diligent exercise of

the will in the attempt to work out the implications of the dis-
closures for the living of life in the everyday, common-sense world).

Nowhere today in Western civilization are these two conditions jointly fulfilled. Churches lack faith in the sense just mentioned; hipsters lack discipline. This might lead us to forget about
the drugs, were it not for one fact: the distinctive religious emotion and the emotion that drugs unquestionably can occasion—
Otto's *mysterium tremendum, majestas, mysterium fascinans*; in a
phrase, the phenomenon of religious awe—seems to be declining
sharply. As Paul Tillich said in an address to the Hillel Society at
Harvard several years ago:

The question our century puts before us [is]: Is it possible to regain the
lost dimension, the encounter with the Holy, the dimension which cuts
through the world of subjectivity and objectivity and goes down to that
which is not world but is the mystery of the Ground of Being?

Tillich may be right; this may be the religious question of our
century. For if (as we have insisted) religion cannot be equated
with religious experiences, neither can it long survive their
absence.

NOTES

1. Philip Kapleau, *The Three Pillars of Zen: Teaching, Practice and
Enlightenment.* Compiled and edited with translations, introductions, and
notes (New York, Harper & Row, 1966).
2. James S. Slotkin, *Peyote Religion,* N.Y.: Free Press of Glencoe,
1956.

SUGGESTED READINGS

R.E.L. Masters and Jean Houston's *The Varieties of Psychedelic Experience* (N.Y.: Dell Publishing Co., 1966, paperback) is a solid, in-depth introduction. The death-rebirth sym-

bolism (p. 188), is particularly interesting. Walter Houston Clark's *Chemical Ecstasy—Psychedelic Drugs and Religion* (N.Y.: Sheed & Ward, 1969) is also rewarding and contains a useful annotated bibliography. He points to studies which suggest that psychedelic therapy often moves successively through stages of insight reminiscent of Freud, Rank and Jung (p. 110). *The Highest State of Consciousness,* edited by John White (Garden City, N.Y.: Doubleday, 1972, paperback), contains three excellent articles by W. Pahnke, J. Houston and R. Masters, and G. Jordan, Jr.: "Drugs and Mysticism," "The Experimental Induction of Religious-Type Experiences," and "LSD and Mystical Experiences." *Altered States of Consciousness,* Charles Tart, editor (N.Y.: John Wiley, 1972, paperback), has an entire section containing valuable articles on mind-expanding drugs. W. Braden's *The Private Sea—LSD and the Search for God* (N.Y.: Bantam Books, 1967, paperback) is a reporter's fascinating, at times sweeping and controversial, summary with many references to Eastern thought. *Drugs and the Other Self—An Anthology of Spiritual Transformations,* edited by C. Nahal (N.Y.: Harper and Row, 1971, paperback), surveys many personal experiences. Carlos Castaneda's books, especially *Journey to Ixtlan* (N.Y.: Simon & Schuster, 1972), are fascinating anthropological studies, written in the form of a dramatic dialogue with a Mexican Indian who teaches Castaneda the first stages through the use of drugs, to become the warrior who sees rather than merely looks. A compelling autobiographical study of a trip beyond LSD to the eternal low-pressure center of the inner cyclone is found in *The Center of the Cyclone—An Autobiography of Inner Space* by John C. Lilly, M.D. (N.Y.: The Julian Press, 1972).

For more critical studies, I would suggest a full reading of Huston Smith's "Do Drugs Have Religious Import?," in *The Journal of Philosophy,* as cited, and also found in R. P. Wolff's *Philosophy—A Modern Encounter* (Englewood Cliffs, N.J.: Prentice-Hall, 1971), pp. 551-562. See also Smith's article, "Psychedelic Theophanies and the Religious Life," (*Christianity and Crisis,* June 26, 1967, pp. 144-147). The author, who is not unsympathetic to controlled drug experimentation, doubts the carryover power of psychedelic experiences, if not shored up by an organized community of the faithful. He finds that the movement lacks a social philosophy, tends to be antinomian, and seems to be unable to integrate the psychedelic experience with daily life. In an interesting analogy in which he compares the psychedelic effect with a microscope: "Does a microscope expand vision? Yes, by enlarging, say, a cell to the point where it fills our visual field. But equally no: it contracts our vision by shutting out everything but the cell we are looking at." Similarly, Stephen Schoen's "LSD and Creative Attention," in *Ways of Growth,* edited by H. Otto and J. Mann (N.Y.: The Viking Press, 1968, paperback), pp. 158-166, presents a perceptive warning about the loss of natural spontaneity and the necessary finite sense of otherness in LSD usage. R. C. Zaehner in *Mysticism, Sacred and Profane* (N.Y.: Oxford University Press, 1961, paperback) presents the thesis that drugs promote natural mysticism, i.e., monistic, impersonal mysticism, but not genuinely Christian mysticism. See also his most recent work, *Drugs, Mysticism and Make-Believe* (N.Y.: Pantheon, 1973). Zaehner discusses Pahnke's experiment and finds there a feeling of oneness with self or nature but not Christian mysticism.

For a general theological approach to religious experience, see Charles R. Meyer's *The Touch of God—A Theological Analysis of Religious Experience* (N.Y.: Alba House, 1972), a semi-popular, sound study which includes an analysis of religious peak experience. See also his work, *A Contemporary Theology of Grace* (N.Y.: Alba House, 1971). Jean Mouroux's *The Christian Experience* (N.Y.: Sheed & Ward, 1954) contains some carefully developed criteriological principles on religious experience (pp. 3-47).

EDITOR'S COMMENT

Perhaps some theologians might believe that the quest of religious experience through drug usage represents a new outbreak of gnosticism. Victor White, O.P., speaking of gnosticism, wrote: "At least tacitly underlying all truly gnostic writings is the assumption of the possibility of liberation, not by faith, love or deeds, but primarily, even solely, by knowledge . . ." (*God and the Unconscious,* p. 197). Here, the knowledge would be the esoteric, experiential knowledge obtained through drug usage. However, this criticism seems to be offset by the conclusions of some of the researchers listed in the readings. In exceptionally prepared persons, for example, the results seem to indicate an increase in faith, in both the human and religious sense, a flight to reality and action, and a growth in charity. But insofar as a movement were to claim that only a given, esoteric experience could "save" or liberate man, this would be gnosticism.

I wish to end by offering for the reader's reflection a few tentative conclusions about drug experience and religious experience:

1. If a person begins with faith in a personal God, this often shows up in these experiences. If he begins without such a faith, the experiences seem to be of symbols in the unconscious, which *may* help to integrate us with ourselves, with others, or with nature. (However some atheists in these experiments have developed a strong sense of personal immortality.)

2. In themselves, these experiences are not conclusive demonstrations of the claims of monotheistic religion. Psychic experiences are experiences of *the-self-in-relation-to—*in relation to what or whom? One's answer will depend on one's philosophy and theology, on one's experience of coherence, on faith. Personally, I believe that many controlled drug experiences *are* genuine experiences of God, but the non-theistic spectator might well interpret them as Freud interpreted the "oceanic feeling."

3. Psychedelic experiences seem to perform the important function of releasing feeling. Thus they may be valuable for uniting religious feeling with cognitive meaning and direction. This would harmonize with Paul Tillich's idea of "meaning," as a sense of direction plus feeling-power.

4. Mystical experience must always be balanced by prophetic and social religion. "Let me have no more of the din of your chanting, no more of your strumming on harps. But let justice flow like water, and integrity like an unfailing stream" (Amos 5, 23-24). Western prophetic religion, while it has included strong mystical spirits, has generally mistrusted an exclusively mystical

approach. It has emphasized justice, charity, and belief in a personal God. Christian guides have always rated mysticism positively or negatively, precisely insofar as it has or has not promoted growth in charity.

5. Judaeo-Christian faith itself *is* an experience, but it is an experience of being transcended by what one experiences.

These suggestions, I believe, are equally applicable as criteria for discerning the religious value in peak experiences, drug usage, or the meditative movements and the Pentecostal experience, which we will later discuss.

9 Transcendental Experiences and Meditation

ROBERTO ASSAGIOLI, M.D.

Peak experiences and plateau states are desirable, life-enhancing and resemble in some aspects mystical states. But the use of drugs to this end is for the general public illegal, dangerous and sometimes a symptom of a lack of inner strength for coping with reality. Is there another way? What about meditation? Andrew Weil in his controversial book, *The Natural Mind* (New York: Houghton Mifflin, 1972), claims that many long time drug users have given up drugs for meditation but that he has not met long time meditators who "give up meditation to become acid-heads." The astonishing proliferation of works in the area of meditation makes most difficult a selection of a representative work. The following excerpts are from the book of Roberto Assagioli, M.D., *Psychosynthesis* (N.Y.: The Viking Press, 1965, paperback).* Assagioli (born 1888) participated in the beginnings of psychoanalysis in Italy around 1910. He has written on the notion of the will (his forthcoming book is entitled *The Act of the Will*) and has developed various visualization and meditative techniques. In the suggested readings, the reader may find a brief survey of books which present contemporary thought on the psychology of meditation, its techniques and its theories. Some readers may profit from experimenting with one of these techniques before moving on. Without such practice, one merely reads and conveys material about experience without experiencing what one transmits.

* From *Psychosynthesis* by Roberto Assagioli, M.D. Published by Hobbs, Dorman & Company, Inc., New York, N.Y. (1965), and reprinted with permission. Excerpts from pp. 194-215.

At this point it seems advisable to explain in what sense psychosynthesis is "neutral" towards religion and philosophy.

First, it must be clearly stated that "neutral" does not mean "indifferent." Religion can be, and has been, considered at two different stages:

1. The "existential religious or spiritual experience"; that is, the direct experience of spiritual realities. This has been realized by the founders of religions, the mystics, some philosophers and, in varying degrees, by many people.

2. The theological or metaphysical *formulations* of such experiences and the *institutions* which have been founded, in various historic periods and "cultural spaces," in order to communicate to the masses of men who did not have that direct experience, its fruits and outcomes. Further, the *methods, forms* and *rites* through which the masses of men may be helped to participate —indirectly—in the "revelation."

From another angle the French philosopher Henri Bergson in his book *Two Sources of Morality and Religion* (New York: Doubleday, 1954) emphasizes the difference between *static* and *dynamic* religion.

Psychosynthesis definitely affirms the *reality* of spiritual experience, the existence of the higher values and of the "noetic" or "noological" dimension [1] (as Frankl aptly calls it). Its neutrality refers *only* to the second phase: that of the formulations and the institutions. It appreciates, respects and even recognizes the necessity of such formulations and institutions; but its purpose is to help to attain the direct experience.

First, it offers its assistance to those who do not believe in religion nor have any clear philosophical conception. To those who refuse to accept the existing historic formulations, psychosynthesis offers methods and techniques towards spiritual realization. But those who have a living faith, those who belong to a Church or are followers of a philosophical school, have no reason to be afraid of psychosynthesis. It does not attempt to interfere with or to change their position; on the contrary, it can help them to make a better use of the methods and teachings of their own religion. Moreover, psychosynthesis can help them to understand that the same experiences may find expression through different enunciations and symbols; and in this way, it can help them to understand formulations dissimilar to their own and to be broadminded towards them. It can even go so far as to make them see the possibility of a "psychosynthesis of the religions"; which does not mean creating a unique religion and abolishing the existing ones; it means that understanding and appreciation between the different religious confessions can be developed, and some fields of cooperation can be established. . . .

The Investigation of the Superconscious

The basic premise or hypothesis is that there exists—in addition to those parts of the unconscious which we have called the lower and middle unconscious, including the collective unconscious—another vast realm of our inner being which has been for the most part neglected by the science of psychology, although its nature and its human value are of a superior quality. The reason for such curious neglect would in itself constitute an interesting piece of psychoanalysis and would shed much light on the psychology of psychologists. This higher realm has been known throughout the ages and, in the last decades, some daring investigators have started to study it in a scientific way, thus laying the foundations for what Frankl aptly calls the "height psychology" (Frankl: *Der unbewusste Gott,* Amandus, Wien, 1949).

Before starting to deal with this subject, it is perhaps necessary to make a clear distinction, in order to avoid the confusion which has often been made, between the superconscious or "higher unconscious" and what has been called "superconsciousness," but which it would be more exact to call "a higher state of awareness or spiritual consciousness." This raises the all important and not often clearly realized difference between "superconscious" experiences and psychological activities and the spiritual Self.

The superconscious precedes consciousness of the Self, because—as we shall see—there are very many people who have had conscious experience of facts or of functions which are generally superconscious; i.e., those that generally do not enter spontaneously into the field of consciousness, but which in some cases make a spontaneous, unexpected, sometimes unwanted irruption into the field of consciousness—parallel to, or in a sense inverse to, the irruption into the field of consciousness of instinctual or emotional drives and forces.

What is necessary is to differentiate this superconscious but previously unconscious material from the type of material that may come from the lower levels of the unconscious which have been extensively studied by Freud and his followers. It seems that in some of the extreme cases of irruption from superconscious levels the material that comes arrives—so to speak—almost ready made, and has very little connection with previous experiences. It is not something which arises in the usual way from the lower unconscious as the result of now released but previously repressed experiential contents; it is something new and, as said above, sometimes has little relationship to precedent personal experiences of the individual.

At this point it is necessary to remember that while there is a difference of quality, the superconscious shares some of the other characteristics of the whole unconscious. The superconscious is only a section of the general unconscious, but which has some added qualities that are specific. On the whole it partakes of the nature of the unconscious and the general possible relationships between the unconscious and the personal consciousness.

Viewed in terms of energy, we may consider the contents of the superconscious as energies having higher frequency than some of the contents of the lower unconscious. We could say, more definitely, that psychodynamics and its laws—and in part the methods derived from them—are the same for the three levels of the unconscious. The difference—and it is very real—consists in what is specific to the superconscious in terms of certain *values,* because—and here we come to the point now being increasingly recognized in psychology—*valuations are unavoidable.* It would be easy and perhaps amusing to show how many implied, unconscious, unrecognized valuations there are in many of the so-called purely objective and descriptive expositions of psychologists. It seems to the writer to be more truly scientific to admit that the function of valuation is a natural, necessary and useful activity of the normal human psyche. . . .

Symbols for Spiritual Psychosynthesis

We now come to the specific application of the technique of symbol utilization with its objective of realization of the spiritual Self. This process is necessarily an indirect one because every symbol constitutes an intermediary, and as such, symbols are particularly useful and for certain individuals necessary because of the great difficulty of a direct realization of a state of awareness which to the ordinary consciousness appears—although mistakenly—as abstract and as lacking in definite qualities. This is a paradox, for the spiritual Self is the greatest reality, the real essence of our being. Therefore, owing to this difficulty, the help of symbols is particularly indicated.

There are two main groups of symbols which can be used to indicate or to evoke the spiritual Self.

1. The first group is composed of *abstract or geometrical and nature symbols.* The first and foremost is that of the sun; and similar to it is the star, and another, a sphere of fire. Among the nature symbols is that of the rose, used for example, by the Persian mystics, by the troubadours of the Middle Ages, by Dante in his *Divine Comedy.* In the Far East, especially in India, instead of the rose the lotus is commonly used as a spiritual symbol—sometimes the lotus with a jewel at the center.

Abstract geometrical symbols are often combined with the symbol of the sun or a star; e.g., the visualization of an equilateral triangle which symbolizes the three aspects of the personality—physical, emotional and mental—and above the apex of the triangle a sun or star, with radiating rays, symbolizing the Self. This is a very apt symbol to illustrate the process towards and the achievement of spiritual psychosynthesis through the action of, the pervasion by, the spiritual Self of the reconstructed or renewed personality.

2. The second group of symbols of or for the attainment of the spiritual Self is of a more or less personified type. In this group we find the Angel, the Inner Christ—in the mystical sense, the Inner Warrior, the Old Sage, and the Inner Master or Teacher. The last symbol, of the Inner Teacher, is particularly useful because it introduces and is an instrument of a technique which is very im-

portant and fruitful in establishing a relationship between the personal self and the spiritual Self. This is the Technique of Inner Dialogue.

The choice of symbols is, of course, governed by the philosophical and religious—or non-religious—background of the patient. Religious symbols such as the Inner Christ would obviously be meaningless to an atheist or agnostic, and in such cases a symbol such as the Inner Teacher or certain nature or geometrical symbols would be indicated.

The Technique of Dialogue

In presenting this technique to the patient he is asked to imaginatively dramatize the following situation: he imagines himself as being in a quandary, having a specific personal or interpersonal problem which he does not feel he can solve by the ordinary rational means of the conscious personality. We then point out to him that if there were a very wise man, a teacher who had the spiritual and psychological competence to take up the problem with him and give him the right answer, he would certainly take considerable pains to obtain an interview with the teacher and seek his wise counsel. To this the patient generally signifies his agreement, and we then explain to him that there is a wise teacher within him—his spiritual Self who already knows his problem, his crisis, his perplexity. Although he need not make an outer journey to reach the teacher, it is necessary to make an inner journey, more exactly an ascent to the various levels of the conscious and superconscious psyche, to approach this inner teacher and then in imagination to simply state the problem, talking to the imagined teacher realistically as if he were a living person and, as in everyday conversation, courteously awaiting a response.

On occasion the answer is immediate and spontaneous; it is received clearly and comes with authority and an absence of all doubt. But this occurs in only the more fortunate cases, for sometimes there appears to be no answer at all. This should not be a reason for discouragement. Sometimes the answer is delayed and comes in an unexpected moment, when the personality is not looking for it and is perhaps occupied with other concerns—a condition that seems to facilitate the reception of the message, because eager expectation and tenseness can constitute an obstacle to receptivity.

There are more indirect and intriguing ways of receiving or finding the answer to the problem. The process or mechanism of this transmission is difficult to understand and often its existence is more than many people realize or are ready to admit. It apparently involves the whole gestalt of a person's life and the subtle unconscious psychological interplay between the patient and his environment. However, it is not necessary to know the mechanism of transmission—the fact is that sometimes the answer comes seemingly spontaneously through a third person or through a book or other reading matter, or through the development of circumstances themselves. In a certain sense this should not surprise us too much, and it might indicate the fact that enlightening impressions or psychological communications are reaching us all the time, even when not consciously sought. It is we who do not recognize the many and varied "signals." But the fact of formulating a question and being in a state of general expectation helps us to register and recognize what would otherwise remain hidden.

In this technique of the inner dialogue we should put the emphasis on the dialogue itself, more than on the "teacher," and experience indicates that what really interests the patients IS the answer, IS the dialogue and NOT the way and means to reach it. . . .

Of the personified symbols of the spiritual Self, that of the Inner Christ is one that we use in cases of individuals who are fairly open to Christian symbolism, in line with the general rule of using as much as possible the subject's own terminology in relation to the whole setting of his beliefs and preferences. As we mentioned earlier, in the case of atheists it is possible to use abstract, geometrical, or nature symbols or that of the inner teacher without going into a laborious discussion as to the existence or non-existence of a deity. In modern life, with the great majority of cases, it is better to stick to the empirical approach of techniques and the actual results of the techniques, eliminating every philosophical or religious question.

With devout Christians who have a certain mystical bent the symbol of the Inner Christ is readily accepted, for often it is not new to them because many Christian writers or mystics have used it, and one is merely calling the attention of the subject to the specific use of the symbol in connection with his own spiritual psychosynthesis. This with many people is the taking up and renewing of an earlier experience.

One may add that the concept of the Inner Christ is not always well defined in the minds of many Christians. There is a certain confusion in their minds between the Inner Christ in its precise restricted sense as a personification of the Self, and the Biblical Christ as the world Figure and Son of God, speaking to their soul inwardly. With this type of person, for practical purposes it is not always necessary or even advisable to make the distinction sharp. If the symbol works—that is the important thing.

In connection with this we draw attention to the famous book *The Imitation of Christ* attributed to Thomas à Kempis. Without attempting to give any religious or theological opinion or judgment on it, from the purely psychological point of view the first three books of *The Imitation of Christ* appear clearly to be a dialogue between the aspiring personality and the Self as the Inner Christ.

One thing that is important to remember is that in spiritual psychosynthesis the mystic experience per se is not the goal; and that the goal of spiritual psychosynthesis has the very practical purpose of increased creativity, of increased ability to give of oneself to some chosen field, and that for certain types of individuals this may be achieved without any mystical experience whatsoever.

It may be useful to make here some semantic observations on the word "mystical" which is very loosely used, both in its positive and negative connotation. Without dealing as amply with the subject as it well deserves, we would say that "mystical" in the good and precise religious sense means: union of love with God, a state of spiritual ecstasy accompanied by bliss, self-forgetfulness, and a forgetting of all outer reality and environment. This is the mystic experience as such, but it is limited and whatever value it may have, it is yet only one stage or episode not only in spiritual psychosynthesis but also in the development of the true perfect Christian. Several Christian teachers have rightly pointed out that the mystical experience is not an end in itself, but from it the subject has to draw the fire, enthusiasm and incentive to come back into the world and serve God and his fellow men. So the mystical experience while having positive value is not an end in itself and is a partial experience of the spiritual life.

There are many ways in which one may have a living contact with the Self, which have no mystical quality at all, taking mystical in the precise sense just mentioned. The dialogue between the spiritual Self and the personality can be unaccompanied by any emotional exaltation; it can be on a clear mental level, in a sense impersonal, objective, and therefore unemotional. This is a fact that it is well to realize, particularly in treating patients who have no strong orthodox religious beliefs or affiliations . . .

Exercise of the Blossoming of the Rose

The flower has been regarded and used as a symbol of the Soul, of the spiritual Self, of Divinity in both the East and West. China adopted the image of the "Golden Flower," while India and Tibet adopted the lotus (in appearance similar to the water-lily), which has its roots in the earth, its stem in the water, and its petals in the air, where they open under the rays of the sun. In Persia and Europe the rose has been extensively used. Examples are to be found in the *Roman de la Rose* of the Troubadours, the mystical rose exquisitely described by Dante in *Paradise* (Canto XXIII) and the rose at the center of the cross that forms the symbol of some religious orders. Usually it has been the already open flower that has served as a symbol of the Spirit, and, although this is a static representation, its visualization can be very stimulating and evocative. But even more effective in stimulating psychospiritual processes is the *dynamic* visualization of a flower, that is, of its transition and development from the closed bud to the fully open bloom.

Such a dynamic symbol, conveying the idea of development, corresponds to a profound reality, to a fundamental law of life that governs the functions of the human mind as well as the process of nature. Our spiritual being, the Self, which is the essential and most real part of us, is concealed, confined and "enveloped" first by the physical body with its sense impressions; then by the multiplicity of the emotions and the different drives (fears, desires, attractions and repulsions); and finally by the restless activity of the mind. The liberation of the consciousness from the entanglements is an indispensable prelude to the revelation of the spiritual Center. The agency for achieving it—and this applies in nature as much as in the realm of the mind—is the wonderful and mysterious action of the intrinsic vitality or "livingness," both biological and psychological, that works with irresistible pressure *from within*. This is why the principle of *growth*, of *development*, of *evolution* has been receiving much attention in psychology and education and will be increasingly applied in the future. It is the foundation of one of the most effective methods of psychosynthesis and forms the basis of the exercise now to be described.

1. Procedure

We describe the exercise as it is presented to a patient or to a group:

Let us imagine we are looking at a rosebush. Let us visualize one stem with leaves and rosebud. The bud appears green because the sepals are closed, but at the very top a rose-colored point can be seen. Let us visualize this vividly, holding the image in the center of our consciousness.

"Now begins a slow movement: the sepals start to separate little by little, turning their points outward and revealing the rose-hued petals, which are still closed. The sepals continue to open until we can see the whole of the tender bud.

"The petals follow suit and slowly separate, until a perfect fully-opened rose is seen.

"At this stage let us try to smell the perfume of this rose, inhaling its characteristic and unmistakable scent; so delicate, sweet and delicious. Let us smell it with delight. (It may be recalled that religious language has frequently employed perfume as a symbol, e.g., 'the odor of sanctity'; and incense is also used in many religious ceremonies.)

"Let us now expand our visualization to include the whole rosebush, and imagine the life force that arises from the roots to the flower and originates the process of opening.

"Finally let us identify ourselves with the rose itself or, more precisely, let us 'introject' it into ourselves. Symbolically we *are* this flower, this rose. The same life that animates the universe and has created the miracle of the rose is producing in us a like, even greater miracle—the awakening and development of our spiritual being and that which radiates from it."

Through this exercise we can effectively foster the inner "flowering."

2. Comments

The results with patients have varied greatly in different cases; but sometimes they have been apparently out of all proportion to the simplicity of the exercise. There has resulted with some patients a true Self-realization, and awakening of hitherto latent inner qualities that certainly speeded up the healing process.

The efficacy of the exercise depends on the ability to introject the rose, to experience the sense of the living symbol, so that the symbol works in us creatively. There is deep similarity between the process of unfoldment in a plant and what happens inwardly in ourselves. Here one could speak at great length—and with some patients one can wisely do so—about the secret of self-realization, of actualization, of the ordinary personality considered as a "seed" of what one can become. There are also many psychoanalytic elements—of resistance, of doubt, of oscillation, and so forth; so the patient is, of course, encouraged to speak freely of his spontaneous reactions, and then these are analyzed again and again until they are dissipated, and the blossoming or unfolding takes place freely and unimpeded.

NOTE

1. "This is another logotherapeutic term which denotes anything pertaining to the spiritual core of man's personality. It must be kept in mind, however, that within the frame of reference of logotherapeutic terminology 'spiritual' does not have a primarily religious connotation but refers to the specifically human dimension." Viktor E. Frankl in his paper read before the Annual Meeting of the American Ontoanalytic Association in Chicago, May 7, 1961.

SUGGESTED READINGS

A most handy discussion of growth movements, which includes much material on growth through meditation, is Severin
Peterson's *A Catalog of the Ways People Grow* (N.Y.: Ballantine
Books, 1971, paperback). Each of the forty-two chapters gives an
incisive introduction to the essentials of one movement.

Two works replete with physiological and some psychological
discussion of meditation and bio-feedback are *Altered States of
Consciousness,* edited by Charles Tart (N.Y.: John Wiley, 1972,
paperback), and *The Highest State of Consciousness,* edited by
John White (Garden City, N.Y.: Doubleday, 1972, paperback).

Some specific techniques: (a) meditation on peak experiences is explained in Paul Bindrim's "Facilitating Peak Experiences," in *Ways of Growth,* edited by Herbert Otto and John Mann
(N.Y.: The Viking Press, 1968, paperback), pp. 115-127; (b)
meditation on "self-symbols," which are allowed to gradually disappear with the intention of moving to a rebirth experience, is
discussed in Jean Houston and R. E. L. Masters' "The Experimental Induction of Religious Type Experiences," pp. 317-320, in
The Highest State of Consciousness; (c) concentration techniques
are discussed in Arthur J. Deikman's "Experimental Meditation,"
pp. 199-218, in *Altered States of Consciousness;* (d) the method
of "twilight imagery" with its Jungian undertones is carefully described in Ira Progoff's *The Symbolic and the Real* (N.Y.: Julian
Press, 1963), pp. 109-168; (e) detailed illustrations of the techniques of visualization, intuition and the use of religious symbols
are found in *Psychosynthesis* by Roberto Assagioli (N.Y.: The
Viking Press, 1965, paperback); (f) tapes on meditative techniques are available from Big Sur Recordings, 117 Mitchell Blvd.,
San Rafael, Calif. 94903; (g) a tape with a metronome sound to
facilitate "alpha conditioning" is available from Silva Mind Control, P.O. Box 1149, Laredo, Texas 78040, together with literature;
(h) the technique of transcendental meditation is learned only by
initiation, but material is available from MIU Administration
Center, Los Angeles, Calif. 90024.

More theoretically: a first-rate study whose emphasis is a bit more psychological than religious is *On the Psychology of Meditation*, by Claudio Naranjo and Robert Ornstein (N.Y.: The Viking Press, 1972, paperback). *The Still Point—Reflections on Zen and Christian Mysticism*, by William Johnston (N.Y.: Harper and Row, 1970, paperback), is both simple and profound. The author makes use of Eastern thought, Jung, T. S. Eliot, and Western mystics such as St. John of the Cross and St. Teresa.

For the technique of the "Jesus prayer," see *Living Prayer*, by Archbishop Anthony Bloom (London: Darton, Longman and Todd, 1966, paperback), and *The Art of Prayer—An Orthodox Anthology*, compiled by Igumen Chariton of Valamo (London: Faber & Faber, 1966). Out of the many books of meditation on Jesus, one might choose Luigi Santucci's *Meeting Jesus—A New Way to Christ* (N.Y.: Herder and Herder, 1971).

Many practical, meditative techniques are also found in *Passages—A Guide for Pilgrims of the Mind* (N.Y.: Harper and Row, 1972, paperback), by Marianne S. Andersen and Louis M. Savary, and in *Daily Life as Spiritual Exercise* (N.Y.: Harper and Row, 1972, paperback) by Karlfried Graf von Dürckheim. See also Bernard Basset's *Let's Start Praying Again* (N.Y.: Herder & Herder, 1972), and F. C. Happold's *Prayer and Meditation—Their Nature and Practice* (Baltimore: Penguin Books, 1971).

10 Therapeutic Meditation and Consciousness

THOMAS HORA, M.D.

Meditation can lead to a sense of wholeness, or union with oneself, with the world, or with God. The following three chapters contain reflections on the psychological, philosophical and religious roots of meditation. These chapters may be read either as three separate units or as a related trilogy.

Chapter X may be read as a meditation on self which leads to the self-awareness arising out of a form of psychotherapy, based on a philosophy of being and on Eastern mysticism. Chapter XI is a meditative consideration of God as the Ultimate Thou, the Ultimate Other. Chapter XII represents an endeavor to reconcile the self-awareness which terminates in absolute consciousness or awareness, characteristic of the East and of certain schools of existential psychotherapy, with the awareness of God as Other.

The reading in the present chapter, "Tao, Zen and Existential Psychotherapy," * is by Thomas Hora, M.D., supervising psychiatrist at Hillside Hospital, Glen Oaks, N.Y., instructor in psychiatry at Rockland State Hospital, Orangeburg, N.Y. and frequent contributor to professional journals. The article is best read as a philosophical meditation on the self, which unites the spirit of Zen, Tao and existential psychotherapy. The therapeutic experience of being and of being a self is shown as a transcendental experience of consciousness which heals the disturbances of consciousness and reaches beyond the duality of I and you.

* From "Tao, Zen and Existential Psychotherapy," by Thomas Hora, M.D., *Psychologia*, 1959, 2, pp. 236-242. Reprinted with the permission of the editors.

Motto:
A man came to Buddha and asked him:
"Tell me Buddha, are you a God?"
"No, I am not a God."
"Are you an angel?"
"No, I am not an angel."
"Are you a prophet?"
"No, I am not a prophet."
"What are you then?"
Whereupon Buddha answered:
"I am awake."

The psychotherapeutic process is a segment of life. Life is an event. Life is happening to man. Existence is reflected in man somewhat like light which becomes visible while passing through a translucent medium. Medard Boss [1] quoting Heidegger speaks of "l'homme clairiere de l'existence." Man participates in existence. He does not cause it to be. Should he, however, fancy himself as the "maker" or "master" of his existence, he will invariably run into conflict with the Fundamental Order of Things. He will find himself in disharmony with the ontological ground of existence.

To think in terms of "techniques" of psychotherapy, or "doing" psychotherapy is a somewhat similar mistake. It is based on lack of understanding of existence as an event. The idea of "managing" or "handling of cases" in psychotherapy represents an objectification which violates the essence of man as an existential phenomenon.

Man is not a "case" and psychotherapy cannot be "done."

Psychotherapy, as life itself, is an event in time. Therefore, we can only talk about a process of psychotherapy or the *way of psychotherapy* somewhat as the Taoist sages spoke of the "Way or Tao of Life." In the psychotherapeutic situation as in all human encounters, patients appear not only as samples of various psychic mechanisms or disease entities, but above and beyond that, as people with specific ways of experiencing life, specific ways of reacting to stimuli coming from the environment, and specific ways of responding to deep stirrings of inner potentialities which demand realization within a *limited and unknown time span*. According to

Heidegger's ontological thesis, human beings have specific ways of "being-in-this-world." [2]

The psychotherapeutic process is then an event in which existence becomes manifest and reveals itself to the participants as being-in-the-world in lived time (Le temps vécu, Minkowski),[3] and in communicative relationship. Heidegger speaks of Existence as a time producing form of temporality. ("Dasein ist eine sich zeitigende Zeitigkeit.") Martin Buber [4] points to the essentially dialogic nature of man.

The event of the existential encounter, however, is phenomenologically characterized by a transcendence of the *temporo-spatial coordinates of existence.*[5] Which means that in the existential encounter itself the experience of the passage of time and the awareness of separation between subject and object are absent.

That which reveals itself is a phenomenon. Phenomena are manifestations of existence. Man's awareness of the phenomena is obscured and limited by his strivings to impose his will upon what is. The pursuit of what "should be" makes man blind to the phenomena of what is. Therefore, a therapeutic process cannot be conducted, intended, managed; it must be *allowed to occur.* The phenomena of existence behave like time of which Cheng-Tao-Ke [6] said:

"It is only when you seek it that you lose it."
"You cannot get hold of it, nor can you get rid of it."

The essence of *existential communication* [7] lies in its nonteleological character. In the light of this realization the concept of "free association" reveals itself to us as a misnomer containing a double contradiction. First, it is not free because it is *intended* to be free; second, it is not free because it is to serve a *purpose.*

For the existential therapist it is of importance to understand the challenging words of Lao-tzu: [8]

"The truthful man I believe,
but the liar I also believe
and thus truthfulness is born."

It seems beyond doubt that Lao-tzu clearly understood the nature of existential communication. In effect he tells us that when "deep calls to deep," or when "Being meets Being" then in "silent whisper" truth does not fail to reveal itself.

To understand himself man needs to be understood by another. To be understood by another he needs to understand the other. When two people understand each other completely, there is *communion*. Communion is that union which makes differentiation possible. Man becomes an individual through union with the other. By losing himself in the other he finds himself as the One. For man is wholly similar and wholly different at the same time. Somewhat like two mosaic pictures may contain the same stone fragments but be entirely different in their overall design.

In the moment of being understood, the patient experiences communion, that is, he experiences a release from his *epistemic isolation*.[9] The subject-object dichotomy between himself and the therapist melts away. This is what Boris Pasternak must have meant when in his Nobel prize winning book "Doctor Zhivago" he wrote: "Communion between mortals is immortal."

The ontological essence and existential meaning of a communication or dream is to be found primarily in the experiencing of its basic climate (Gestimmtheit) and only secondarily in its symbolic content.[10]

Since striving and intentionality are self-defeating therapeutic attitudes, we tend to arrive at the conclusion that passivity may be a desirable one. This is a mistake. For striving to be active or striving to be passive is the same. This points up the futility of the perennial disputations between the so called active therapists and the adherents to the traditionally passive approaches. The issue is neither activity nor passivity, (neither directiveness nor nondirectiveness) but *awareness,* that is, *being in a condition of wakeful receptivity and responsiveness to the phenomena.* This condition of being is vitiated by striving and intending, evaluating, judging, categorizing, pigeonholing into conceptual schemes and psychodynamic patterns. Freud, interestingly enough, wrote about this problem quite clearly in his Collected Papers: [11]

For as soon as attention is deliberately concentrated in a certain degree, one begins to select from the material before one; one point will be fixed in the mind with particular clearness and some other consequently disregarded, and in this one's expectations or inclinations will be followed. This is just what must not be done, however; if one's expectations are followed in this selection there is danger of never finding anything but what is already known, and if one follows one's inclinations anything which is to be perceived will most certainly be falsified.

He recommended the attitude of "free floating attention." It is of great significance that his recommendation was interpreted as passivity. This is easily understood, however, if we consider our propensity to dualistic thinking.

Heidegger speaks of "letting-be." He describes letting-be as a relationship in which all that is can reveal itself in the essence of its being.[12] The essence of a being is his true self. Truth can only reveal itself under conditions of freedom. Freedom is letting-be; therefore the essence of truth is freedom. Essence is the inner potentiality of something existing.

Letting-be must not be mistaken for quietism, passivity, nondirectiveness, or leaving alone. The concept of letting-be means affirmation of the existence of another person. It connotes an attitude which favors the free emergence of the inherent creative potentialities of all. Letting-be expresses a therapeutic attitude of the highest ethical order inasmuch as it refrains from treating the patient as an object of exploration and manipulation, but relates itself to the patient as an *existent* in an affirmative and perceptive way. Affirmation of a person's freedom to be what he is, is an act of love. Love is reverence. Being with a person in the spirit of letting-be makes it possible to comprehend this person in a transjective, i.e. experiential way. The experience of being thus understood is therapeutically beneficial in itself for it is a *transcendental experience*.

It is of utmost importance to *understand understanding*. Understanding is not an act of the will. It is an *event. Understanding happens to man in the openness of the existential encounter.*

The Zen masters lead their students to an experiential realization of "letting-be" or "non-attachment" with the aid of the famous koan: "Can you hear the sound of one hand clapping?" [13]

The Taoist sage Lao-tzu was able to resolve the problem of resistance by the simple statement: "The wise man does not contend, therefore, no one can contend against him." [14]

The striving intentional man lives in the sphere of discursive-inductive modality of knowledge. The open, receptive man is reached or "grasped" by reality. He is accessible to the phenomenological-empirical modality of knowledge which is vibrant with life and truth of Being. The former is the arid intellectually thinking rationalist, the latter is the creative meaningfully thinking "essentialist." [15]

Intellectual thinking compares to essential thinking as playing the piano with one finger compares to the fully harmonic music created by the use of the fingers of both hands. The pure intellectual thinker is an outsider and an onlooker who perceives but the surface of things in the world. The essential thinker is a person who exists in-the-world the totality of his being. The intellectual thinker is motivated by curiosity, the essential thinker seeks to experience the truth. The intellectual thinker is an observer, the essential thinker is a participant. The intellectual thinker analyzes, dissects, takes things apart in order to explore ever so small details and to organize his information into systems and categories of knowledge *about* things; the essential thinker is creative and concerned with the totality, integrity and wholesomeness of all things existing.

The existential psychotherapist does not "do" psychotherapy, *he lives it.* He meets his patient in the *openness* of an interhuman existential encounter. He does not seek to make interpretations, he does not evaluate and judge; *he allows what is to be in order that it could reveal itself in the essence of its being, and then proceeds to elucidate what he understood.* In contrast to the interpretative approach, this is a hermeneutic, that is, clarifying mode of being with a patient (Binswanger,[16]).

Nonevaluative, "choiceless awareness of what is" (Krishnamurti,[17]) leads to an elucidation of the patient's mode of being-in-the-world with an enlightened understanding of the implications for his existence. Complete understanding of one's mode of being leads to a spontaneous shift in world view, that is, a changed attitude towards life. Change occurs the moment man can see the totality of his situation. *Change is the result of expanding consciousness.* Where light enters, darkness vanishes.

It is to be emphasized that contrary to general belief, man cannot change himself. *Change happens to man.* Darkness cannot be removed from a room. It vanishes when light enters.

It is therefore naive for us to claim or to aspire to cure a patient. There is no such thing as a cure. As Sartre said: "It is absolutely impossible to prove that a cure has ever cured a patient." Healing occurs through a meaningful shift in the world view of an individual brought about through genuine understanding of the structure of his existence, that is, through enlightenment. As mentioned above, understanding is an event which happens in the openness of the existential encounter. *This openness (wakefulness) is the therapist's main qualification.* It makes him available for comprehension of the phenomena through which the patient's mode of existence is revealed to him. *Openness* for the existential meeting is then the prerequisite for understanding to happen. Understanding can be spoken of as "action which is non-action," it is a modality of cognition which constitutes the essence of love. For love is neither giving nor getting, neither doing nor not-doing. *Love is a condition of being* in the presence of which constructive events have the freedom to occur. As Chuang-tzu [18] said: "To surrender oneself to the Tao is to renew creation. He who performs this action which is non-action is in harmony with the essence and destiny of All Things."

Thus, the existential psychotherapeutic process can be described as a meeting of two or more beings in the openness and wakeful receptivity to *what is,* leading to a *broadening of consciousness* through revealment of that which hitherto was obscured. The broadening of consciousness and understanding of what is brings man into harmony with the essence and destiny of All Things. Personality integration becomes an expression of *Ontic Integration.*[19]

The existential therapeutic relationship is neither operational nor explorative, neither reconstructive nor interpretative, neither directive nor nondirective; it is experiential and hermeneutic, i.e. enlightening.

Since it is *phenomenological-transcendental,* that is, since the mode of cognition is such that the subject-object dichotomy is transcended, the so called psychic mechanisms of transference, countertransference, projection, introjection, identification, resistance, empathy lose much of their significance and reality. The patient participates as a total human being, not as Ego, Id, Superego. He is an existent in encounter with an other. His relationship with the therapist is expressed by Buber [20] as "intersubjectivity," by Marcel [21] as "mutual spiritual inclusion," by Heidegger [22] as "being-in-the-world as transcendence," and by Carl Rogers [23] as "total presence" which he describes as total organismic sensitivity to the other person. Sosan in his Shinjinmei [24] writes:

> In the higher realm of true Suchness
> There is neither "self" nor "other."

When direct identification is sought
We can only say "Not two."

The therapeutic process moves in the temporality which is absolutely real and that is the eternal present. The present contains the past. The proper elucidation of the present reveals the past. This, however, is only a byproduct and of secondary significance. As a French psychiatrist put it:

On ne guérit pas en se souvenant
Mais on se souvient en guérissant.
(One does not heal through remembering
but one remembers through healing.)

In the existential therapeutic process there is little stress laid on causality and pathogenesis even though these tend to emerge spontaneously in the course of the elucidation of the patient's worldview and the structure of his existence. The patient's attitude towards the past, present and future invariably expresses his attitude towards existence in general. Time is the "existential horizon" (Heidegger,[25]) upon which man's mode of being-in-the-world discloses itself.

The capacity to be aware of the experiential impact of others upon oneself and vice versa, tends to open up a new *dimension of consciousness* which leads to a growing understanding of one's own structure of being-in-this-world or failing to be-in-this-world because of various defensive attitudes and strivings. As one patient put it: "I can feel myself standing in my own way. I understand how isolated and lonely I am."

The experiential awareness of one's own defensiveness converts the meaning of the defenses from comfort to obstacle and impediment. The moment one experiences one's own defenses as impediments, they tend to fall away.

The moment one experiences one's own strivings and avidity as sources of stress, anxiety and conflict, one becomes aware of their self-defeating nature. The moment one becomes aware of one's temporality and spatiality (that is, one's own relationship to time and space), one becomes sensitive to conflicts which arise in contact with others whose temporality and spatiality may be different from one's own.

The moment one realizes that every assertion of "I" carries with it an implication of "not you" and thus represents annihilation of the other, one tends to appreciate nonduality as the "realm of True Suchness." The French have a saying: "Le moi c'est haissable," which means the "I" is loathsome.

The therapeutic situation provides the opportunity for experiencing the self-defeating nature and burdensomeness of defensive attitudes and strivings, In connection with this, Maurice Friedman in quoting Buber [26] writes:

"If man tries to get rid of his insecurity by constructing a defensive armor to protect himself from the world, he has added to his exposedness. Conversely, if he accepts his exposed condition and remains open to those things which meet him, he has turned his exposedness into *"holy insecurity."*

"The defensive man becomes literally rigid with fear. He sets between himself and the world a rigid religious dogma, a rigid system of philosophy, a rigid political belief and commitment to a group, and a rigid wall of personal values and habits. The open man, however, accepts his fear and relaxes into it."

One patient who was so sensitive to coercive and demanding people that she habitually reacted to them with breathing difficulties, depressions and states of depersonalization, having understood her reactions to be of defensive character, one day made a surprising remark: "I wish I were a glass window pane!" At first it was not clear what she meant. But from that day on, this patient began to let-go of her defensiveness and began to allow coercive stimuli to pass through herself like light passes through a window pane. She remained perceptive of the nature of the stimuli, but having ceased to defend herself against them, became immune to them.

Interestingly enough, some time later she did not remember having made the remark about the window pane, but when reminded of it, she said: "A window pane is really a good symbol for a human being. It is brittle, easily destroyed, yet enduring. Its function is to be translucent, to shed light. The cleaner it is the more invisible it is and yet the more light it sheds. The dirtier it gets, the more "ego" it acquires, that is, the more visible it becomes itself, the less light it sheds."

This is particularly interesting because of the similarity of this patient's spontaneous notion to the Taoist Chuang-tzu's [27] saying: "The perfect man employs his mind as a mirror; it grasps for nothing; it receives, but does not keep." In Chinese metaphysics this is called "wu-hsin" or "idealness," signifying a state of consciousness in which one simply accepts experiences as they come without interesting with them on the one hand, or identifying oneself with them on the other. We can add: One lets experiences come and go freely like the air one breathes. For what we oppose, we confirm. What we avoid, we oppose. What we grasp, we violate. What we cling to, clings to us. What we destroy, destroys us.

We must beware of the tendency to conclude that the alternative to opposing, avoiding, grasping, clinging, etc. is accepting. This would be a mistake of falling into a dualistic trap. The alternative to all the above attitudes is *letting-be*. (Not to be mistaken for leaving alone.)

Cognition and consciousness are fundamental criteria of mental health and along with authenticity of Being they constitute the central issue in existential psychotherapy.

One patient whose prevailing attitude toward his therapist was a hostile and provocative one, having realized after a while the futility of his strivings, changed his attitude to a friendly, ingratiatingly cooperative one just to discover to his surprise that it really made no difference in what manner he was striving "to get at his therapist." For as long as he was striving to be good or bad, to agree or disagree, to oppose or to cooperate he had a closed mind. His state of consciousness was such that his cognition was impaired.

In contradistinction to the traditional psychoanalytic interest in the content of unconscious motivation and its historical context, existential analysis points to the epistemological problem which arises as a result of the mind's tendency to attach itself to mental images and motivations in general. In other words, the content of the mental preoccupation, or attachment, or striving is secondary. The primary problem is the disturbance of consciousness which results from it.

For *as man is, so is his cognition; and as man's cognition is, so is he.*[28]

We can thus arrive at a conception of *mental health as a state of consciousness characterized by the capacity "to see what is,"* i.e., to cognize reality in its true essence.

BIBLIOGRAPHY

1. Boss, M. "La Psychoanalyse de Freud et l'analyse existentielle de Heidegger." Paper read at the International Congress of Psychotherapy in Barcelona, Spain. 1958.
2. Heidegger, M. *Existence and Being.* Chicago: Henry Regnery, 1949.
3. Minkowski, E. *Le temps vécu.* Paris: J. L. L. d'Artrey, 1933.
4. Buber, M. *Between Man and Man.* Boston: Beacon Press, 1955.
5. Minkowski, E. Encounter and Dialogue. Paper read at the International Congress of Psychotherapy, Barcelona, Spain. 1958.
6. Chang Tao Ke, as quoted by D. T. Suzuki in: *Manual of Zen Buddhism.* Kyoto, 1935.
7. Hora, T. Existential Communication and Psychotherapy. *Psychoanalysis,* 1957, 15, No. 4 (Winter).
8. Welch, H. *The Parting of the Way.* London: Methuen, 1957.
9. Hora, T. Epistemological Aspects of Existence and Psychotherapy. *J. Indiv. Psychol.,* 1950, 15, No. 2.
10. Hora, T. On Being-in-the-Group. Paper read at the International Congress of Group Psychotherapy, Barcelona, Spain. 1958.
11. Freud, S. *Collected Papers.* Vol. 2. London: Hogarth Press, 1924.
12. Heidegger, M. (2)
13. Lissen, R. *Living Zen.* New York: Macmillan, 1958.
14. Welch, H. (8)
15. Hora, T. Existential Group Psychotherapy. *Amer. J. Psychother.,* 1959, 13, No. 1.
16. Binswanger, L. *Grundformen und Erkenntnisse menschlichen Daseins.* Zürich, 1952.
17. Krishnamurti, J. *Commentaries on Living.* New York: Harper, 1956.
18. Lin Yutang (Ed.) *The Wisdom of China and India.* New York: Random House, 1942.
19. Hora, T. Ontic Integration. Paper read at the International Congress of Psychotherapy, Barcelona, Spain, 1958.
20. Buber, M. (4)
21. Marcel, G. *The Philosophy of Existence.* London: Harvill, 1948.
22. Heidegger, M. *Sein and Zeit.* Tübingen: Max Niemeyer, 1953.
23. Rogers, C. Persons or Science? A Philosophical Question. *Amer. Psychologist,* 1955, 10, No. 7.
24. Sosan as quoted by D. T. Suzuki in: *Manual of Zen Buddhism.*
25. Heidegger, M. (2)
26. Buber, M. as quoted by M. Friedman in: *The Life of Dialogue.* Univ. of Chicago Press, 1956.
27. Lin Yutang (Ed.) (18)
28. Hass, W. S. *The Destiny of the Mind.* New York: Macmillan, 1956.

SUGGESTED READINGS

Thomas Hora presents an approach to God, in a manner similar to Buber's, in "Psychotherapy, Existence and Religion," *Psy-*

choanalysis and Existential Philosophy (N.Y.: E. P. Dutton and Co., 1962, paperback) pp. 70-80. Many authors today relate psychotherapy to Eastern insight. For example, the readei might try Erich Fromm, D. T. Suzuki and Richard de Martino's *Zen Buddhism and Psychoanalysis* (N.Y.: Harper and Row, 1960, paperback) and Alan W. Watts' *Psychotherapy East and West* (N.Y.: Ballantine Books, 1961, paperback). On a more specifically religious plane, see Rudolph Otto's *Mysticism East and West* (N.Y.: Meridian Books, 1957, paperback); D. T. Suzuki's *Mysticism Christian and Buddhist* (N.Y.: Harper and Row, 1971, paperback) and William Johnston's *The Still Point* (N.Y.: Harper and Row, 1970, paperback). Norma Haines, "Zen Buddhism and Psychoanalysis—A Bibliographic Essay," *Psychologia* (1972, 15, pp. 22-30), gives an annotated survey of the literature. (*Psychologia* is an English language journal dedicated to the relationship between psychology and Eastern thought.) See also J. M. Déchanet's *Christian Yoga* (N.Y.: Harper and Row, 1959, paperback). William Johnston's *Christian Zen* (New York: Harper and Row, 1971) is a fine, simple presentation of Zen practice which remains Christocentric.

11 Martin Buber's Meditation on the I-Thou Relationship

PATRICIA B. HEANEY AND JOHN J. HEANEY

In the following essay, the editor, in collaboration with his wife, Patricia Bree Heaney (Associate Professor of Religious Studies, Elizabeth Seton College, Yonkers, N.Y.), offers a reflective synthesis of Martin Buber's thought on the I-Thou relationship. This relationship is founded upon and culminates in an encounter with God. All encounter, according to Buber, issues not in "union" but in the affirmation of otherness deep in the intimacy of relation. Buber's I-Thou model has had a strong impact upon many schools of psychotherapy.

The positions of Buber presented in this chapter and those of Thomas Hora as found in the previous chapter point up the contrasting experiential resolutions of psychotherapeutic and Judaeo-Christian meditation. In chapter XII we will see a possible integration of the two experiences.

For the moment, I would suggest that the differences in the experiences described by Hora and by Buber are radical only in superficial appearance. This suggestion is supported by the fact that Hora himself has written within a theistic framework, while making use of Buber's thought. (Cf. the readings for chapter IX.) One reason for the different "feel" of the two experiences is that the two authors have different purposes. Hora's purpose is primarily therapeutic; Buber's is religious. Hora's article suggests a movement to a state of consciousness which allows one to see what is (characteristic also of certain

151

aspects of the spirituality of Eastern religion). Buber
suggests a movement to seeing-what-is from seeing-
how-beings-are-in-relation to the thou and the Thou.

"Thou" together with "relationship" are
central symbols for Buber's thought. The
word "Thou" is rich with connotation and allusion. A seemingly
simple word, it carries in itself an extremely subtle and supple
creative system.

"Man with man—the unity of I and Thou—is God." [1] This
quotation is not from Buber but from Feuerbach. Buber was
strongly influenced by Feuerbach whom he both resembles and
radically differs from. The difference is that Feuerbach inverted
theology into anthropology in order to save the dignity of man who
alienated the best in himself by projecting his highest ideals into
"God." But Buber preserves man's dignity without rejecting theology through the use of the "Thou" model. The similarity is that
both Buber and Feuerbach, unlike Kant, wish to make the whole
being, not human cognition, the beginning of philosophizing. [2]

A person's key metaphors and models direct the cast of his
thought. Buber draws his main model from interpersonal relations.
"Thou" is a term of address. Evidently then, human relations can
never fade into an alienated background in his system.

What is this "Thou"? If "all real living is meeting," [3] then
thou is not an object or person in isolation in itself. Thou does not
exist except in combination. Man has two "primary words" or "attitudes." [4] Both attitudes or primary words are combination words,
I-Thou and I-It. "Primary words do not signify things, but they
intimate relations." [5]

Thou in the I-Thou combination cannot be separated from
the I. "If Thou is said, the I of the combination is said along with
it." [6] Similarly there is no I taken in itself. There is only I of the
primary word I-Thou and the I of the primary word I-It. "As I
become I, I say Thou." [7] It is a relationship of suffering and action.

Buber says that the primary word I-Thou can be spoken only
with the whole being. The primary word I-It can never be spoken
with the whole being. This latter statement of Buber can be misunderstood. It does not mean that man cannot relate to even the

non-personal with his whole being. It does not mean that man cannot relate to *nature* with his whole being. As we will see, man can say Thou to a tree or a cat. Thus *It* does not signify primarily a thing but an attitude (of accumulation of information, of mastery, of use, of isolating aspects).[8] If this is true of It, it must also be true of Thou. Thou does not signify an object, or even exclusively a person. It signifies primarily an attitude *of relationship*.

To understand Buber's primary words, let us look first at how they fit into man's relationship with nature and with man. Man looks at a tree. He can look at it as an object for a photograph, as something to be cut for lumber, as a thing to be classified. In all this there is an I-It relationship. But with this tree I can also have an I-Thou relation. Without rejecting all the former objective elements, I can "become bound up in relation with it." I can become seized by the power of its exclusiveness.

This is a difficult concept in Buber's thought. It is close to poetic intuition. (Perhaps Gerard Manley Hopkins' "inscape," the grasping of something in its surprising uniqueness and in its individual essence, is a similar concept.[10]) Buber does not like the word experience to describe this relationship. Experience depends on moods. But the tree is before me despite my moods. The attitude involves both sensuality and asceticism. I am caught up in the exclusiveness of the tree. I let it "step forth in its singleness." The only word for the event is relation. Yet how is this relation mutual? Precisely because the tree reveals itself always to one who has the I-Thou attitude.

When I face a human being with the I-Thou attitude, the other is not a "he" or a "she." (Notice that writing about someone, where we must say "he" or "she", immediately moves us into the "I-It" atmosphere.) The Thou is not a thing, an object (he, she), or even a thing among things for, as Buber says, the Thou "fills the heavens." This does not mean that nothing else exists except the Thou but that "all else lives in his light." [11] Here for the first time in Buber the Thou comes in trailing clouds of infinity. Does the Thou in Buber mean more than the other person? We have already hinted at this where it was shown that the Thou is not exclusively the other person. It includes the other person but it is primarily an attitude, and the last question implies that there are intimations of an Absolute in it. Later, we will discuss this point at greater length.

To say the primary word Thou to another does not mean for Buber "to *experience* another person." For Buber, to experience another means to move out of relation, to become self-seeking, to use, to measure according to one's own feelings exclusively. "In the act of experience, Thou is far away." [12] But to take my stand in relations involves risk and sacrifice since I speak the relational word with my whole being. "Thou" means not experience but knowledge. Experience is self-isolation for Buber and knowledge involves a relational web which is concrete and existential. In knowledge of the Thou, "we know nothing isolated about it anymore."

Let us make a tentative summary of the qualities of the Thou thus far presented. (1) Thou never exists alone; it is relational. (2) It signifies the other person but more primarily it involves an attitude. (3) It involves my whole being and involves risk. (4) It does not depend on my moods. (5) It is cosmic in scope; it "fills the heavens." (6) It is "the condition of the possibility of all authentic living." (7) It is not, like the intellect or experience, centripetal, yet it is the knowledge of all knowledge, existential.

Let us continue with our analysis. The relation to the Thou is not in Platonic timelessness. It exists always in time, but always in the present, not in chronological time but in the real, filled present as actual presentness, meeting and relation. Present time exists only because the Thou becomes present. The Thou does not exist in time but time exists in the Thou since the heaven of Thou spreads out over all.[13]

The Thou relation is *not* an idea, for that would lead only to expressing an idea, an abstraction, an I-It word.[14] The Thou relation is not mediated by foreknowledge or fantasy, as in romantic love for example. Neither lust nor goals intervene between the I and the Thou. This needs more explanation.

Since the Thou relation is direct, it would seem to be a *feeling*. But Buber says "feelings accompany the metaphysical and meta-psychical fact of love, but they do not constitute it." [15] When we read the phrase "fact of love," we might surmise that when Buber refers to the Thou attitude, he has simply meant love. This is the first time he has used the word. It is as if he is afraid of such debased coinage. He is so cautious about the word love that he even goes so far as to say:

Nor is dialogic to be identified with love. I know no one in any time who has succeeded in loving every man he met. Even Jesus obviously loved of "sinners" only the loose, lovable sinners against the Law; not those who were settled and loyal to their inheritance and sinned against him and his message. Yet to the latter as to the former he stood in direct relation.[16]

Whether Jesus who said, "Love your enemies" would accept the distinction between love and direct relation is questionable. But the quotation illuminates the meaning of a difficult statement in *I and Thou:* "Yet the man who straightforwardly hates is nearer to relation than the man without hate and love" (p. 16). It also suggests that the I-Thou attitude is identical with Jesus' idea of love.

The Thou relation is love-as-*responsibility* of an I for a Thou. In this, not in feeling, is how I recognize the Thou—though feeling is there. Furthermore, the Thou relation has a "dreadful point" of climax—to love all men.[17] This consistently involves an affirmation of the one being addressed.

The Thou relationship actually forms the I or person because the I-Thou relationship precedes the recognition of self as self. Relation, Buber says, is in fact the inborn Thou. Here we again see that Thou is more strictly the relation than exclusively the other. "Through the Thou a man becomes I." [18]

But the direct Thou relation cannot continually persist. It constantly falls back again into the He, She or It relation, which Buber calls the "eternal chrysalis" of the Thou. Buber does not center upon "alienation" but the event is described. Whenever the I of the relation steps forth and takes on a separate existence, it then moves in a strange, reduced, tenuous, functional activity, separating the body from the world around it. Thus the Thou attitude involves union with the world. Undoubtedly this is not Eastern cosmic consciousness for the body is considered to be intensely involved. It should be more like Norman O. Brown's idea of the erotic, but highly disciplined. Buber always avoids the word "union," which seems to him to dissolve otherness and brings about the absorption of either the I or the Thou. He prefers the word "relation." Relation, it is true, is present even in the I-It attitude but only as experiencing, using, relieving and equipping human life.[19]

In Buber, "spirit" is a response of man to his Thou. Here we meet the convergence of the terms "mystery," "spirit" and "Thou." Man speaks in many tongues but the Spirit is one, the response of the inborn Thou which appears and addresses him out of the mystery. Spirit is not the I but *betweenness* between I and Thou. It seems that Thou is the mystery but precisely as the "between." The relational event is the mystery which Spirit responds to and lives in. The stronger is the response, the more there is *silence* before the Thou. This is the silence of the mystery, of the presence, and presence is power. But I-It always returns again in a dialectical creative tension. I-It creates objective knowledge and work. It presents the field which breeds the new I-Thou response and man cannot live without the I-It attitude.

Before moving on, it may be helpful to summarize the preceding section:

(1) I-Thou exists in the lived present. (2) It is not an idea. (3) It involves feeling but does not originate with feeling. (4) It is love as responsibility; its goal is the love of all men. (5) The Thou relationship constitutes the I or person. (6) It is undulating, cyclic, dynamic, dialectic. (7) It involves relation with the whole world. (8) The inborn Thou of relation constitutes Spirit, addressed out of the mystery.

The relationship of feeling to the I-Thou relation is subtle and very revealing. "Living mutual relation includes feelings but does not originate with them."

Our relations in charity often seem dead and without feeling. How can a man's whole being become involved in the I-Thou relation? Buber explains this by using the Hasidic idea of the "evil impulse" in every man. If one wishes to find his central wish, that which stirs his inmost being, the recognition comes in the form of the "evil urge" which seeks to lead him astray. Man has become so alienated from his strongest feelings that he knows them only hidden in what can lead him astray.[20] "The man who lets the abundant passion of what is rejected invade the growth to reality of what is chosen—he alone serves God with the evil impulse."

The "evil impulse" then is the feeling, the passion, which is guided by and into the relation. It gives the relation power but it serves it and always accompanies it, yet does not primarily constitute it. When guided, the "evil impulse" leads to a relationship which is both sensual-passionate and ascetic.

The feeling problem becomes most clear when the I-Thou relation moves out to world community, "the dreadful point." When men realize, Buber says, that I-It relations to institutions yield no life, they try to loosen them asunder by the introduction of freedom of feeling. They think that the community of love will arise out of free, abundant feeling. But, he insists, "the true community does not arise through peoples having feelings for each other (though indeed not without it) but through, first, their taking their stand in living, mutual relation with a living Centre, and second their being in living, mutual relation with one another." [21]

This is a crucial sentence. Buber has not *logically* justified his introduction of the "Center" which is the builder of community. That is he has no strict natural theology. It seems he begins from biblical faith through Hasidic interpretation.[22] God, he says, is not an idea as for Kant.[23] Buber's notion of the "Center" coincides with the biblical experience of God, which is not primarily conceptual but concrete and existential. Yet, Buber considered himself not a theologian, or even a philosopher of religion, but a philosophical anthropologist, an investigator of the problem of man.[24] Therefore, it seems that Buber's source for the Center is *both* philosophical anthropology *and* biblical faith.

How does the Center arise from Buber's philosophical anthropology? Robert Johann in *The Pragmatic Meaning of God* uses John McMurray's thought (which is very close to Buber's though he did not use him) to show that since feelings in relation are not always reciprocal, a Personal Center, God, who responds in feeling, is needed to sustain love.[25]

Buber's approach is somewhat similar to this. However, he avoids the word "feeling" which has too many selfish connotations for him. Rather relationship is a metaphysical process in which feeling in our normal sense of the word is a by-product. Further-more, the Thou feeling can become universal. In fact, contrary to Harvey Cox's interpretation of Buber in *The Secular City,* the I-Thou relation does not have to be with a person one feels uniquely for and knows well. It can be with a movie cashier.[26] But rela-tion, as for example in one of its higher forms, marriage, does not come to life from free feeling. Rather it arises from "the revealing by two people of the Thou to one another." [27] The Thou which is revealed goes beyond the other; it fills the heavens. "The extended lines of relation meet in the Eternal Thou." [28] It is "the condition of the possibility of all authentic living." Here Buber widens Kant. The condition of the possibility of knowledge is not the Kantian categories but the presence of the Thou attitude. (Cf. the intro-duction to chapter XVII for a discussion of the Kantian position.)

Buber has moved to his silent, dynamic basis, God, the Eternal Thou. This is not a move to mysticism, which he rejects as not respecting otherness, personhood, but to relationship, in betweenness. Buber might seem to be speaking of an eternal Thou which the atheistic existentialists have believed always brought alienation. But Buber avoids alienation in speaking of the Eternal Thou. For him, there is no heteronomous norm of morality. No one has ever understood the Ten Commandments unless he has heard the Thou of the command as addressing himself in his par-ticular situation.[29] "He who approaches the Face has indeed sur-passed duty and obligation."

Similarly with regard to human love. A man who loves a woman, it is true "is able to look in the Thou of her eyes into the beam of the Eternal Thou." But a man would be coarse, he says, who, while lovemaking, tells his woman that he sees the eternal Thou in her. It would be foolish because "there is nothing in which God cannot be found." Buber reacted to Kierkegaard, who rejected Regina Olsen for God, with the remark that God wants to come to us by means of the Reginas he has created and not by the renunciation of them.[30]

God then is the Thou present to the spirit from the begin-ning. This Thou is the source of mystery, of relation, of spirit, of powered presence. But Buber's anthropology does not tell him what God is in himself, only how we are related to him. He is not an idea. He cannot be experienced but he can be "done." [31] He cannot be inferred. He yields himself as there from the beginning. He is the Absolute Person whom we know only in relation to us. He cannot be understood. He can be addressed, "Thou." Perhaps the best definition would be a paraphrase of what Buber says of reality: God cannot be comprehended but he can be embraced. God cannot be expressed but only addressed. In one sense, this is the "death of God," the death of all images.

Buber's Thou, then, has all the qualities mentioned under the two summaries. The pre-condition of the I-Thou relation is the eternal Thou, the eternal face in every face. It does not alienate us from the world because "meeting with God does not come to man in order that he may concern himself with God, but in order that he may confirm that there is meaning in the world." [32]

In one sense Buber's eternal Thou is in process. But he opposes the idea of a God becoming. This is perverted, he says, because "only through the primal certainty of divine being can we come into contact with the mysterious meaning of divine becoming . . . If God were entirely in process, man could not know where the process might lead. What turgid and presumptuous talk that is about the 'God who becomes,' but we know unshakably in our hearts there is a becoming of the God that is." [33] Buber thus opposes the concept of God as pure becoming but not a becoming of God in the world, his ripening in man. But elsewhere he says that we must avoid the pretention to know God in himself. Man cannot know God but can imitate him. Man can know God only in relation. But in relation, the eternal Thou co-suffers in every face. There is process in relation, in dynamic reciprocity, and perhaps that is more than enough to know. There is growth in meaning in the "lived concrete."

What does Thou mean in Buber? Thou can only be indicated or suggested. Thou cannot be expressed. Yet Thou can be addressed, "Thou."

Buber's I-Thou presentation is an incomparable approach to meaning, creativity and liberation from alienation. The other, whether human or divine, can never as in Sartre, make me into an object. Through his prose-poetry, Buber moves his reader into the realization that what he now recognizes was there all the time. It is not an argument. It is more powerful. It is a presentation of the lived concrete. Since the I-Thou relation must grip one's whole being, "evil" itself comes to mean passion without direction or action without passion. Whether Buber's I-Thou philosophy leads to this passion one can say only from an attempt at living it.

Buber's Thou is an attitude of spirit in relation to God. God, in Buber's thought, must be described as a person, an Other, for he says that he does not mean by God an idea or a principle but who, "whatever else he may be—enters into a direct relation with us men in creative, revealing and redeeming acts, and thus makes it possible for us to enter into a direct relation with him. This ground and meaning of our existence constitutes a mutuality, arising again and again, such as can subsist only between persons." Since the concept of personal cannot fully adequate God's essential being, Buber says it is "both permitted and necessary to say that God is *also* a Person." [34] As he presses the aspect of otherness required for mutuality, Buber says: "What the ecstatic man calls union is the enrapturing dynamic of relation," but not a unity which dissolves the I and Thou. "God comprises, but is not, my self." God for Buber is the wholly Other, "but He is also the wholly same, the wholly Present. Of course He is the *Mysterium Tremendum* that appears and overthrows; but He is also the mystery of the self-evident, nearer to me than my I."

Buber stated it well in *Israel and the World* (p. 17): "According to the logical conception of truth only one of two contraries can be true, but in the reality of life as one lives it they are inseparable. The person who makes a decision knows that his deciding is no self-delusion; the person who has acted knows that he was and is in the hand of God. The unity of the contraries is the mystery at the innermost core of the dialogue."

NOTES

1. L. Feuerbach, *The Essence of Christianity,* tr. by George Eliot (N.Y.: Harper Torchbook, 1957), quotation from introduction by Karl Barth, p. xiii.
2. M. Buber, *Between Man and Man* (N.Y.: Macmillan, 1965), p. 146. On Buber and Feuerbach, cf. M. Friedman, *Martin Buber—The Life of Dialogue* (N.Y.: Harper Torchbook, 1960), pp. 29, 48, 128, 164.
3. M. Buber, *I and Thou* (N.Y.: Scribner's, 1958), 2nd ed., p. 11.
4. *Ibid.,* p. 3.
5. *Ibid.,* p. 3.
6. *Ibid.,* p. 3.

7. Friedman, *op. cit.*, p. 59.

8. Friedman, pp. 64, 68.

9. *I and Thou*, p. 126.

10. "There is one notable dead tree, . . . the inscape markedly holding its most simple and beautiful oneness up from the ground through a graceful swerve below (I think) the spring of the branches up to the tops of the timber." *Gerard Manley Hopkins—A Selection of His Poems and Prose* by W. H. Gardner (N.Y.: Penguin, 1953), p. xxi.

11. *I and Thou*, p. 8.

12. *Ibid.*, p. 9.

13. Cf. p. 9.

14. Probably Buber should have said, "not *simply* an idea." On the problem of totally eliminating the cognitive (which probably Buber does not intend), cf. R. W. Hepburn, *Christianity and Paradox* (N.Y.: Pegasus, 1958), pp. 48ff.

15. *I and Thou*, p. 14.

16. *Between Man and Man* (N.Y.: Macmillan, 1965), pp. 20-21.

17. *I and Thou*, p. 15.

18. *Ibid.*, p. 29.

19. *Ibid.*, p. 38.

20. For a good treatment of the evil urge, see M. Friedman, *To Deny Our Nothingness* (N.Y.: Delta, 1967), pp. 302ff.

21. *I and Thou*, p. 45. Here Buber radically diverges from the eros movement as portrayed, for example, in Brown's *Life Against Death*. Rollo May in *Love and Will* is closer, but Buber, we think, is clearer.

22. Cf. Friedman, *Martin Buber*, pp. 16-26.

23. *The Eclipse of God* (N.Y.: Harper, 1952), p. 54.

24. Cf. *Between Man and Man*, where the statement by Buber is mentioned in Friedman's introduction, p. xviii.

25. *The Pragmatic Meaning of God* (Milwaukee: Marquette University Press, 1966), pp. 51ff.

26. Cf. Philip Troy, "Buber in the Secular City," *Listening*, Winter 1968, pp. 55-61.

27. *I and Thou*, pp. 46, 81.

28. *Ibid.*, p. 76.

29. *To Deny Our Nothingness*, p. 290.

30. *Between Man and Man*, p. 52.

31. *I and Thou*, p. 110. Here Buber comes close to Blondel's philosophy of action (cf. chapter 17 *infra*).

32. *Ibid.*, p. 115.

33. Friedman, *Martin Buber*, pp. 52-53.

34. *I and Thou*, p. 135.

SUGGESTED READINGS

The basic book, of course, is Buber's *I and Thou*. In the previous essay, the references are to the second edition, translated by Ronald G. Smith (N.Y.: Charles Scribner's Sons, 1958, paperback). However, I would recommend the later translation, including an excellent introduction, by Walter Kaufmann (N.Y.: Charles Scribner's Sons, 1970, paperback). The fine comprehensive survey by the Buber scholar, Maurice Friedman, *Martin Buber—The Life of Dialogue* (N.Y.: Harper and Row, 1960, paperback), relates the I-Thou concept to the corpus of Buber's writings, and it has a pertinent chapter on Buber's approach to psychotherapy. For other works by Buber, see Friedman and the notes to the preceding essay. Two short introductions to Buber's thought are: Lowell Streiker's *The Promise of Buber* (N.Y.: J. B. Lippincott Co., 1969, paperback); R. G. Smith's *Martin Buber* (Richmond, Va.: John Knox Press, 1967, paperback).

12 The Self in Eastern and Western Thought

W. NORRIS CLARKE, S.J. AND BEATRICE BURKEL

This chapter * is presented as an effort to bridge the two experiences described in Chapter 10 and 11. While the following article contains a discussion of the notion of Self in Eastern and Western religion, it is relevant to the dialogue between religion and psychology, especially with regard to those psychologists who resort to the insights of Eastern mysticism.

The article is co-authored by W. Norris Clarke, S.J., of Fordham University, and Beatrice Burkel (Bruteau). Father Clarke, who has published many articles on the experience of God, is an expert on the philosophy of theism, and is a devoted observer of Eastern thought. Beatrice Burkel (Bruteau) is the author of *Worthy is the World: The Hindu Philosophy of Sri Aurobindo* (1972) and is preparing a work on Teilhard de Chardin and the Hindu Tradition.

The authors endeavor to illuminate the relationship between absorption of self in the Absolute (whether consciousness or God) and the love of God as a self-confronting Thou. The study of the psychology of religion will be greatly enhanced when and if we are able to reconcile the self-losing of Eastern and even of much Western mysticism with the self-affirmation of Western humanistic psychology, and with the love of God as Other found in biblical religion.

* From "The Self in Eastern and Western Thought: The Wooster Conference," by W. Norris Clarke, S.J. and Beatrice Burkel. *International Philosophical Quarterly,* March 1966, pp. 101-109. Reprinted by permission of the editors of *IPQ.*

During the last three days of Easter Week, 1965, the College of Wooster, Wooster, Ohio, played host to a newly formed Conference on Comparative Philosophy and Culture which took as its first problem "The Self in Eastern and Western Thought." The initiator and guiding hand of the Conference was the distinguished Indian philosopher, P. T. Raju, for some years now a professor at the College. Seventeen panelists were invited as main speakers and discussants, with some forty other invited delegates. The participants came from thirty-five institutions, twenty-three states, and five foreign countries.

Despite a somewhat crowded schedule, which did not permit ample time for discussing the rich content of the many papers, the Conference stands out in the memory of this participant as one of the most interesting and fruitful of the vast number of philosophical meetings he has attended. The idea behind the Conference was an excellent one: to get together a fairly small and manageable group of representative scholars to discuss for several days one topic of central importance in both Oriental and Western traditions. This type of meeting, which can be held more often and on a less elaborate basis than the already well-established East-West Philosophy Congress held in Hawaii every five years, is not, of course, a substitute for the latter but only a creative complement to it.

The scope of the Conference can be gathered from the following list of papers: F. S. Northrop (Yale), "Towards a More Comprehensive Concept of the Person"; Peter A. Bertocci (Boston), "Personal Freedom, Natural Law, and Creativity of God"; M. Q. Baig (Pakistan and Toronto), "Unity: Appearance and Reality in the Light of the Sufi Doctrines of Ibn' Arabi and Ahmad Sarhandi"; James Norton (Wooster), "The *Book of Job* and the *Bhagavadgita*"; Richard McKeon (Chicago), "Love, Self, and Contemporary Culture"; I. R. Faruqi (Lebanon and Syracuse), "Self in Mu'tazilah's Thought"; A. K. Sarkar (Ceylon and New Mexico), "Sankara's Interpretation of the Self and Its Influence on Later Indian Tradition"; Richard Hocking (Emory), "Other Persons, Other Things"; K. V. Ramanan (India and Boston), "The Concept of Personality and Morality on the Basis of the *Prajñāpāramitās*"; Alburey Castell (Wooster), "The Rational Animal"; Harold B. Smith (Wooster), "Variants in the Concept of the Self in the Islamic Tradition"; Paul Tillich (Chicago),

"The Problem of Immortality"; Karl Potter, "The Agent or Empirical Self: An Investigation of Some Assumptions Characteristic of Some Indian Philosophies"; Archie Bahm (New Mexico), "Soul or No Soul? Why Buddha Refused to Answer"; Troy Organ (Ohio U.), "Self as Discovery and Creation in Western and Indian Thought"; P. T. Raju (India and Wooster), "Approaches to the I-Consciousness; Its Depths, Normal and Abnormal"; Sterling McMurrin (Utah), "Concern for the Person."

Since we have not the space to discuss each one of these papers—to be published later in a volume of *Proceedings*—let us concentrate on what seemed to us to emerge as the central issue in the dialogue between East and West. This was not the Humean or empiricist-positivist issue of whether or not there is a genuine unity in man which is not a mere sum or sequence of particular acts, or events, or lower physical components of some kind. The Western thinkers present seemed all, save perhaps Professor Northrop, to hold for the reality of a permanent unitary self of some kind, however it is to be explained metaphysically. Prof. Castell's humorous and incisive paper, drawn from his new book, *The Self in Philosophy,* staked out the anti-Humean position perhaps the most clearly and decisively for the Western thinkers present, or at least marked a general minimum agreement from which to proceed to further dialogue with the Eastern traditions.

The real issue was whether or not in its ultimate depths the human self is—and will always remain in any future mode of existence—finite, determinate, and ontologically distinct from the Absolute Ground of all reality; or whether at its deepest level the human self is really identical (or at least continuous) with the Absolute, hence in its ultimate root indeterminate, infinite, non-multiple. Although this was not most of the time the main explicit topic of discussion, still it seemed to us and to others that it implicitly underlay most of the explicit confrontations between Eastern and Western lines of thought both in the formal and informal exchanges. Professor Northrop first spelled out this basic issue in a challenging manifesto of agreement with the fundamental Buddhist principle that all determinate entities are transitory and that the only permanently abiding reality is the Whole, the all-enveloping Ground of pure Being and Consciousness, which is one, non-particularized, all-embracing, continuous, hence indeterminate and supra-personal, an infinite ocean of pure consciousness, from which and within which all particularized and phenomenally discontinuous entities arise and into which they will all in turn be reabsorbed, like individual waves on the surface of the one ocean.

One particularly interesting reflection of this problem was the rather sharp split that appeared within the Islamic tradition on this point. Professor Baig from Pakistan presented two key examples of the Sufi mystical tradition, with its strong leaning toward identification of the deeper self with God. Professor Faruqi from Lebanon maintained, on the other hand, that the authentic orthodox Islamic tradition (determined by the clearly expressed consensus of the total Moslem community down through its history) is uncompromisingly dualistic and anti-mystical in its understanding of the relations between the human and the divine. Professor Smith of Wooster, finally, defended the position that both the mystical and the anti-mystical traditions were authentic, existing in polar tension within the overall unity of Islam.

The contrast between the typical Eastern and Western approaches was brilliantly highlighted in the paper of Professor James Norton on *The Book of Job* and the *Bhagavadgita*. He pointed out how the heroes of each, Job and Arjuna, both started out as rational, morally autonomous selves quite distinct from God and in dialogue with Him. But Arjuna moves to true self-knowledge by turning within, penetrating through introspection to the limits of the finite self, then transcending beyond into identity with the pure consciousness of the all-embracing infinite Self of God. His growth is through dialogue to identity.

Job, on the other hand, advances to authentic self-knowledge, not by solitary introspection, but through interpersonal dialogue with his would-be human comforters to a final stage, not of identity with God, but of a trusting, I-Thou personal relation with Him, retaining his own full personal identity and moral autonomy but going beyond merely rational analysis to a loving, obedient acceptance of God in mystery.

The first of these ways to God is represented in the West by the figure of Jung; the second, by Buber. According to Professor Norton, though each vision of the human self is consistent in itself, they are incompatible, and we must choose between them.

A significant contribution toward bridging this gap was made by Professor Ramanan, in his outline of the process of growth into the perfect person according to the *Prajñāpāramitās* in the Maha-yana Buddhist tradition, on which he is a specialist. Here the central principle is that human self-consciousness is not a substance or thing but an activity, an activity of self-expression, whose goal is to attain the Limitless, not to merge into it in indistinctness, but so to live that one is rooted in the Limitless while expressing it in the determinate or finite. The false sense of the self consists in clinging to the determinate, the conditioned, as though it were the ultimate. The realm of the determinate, however, is not to be scorned as illusion but set in its proper perspective as radically dependent.

Thus the self grown to authentic spiritual maturity shares two orders of being at once: infinite and unconditioned in its root, it is at the same time dependent and conditioned in its phenomenal expression. It is a living dynamic relation of rooted-ness of the conditioned in the unconditioned. Hence it cannot be said to be *either* one *or* many exclusively, but both at once, or transcending both. Its ultimate state of self-realization is one of full freedom, full awareness of relatedness to other persons, yet as ulti-mately rooted in the Absolute with no clinging to the determinate through which it expresses the Infinite. The possibilities of fruitful dialogue between East and West in terms of this richly nuanced conception of the self seem to us highly promising.

We must regretfully pass over the many other interesting and valuable contributions to particular aspects of the self in Eastern and Western thought. Let us conclude with a few reflections of our own on the possibility of further dialogue between East and West on the central problem of the relation of the human self to the Absolute.

(1) The most fruitful meeting ground between Eastern and Western thinkers is the existential plane of spiritual experience, rather than the philosophical or theological level of conceptual formulation and interpretation of this experience. On the latter level we are still very far apart and often talk at cross-purposes without realizing it. On the former, we are much closer in many cases than we suspect. There is to my mind a profound affinity on the level of basic experience among men of spiritual depth in all cultures which affords a sound basis of optimism for increased

mutual understanding between the great spiritual traditions in the future. This may, in fact, turn out to be the most significant spiritual discovery of our day. This experiential level should therefore be the starting point of dialogue, not the second-level elaboration into theories. But it does require men of some depth of personal spiritual experience to meet on this ground. And such encounters will remain difficult and rare as long as Western philosophers (more given to this than Orientals) are reluctant to reveal more of themselves than the technical academic face of the professor objectively analyzing conceptual schemes.

(2) In attempting to interpret the characteristic spiritual experiences of East and West we do not think we should settle too quickly for a radical or unbridgeable opposition between the so-called impersonal monistic Oriental interpretations and the personal dualistic Western ones. It seems to us that if one keeps his eyes focused carefully on the actual experiences of the great figures in each tradition—as well as one's own experience—certain constants emerge, which should force both sides to yield partially in the unqualified character of their assertions. Thus in all the classic descriptions of the mystical experience of union with God, whether in East or West, one of the constants is the sense of a dissolving of the barriers of the human self as particular, limited, set off from all others, as self-identical by *exclusion* of others. There is a sense rather of being invaded, immersed, drawn out of one's limited self into the great ocean of pure unlimited consciousness that is the Absolute, however one may name it, so that the explicit consciousness of self as distinct from the Absolute disappears and any act of reflexive self-consciousness is impossible, though consciousness itself is by no means blotted out but greatly intensified.

Now it seems to us that as long as one remains on the psychological level of consciousness or spiritual experience philosophers of both East and West can legitimately describe this experience of mystical union with the Absolute as a transcending of the determinate, finite, particular, or phenomenal self—hence, too, of the "personal" self as understood by many Eastern thinkers. For finitude, determination, and particularity in the strong sense all imply distinction from other selves by negation and exclusion. *Omnis determinatio est negatio.* This is self-identity by exclusion. I am myself because I am *not* you, because I somehow stand over against you and exclude you. The priority here lies with the principle of contradiction.

But this mode of distinction by negation or exclusion of others is not experienced at moments of intense spiritual union with the Absolute, perhaps not even in really profound and intense experiences of human love. There exists, at least on the conscious level, a complete standing-out-of-one's-consciousness-of-self (ecstasy) to be totally absorbed in the object of one's knowledge and love. And anything less could hardly be the ultimate state of fulfillment of the human self with its profound drive toward union with all things, toward becoming what it knows. Hence all determinations, limits, or barriers between the self and the rest of being must vanish when consciousness reaches its full perfection. So much, it seems to us, should be admitted even by Western pluralistic personalist thinkers. And in this mode of thinking it is the principle of identity which takes the priority: all distinction is conceived within a prior more profound unity of being.

But let us turn now to the other side of this picture. To admit thus with Eastern thinkers that determination, finitude, and self-identify by exclusion of others is not the only possible or the highest state of human consciousness does not necessarily commit us to conclude, as many of them do, that therefore the *plurality* of selves —both human and human-divine—is also a transitory state. Here lies the crux of the matter. We suggest as an hypothesis for philosophical exploration that it is possible also to have distinction not merely through determination and exclusion of the other but through affirmation of the other in love. This would be a purely positive plurality through pure affirmation, without implying any determination, limits, barriers, or exclusion between the lover-affirmer and the loved-affirmed, at least within the field of consciousness, if the mutual response were total on both sides. Such a total interpenetration of consciousness would, of course, be possible only in the realm of the strictly spiritual, since it is of the very nature of matter as we know it to be dispersed parts outside of parts, mutually exclusive of each other.

We might add that we already have in the West a theological model of such plurality through pure affirmation by knowledge and love in the Christian notion of God as a Trinity of Persons in the same simple unity of being or nature. Since each Person possesses the identical same nature with all its infinite perfection, there can be no question of any determinations, limits, or barriers within any of the Persons or between them. The plurality derives purely from the irreducible relations of giving and receiving in a context of self-expression. It is true that Christian theologians do say that considered strictly as Persons (as terms of the relation of giving and receiving the divine nature) the Father "is not" the Son and the Son "is not" the Father. But this negation is only a very qualified one within the deeper enveloping unity of the divine being, and involves no determinations, limits, or barriers in the Persons thus distinguished.

Our point is not that we can get a clear concept of the union of one-many in the Christian notion of God as both One and Triune, which Christians also believe to be a mystery that can only be pointed to, not grasped, by unaided human intelligence and can be expressed only in dialectical language. Nor are we asserting that the union of the human self with the divine can be as intimate as that between the Persons of the Trinity. But the point is that a mode of being at its highest perfection is here being positively asserted within the ambit of Western thought which unites unity and plurality without contradiction and in which the human self is invited to share at its own ultimate stage of perfection, at least on the level of knowledge and love. (In the Trinity itself, of course, the unity and freedom from limit are held to exist not only on the conscious but also on the ontological level.)

There are, then, within Western thought itself sufficient foundations for a carefully qualified but significant agreement with Eastern thinkers that on the level of spiritual consciousness at its ultimate depth and perfection all spiritual consciousnesses or selves are so deeply rooted in the Absolute Self or Pure Consciousness that all determinations or limits of the former which would set any barrier or exclusion between them (what Oriental traditions usually mean by "individual personality") are dissolved.

Can Western thinkers go on further and agree with the "monistic" Oriental traditions that the same dissolving of limits and determinations also holds on the underlying ontological level itself, so that the only real truth is the unity of all being? Here is where the real dispute seems to us to be located. But it may be that this sharpened-up form of the problem, with its clear distinction of conscious and ontological levels, really exists so far principally in the minds of Western thinkers and has never become quite as distinct a live option for most Orientals. One of the first things one has to learn, it is pretty generally admitted, in trying to penetrate into Oriental philosophy is that the primary meaning and the primary source of evidence of what look like straight metaphysical or ontological statements about reality itself are to be sought in the order of *spiritual experience*. Oriental philosophy is primarily what might be called a phenomenology of spiritual experience, and only secondarily a metaphysical analysis of the "objective" nature or being of reality itself. And because for them reality at its ultimate depth is simply identical with, or constituted by, consciousness itself, they might well be reluctant on principle to admit any clear-cut distinction between the two aspects of reality, consciousness and being. The phenomenology of spiritual consciousness in depth would, in the last analysis, be identical with metaphysics or knowledge of the ontological structure and interrelations of reality itself. It seems to us that one of the most notable characteristics of Oriental thinking as contrasted with Western (though there are many exceptions on both sides) is this tendency to pass back and forth from phenomenological description to metaphysical explanation without any apparent clear awareness of the distinction between the two modes of thinking. At least that is the impression we get, along with many other Western thinkers, and we tend to feel uneasy and critically unsatisfied in the presence of such a procedure. Yet we have heard impressive defenses of this Oriental methodology from those who have a much more profound feel for it than we have. And the point they make is that spiritual experience at the deep level of union with the Absolute flowers into an intuition from within of the very inner structure and unifying bonds of all reality, as though viewed from the perspective of the divine creative source itself. If this actually is the case—and it would be presumptuous to deny its possibility or actuality—then, of course, phenomenology would be identical with metaphysical explanation or simply replace it by vision.

Even granting, however, such an intuitive vision into the inner ontological structure of reality and its relation to the Absolute

Source and Center, it would seem to me impossible to dispense with negation and limitation (determination) of some sort as a necessary condition of possibility for the initial *ontological* situation of plurality of being, at least on *lower* levels (plurality without determination by negation, as in the Trinity, holds only on the level of Infinite Being). For whether one calls such multiplicity illusion, *maya,* or lower levels of the real, in every such case it seems apodictically impossible to reach anything lower or less perfect than the Absolute except through some kind of negation. This would involve an act of partial affirmation and partial negation on the part of the Absolute as originating source, resulting in limitation or determination. This initial indispensable ontological negation, however, would only be in view of, ordered towards, the affirmation of the multiple in knowing-love, which, when fully responded to by finite centers of consciousness, would in turn overcome in the order of consciousness the initial ontological barriers of limitation excluding one from the other, and would tend toward the total interpenetration of the One and the many in a single unitive field of blissful consciousness that transcends without abolishing the opposition of One to many.

Western thinkers, on the other hand, tend to distinguish more sharply the activity of man's consciousness from his "previously" given or presupposed finitely determined nature and being, though the two are of course inseparably intertwined. And yet even a Western metaphysician like Thomas Aquinas, who insists so strongly on the real multiplicity of beings and the distinction of creature from Creator, also holds with equal explicitness—though the implications of this are less widely recognized—that the power of knowledge and love is given to finite beings precisely in order that they may transcend on this "intentional" level the limits of their essential being which cannot be overcome on the ontological level itself. (See *De Veritate,* q. 2, a. 2.)

Perhaps if these differences of emphasis, now on the ontological, now on the consciousness level, were kept more explicitly in mind by both Eastern and Western thinkers, the areas of authentic possible agreement between them might be widened and the area of authentic remaining disagreement be brought more sharply into focus. And in a sense, since the destiny and ultimate happiness of man are to be worked out on the level of knowledge and love, the areas of agreement might well turn out to be humanistically more significant than those of disagreement.

SUGGESTED READINGS

The bibliographies for Chapters 10 and 11 will also be helpful here. *The Journal of Ecumenical Studies* has had many articles which are germane to the present topic, e.g., P. Kreeft's "Zen Buddhism and Christianity: An Experiment in Comparative Religion," Summer 1971, pp. 513-538.

Of particular significance is "East and West, Phenomenologies of the Self and the Existential Basis of Knowledge," by John T. Marcus, *International Philosophical Quarterly,* IX, 1971, pp. 5-48.

Claudio Naranjo's *The One Quest* (N.Y.: The Viking Press, 1972) is a remarkable effort to find a unifying thrust in psychotherapy, mysticism and experimental education. Much of the book is relevant to the present chapter.

13 Pentecostalism: The Spirit and the Community

CHARLES DE CELLES

The preceding five chapters have centered on peak experiences, experiences of wholeness and oneness with the self, the world and God. An experience, however, which has not emerged in any vivid light from these discussions is the experience of a specific historical sense of community as contrasted, for example, with the sense of cosmic oneness. Yet many sociologists of religion point to the experience of historical community as most important for psychological and religious self-identification, and as a protection against *anomie* (a state of being socially lost because of the breakup of social, cultural and religious forms). From this point of view alone, Pentecostalism is an important phenomenon to consider in relating psychology and religion. Furthermore, it opens up questions with regard to conversion, the experience of glossolalia or speaking in tongues and the psychology and theology of the operation of the Spirit.

It might also be mentioned, though the point is not treated in the following article, that Pentecostalism, unlike many of the experiences already presented, addresses itself to the tragic sense of life. The sick, the isolated, the dying, the distressed—all these have joined with the young and the healthy, and in community have shared what St. Paul considered one of the criteria of the presence of the spirit, joy despite suffering. (The necessary precautions in such a situation are pointed out by authors cited in the suggested readings.)

The following article * is concerned mainly with the
Catholic Pentecostal movement but the remarks are
generally relevant to the Pentecostal "movement" as
a whole. The author, Charles de Celles, received his
doctorate in theology from Fordham University and
is presently teaching at Marywood College, Scranton,
Pa.

The Acts of the Apostles records the first
experiential outpouring of the Holy Spirit
upon the newly formed Christian community. About one hundred
and twenty brethren (Acts 1:15), including Mary, the mother of
Christ, and the twelve apostles, among whom Matthias was now
numbered, were gathered together in a large house. Suddenly the
sound of mighty winds penetrated the entire dwelling. Tongues of
fire appeared. They split and descended upon the head of each
person present. "All were filled with the Holy Spirit and began to
speak foreign languages as the Spirit gave them the gift of speech"
(Acts 2:1-4). The day was Pentecost.

From that moment on the disciples were charged with the
power of God in accordance with the promise of Jesus: "You shall
receive power when the Holy Spirit comes upon you, and you
shall be witnesses for me. . ." (Acts 1:8). Their personalities
were deeply transformed. They could now manifest courage in the
face of Jewish threats, peace in the midst of turmoil, joy when
confronting pain, calm in oppression. They healed, performed
miracles, prophesied, taught, spoke in tongues. As Jews and Gen-
tiles were added to their ranks, they too experienced many of these
gifts of the Spirit of Christ.

Charismatic Gifts

There is good reason to believe that all the charismatic gifts,
including prophecy and tongues, persisted beyond apostolic times.
Some of them, however, were not publicized, such as tongues.

* From "The Catholic Pentecostal Movement," *Cross and Crown*, De-
cember 1971, pp. 403-416. © 1971 by *Cross and Crown*, 6851 S. Bennett,
Chicago, Ill. 60649, and reprinted with permission.

Glossolalia would have made Christianity appear irrational at a time when much of the persecution endured by Christians was due to unsavory charges of irrational conduct being levied against the members of the new faith. One common charge was that Christians sacrificed new-born babies and drank their blood.[1] Eventually, though, many of the charismatic gifts which characterized the early community disappeared, for all practical purposes, from the mainstream of Christianity. So much so that prophecy and tongues were almost unheard of in Catholicism a decade ago.[2]

Today a minority group within American Catholicism, calling themselves Pentecostals, claim that there is a new outpouring of the Holy Spirit with all his charismatic gifts upon the Roman Catholic Church. Many Catholics are skeptical concerning such unusual claims. They are in good company. St. Augustine manifested a similar skepticism, especially as regards glossolalia. He felt that the extraordinary manifestations of the Spirit were indeed necessary in the early Christian community in order to make manifest the authenticity of the gospel message, and thereby launch Christianity. But that purpose had long disappeared, so tongues and like phenomena were no longer needed.[3]

Kevin and Dorothy Ranaghan, leaders of the Catholic charismatic renewal, suggest reasons why the present age is suitable for a power-filled outpouring of the Spirit of God. "There is an openness of the whole Church to everything Jesus would have it be. In such an atmosphere Jesus is able to break through the walls of human weakness with the result that the charismatic life of the Church grows once again." [4]

A second reason proposed by the Ranaghans is the need to draw attention to a Church which has lost its relevance for the contemporary world. The charismatic gifts might well awaken the consciousness of the world to the existence of Catholicism, thereby enabling it to communicate effectively its message of salvation. We might add to these reasons the fact of Pope John's famous prayer pronounced in the name of the Church: "Renew thy wonders in this our day, as by a new Pentecost. . . ." [5]

The Pentecostal Sects

All well and good except for one thing: the outpouring now being claimed by Catholic Pentecostals was already claimed seventy years ago by the fathers of the modern Pentecostal sects. How can this be if Roman Catholicism alone is supposed to enjoy the fullness of the Church? How could separated Christians receive from the Holy Spirit blessings not yet enjoyed within the Catholic Church? Could it be that the authentic Church of Christ was spiritually bankrupt, as the Pentecostal sects claimed? Not very likely. Might it be that the claims to the power of God's Spirit outside of Catholicism are fallacious? There are no grounds for such reasoning.

Father Edward O'Connor suggests that possibly the reason why the Pentecostal experience would have been enjoyed first by non-Catholic Christians is precisely because they had greater need of it. "Those who lack the support of the institutional Church and the grace of the sacraments have a special need of manifest signs from God." [6] He also points out that God may have chosen to manifest to Catholics his absolute sovereignty and freedom as regards the offering of salvation, that he is in nowise hemmed in or restricted by any institution, not even by the Catholic Church.

Whatever the explanation, the fact is that contemporary Pentecostalism as a movement begins outside the confines of the Church of Rome. It dates back to the turn of the century and arises "out of the social disorganization and spiritual rootlessness that accompanied the great waves of immigration to America." [7]

Charles F. Parham is considered to be the father of what might be labeled classical Pentecostalism. Discouraged with his own arid spiritual life, as he saw it, the Reverend Parham, a Methodist minister, initiated a bible school in Topeka, Kansas. He and forty students began an intensive study of the Scriptures which resulted in the conviction that the one reliable sign of having received the baptism of the Spirit was the gift of tongues. Soon thereafter all the members of the study group gained the experience of tongues, each in turn. Five years later Parham opened a bible school in Houston, Texas. One of his students, William Seymour, a black preacher, carried the "full" gospel message to Los Angeles, California. He conducted a three-year revival which attracted people from all over the nation. These people seeded Pentecostalism throughout the United States, as well as in parts of Europe and South America.

At present the Pentecostal sects count ten million adherents.

Two million of these are located in the United States. The largest Pentecostal Church in this country, the Assembly of God, claims more than a million members.[8]

There is very little doctrinal unity among the Pentecostal sects. The only clear-cut unifying factor among them is the enormous stress laid on the action of the Holy Spirit in the lives of Christians, and upon tongues seen as the sure sign of having received the baptism of the Spirit.[9] Pentecostals generally have a deep appreciation for, and a profound knowledge of, Scripture, but their interpretation is fundamentalist.

Neo-Pentecostalism

During the mid-fifties, a mutation in the Spirit-filled churches, known as neo-Pentecostalism emerged. Significant figures include Demos Shakarian, a millionaire who founded in 1953 the *Full Gospel Business Men's Fellowship International,* an ecumenical organization for men, to which numerous Catholics have recently been attached. Another important person is Dennis Bennet, the rector of St. Mark's Episcopal Church in Van Nuys, California, who was deposed after he initiated many of his parishioners into the Pentecostal experience.

Neo-Pentecostalism has one significant difference from the classical Pentecostalism we have just described. It is a movement but not a sect. Its membership consists of Baptists, Lutherans, Presbyterians, Anglicans, and others who remain in the practice of their respective faiths. The only element binding neo-Pentecostals together is the firm conviction that the fullness of the life of the Spirit with accompanying charismatic gifts is a state to which all Christians are called.

Catholic Pentecostalism

Catholic Pentecostalism did not appear until 1966 when several students and faculty members at Duquesne University jointly investigated the phenomenon of tongues and the meaning of the baptism of the Spirit. They began meeting with neo-Pentecostals for common prayer. In February of 1967 four members of the study group claimed to have received the gift of tongues. From Duquesne University the Pentecostal experience spread to Notre Dame, which since has become the center of the movement within Catholicism. From Notre Dame it reached out to Newman Centers at the University of Michigan and Michigan State. Soon the movement made its way to numerous other colleges: Holy Cross, Fordham, Catholic University, Iowa State, and others. Presently over thirty thousand Catholics have received the baptism of the Spirit.

Although Catholic Pentecostal meetings generally take place on college campuses, it would be false to assume that the majority of participants are college students. From my experience of meetings at Fordham and Catholic University and at Marywood College, I can confidently say such is not the case. Faculty members, graduate students, priests, sisters, religious brothers, and townspeople form the bulk of the assembly.[10]

The Prayer Meeting

The best way to be introduced to Catholic Pentecostalism is to be ushered into a prayer meeting. The prayer meeting might well be described as personal communication with God in a community setting. The background of the meeting is private meditation. Two or more Christians are gathered in the name of Christ, confident that he is in their midst through his Spirit. Each member of the assembly prays in his own way to the Father in silence. Constantly emerging from the background of meditation are vocal gestures for public edification. Someone will utter a prayer of praise or thanksgiving. His neighbor will read a Scripture passage. He may then formulate a prayer based on the chosen text. Someone may lead in the singing of a religious song, or simply sing a song himself. A formula prayer may be recited. There may be a doctrinal teaching given. Someone may relate an incident in his life that has helped him to experience the presence of God.[11] If a member feels a strong urge to sing out in a language that he is unfamiliar with, he is welcome to do so. He may interpret his own words, or join the other members of the community in praying for an interpretation. Someone may prophesy. Guitar music is welcomed; so are drums. The only rule is that there are no rules. A person simply allows himself to be guided by the action of the Holy Spirit within him and within the group.

Often a doctrinal theme develops in the prayer meeting. Everybody present must be sensitive to the developing theme. A good prayer meeting is permeated by the feeling of love and affection, and generally undergirded by a sense of bubbling joy. There is a definite sensation of restfulness in the Lord.[12] For the most part, the meetings are not emotionally charged.[13] Many prayer groups reserve the last portion of the meeting for the prayer of petition, but no one is prohibited from the utterance of such prayers during the other portions of the meeting. Pentecostal prayer in general has a marked Trinitarian character.

The Baptism of the Spirit

One thing that is kept separate from the prayer meeting but which plays a significant role in the Catholic Pentecostal movement is the baptism of the Spirit. The term baptism is used here in the sense of "initiation." It is probably not well chosen.[14] The baptism of the Spirit generally refers to a publicly made symbolic gesture in which a baptized Christian, in union with several members of the Pentecostal community, petitions the Holy Spirit to transform his life, to strip him of all resistance to the will of God, and to make him a more perfect image of Christ. Because the individual prays for an outpouring of the Spirit upon himself in a community setting, his request is granted. He comes to experience a deeper relationship to the Holy Spirit, new guidance from him, new joy, peace, love and some charismatic gifts.[15] Often he receives the gift of tongues. The transformation of life described rarely takes place instantaneously, but it usually does occur. The symbolic gesture which is the baptism can be a highly charged emotional experience but it need not be.[16] It is performed but once.

The baptism of the Spirit can also be received in a more dramatic fashion. For example, if someone, after deciding to dedicate himself totally to Christ, is tossed out of bed in the middle of the night and finds a strange tongue on his lips, he is considered to have received the baptism, even though no community has prayed over him. The reception of any unusual charism is evidence of the baptism.

Imposition of Hands

Whenever the baptism of the Spirit is received in the more common manner, that is, in the midst of the community, it is always through the instrumentality of a given physical action. This action is known as the imposition of hands. Although the reception of the baptism occurs only once, an individual may request the laying of hands by the Pentecostal community several times. Many causes prompt the use of this gesture. Some people request the imposition as a preparatory step to the baptism. Others use the symbolic action as a means of rededicating themselves to God. A sickly person may ask the community to lay their hands upon him that he might be made whole. At times members will stand in proxy for a sick person desiring a cure. In a word, the laying on of hands is a commonly used gesture.

Oftentimes the imposition of hands by the community occurs in the absence of an ordained priest. What kind of status does such a gesture enjoy within the Church? The imposition can rightly be compared to sacramentals. Sacramentals do not produce grace of their own strength, *ex opere operato,* but they do provide for the augmentation of grace if utilized through love and in faith.

Two types of sacramentals can be distinguished: things, such as rosaries and medals; actions, like blessings and the sign of the cross. The laying on of hands would be comparable to a sacramental in the second category. It is not technically a sacramental because it does not have official approval from the Church. But if we examine the present-day sacramentals historically, we notice that they were used commonly by the people before gaining official recognition. The recognition did not change their essential character. The fact is that there is an excellent motive prompting the Church to recognize the imposition of hands by the faithful as a sacramental. The religious gesture was commonly used in Old and New Testament times and in the early Church.

Life in the Spirit

Prayer meetings and impositions of hands are observable phenomena associated with Catholic Pentecostalism, but they are not the essence of it. The central issue of Pentecostalism is "fullness of life in the Holy Spirit, openness to the power of the Spirit, and the exercise of all the gifts of the Spirit." [18] Pentecostals experience the presence of the Holy Spirit on two levels: the charismatic and the contemplative. The latter form of experience is recognized as the more significant. In the understanding of Catholic Pentecostals, charisms

are not nearly so important as the other level of the Spirit's activity, which consists in bringing people to a personal encounter with God, a deep and moving experience of his presence and love that fills them with a new peace and joy and arouses in them a lively and affective love for God and neighbor and a hunger for giving praise to God.[19]

Variety of Gifts

Nevertheless, the charismatic gifts of the Holy Spirit are sought eagerly and are recognized as meaningful. What are these charismatic gifts? A listing of them is found in St. Paul's First Epistle to the Corinthians (12:4-11). They include the utterance of wisdom, the utterance of knowledge, faith, healing, miracles, prophecy, the ability to distinguish between spirits, various kinds of tongues, the interpretation of tongues. It is possible to divide these charismatic gifts into three groups.

The utterance of wisdom and the utterance of knowledge are instructive charismata. The gifts of faith, healing, and the working of miracles are sign gifts. They manifest in a striking way the power of God in the world. Faith here does not mean commitment to Christ. Such faith is something possessed by all true Christians, not just by some. The charismatic gift of faith is a prayer made with the overwhelming confidence that whatsoever has been requested of God will be received. It is the kind of faith of which Christ spoke in Mark's gospel. "Truly I say to you, whoever says to this mountain, 'Be taken up and cast into the sea,' and does not doubt in his heart, but believes that what he says will come to pass, it will be done for him" (Mark 11:23).

In addition to teaching gifts and sign gifts, there are also revelatory gifts. Prophecy, the ability to distinguish between spirits (commonly called the discernment of spirits), tongues, and the interpretation of tongues are included among these.[20] Through these charismata God makes known many things to his people, things about himself, about their relationship to him, about their present situation.

The Gift of Tongues

Among the revelatory gifts, the one that is the most dramatically associated with Catholic Pentecostalism is the gift of tongues. Glossolalia can be described as the utterance of strange sounds according to a rhythm that resembles a language. The revelatory gift of glossolalia occurs in a setting of community prayer and is followed by an interpretation. St. Paul explains that tongues must be followed by an interpretation if they are to be genuinely beneficial to the community (1 Cor. 14:13).

The uninformed often imagine that when Catholic Pentecostals gather for prayer meetings there is much speaking in tongues. This is not so. The utterance of strange sounds with volume enough to be heard by the entire prayer gathering is relatively rare. Seldom are there more than two or three occurrences at one meeting. Such seems desirable if weight is given to the recommendations of St. Paul. "If anyone speaks in a tongue, let it be by twos or at most by threes, and let them speak in turn, and let one interpret. But if there is no interpreter let him keep silence in the Church, and speak to himself and to God" (1 Cor. 14:26-28).

The first time I witnessed tongues in public was at a prayer meeting on the campus of Catholic University of America. A young sister sang out in a loud, clear, and beautiful voice a series of incomprehensible sounds. When she had finished, everyone stood in amazement. The leader of the meeting requested an interpretation. After a long period of silence a young woman came forth with an interpretation. "Your angel of deliverance is at hand." [21] Seconds later the woman's husband, who stood beside her, admitted with an astonished look on his face that he had had the same interpretation.

The charism of tongues is not always to be classified among the revelatory gifts. Tongues can be a gift of prayer for the individual. When Catholic Pentecostals speak of the gift of tongues, they generally mean it in this second sense. A person finds himself praising God in a room or in a car when suddenly he runs out of suitable words with which to glorify his Lord. Then a flood of words tumble from his mouth, words which transcend his intellect. He is allowing the Holy Spirit to speak through him. This is the theory. In practice many Pentecostals encourage new members to "try" speaking in tongues.

Among Catholic Pentecostals glossolalia is very common [22] and usually follows the baptism of the Spirit for those who persist in attending prayer meetings. But the gift is not considered an essential element of the Pentecostal experience. It is to be noted that there are Catholic Pentecostals who have been involved in the charismatic renewal movement for years and have never experienced tongues. I number myself among these.

Authentic Languages?

A question that is often posed concerning glossolalics is: Do they speak in authentic languages? Stephen Clark relates a story he received from a choir singer who gave a performance in a Protestant Church while accompanied by several persons enjoying the Pentecostal experience.

During the concert, at a moment of silence, one of the choir members spoke in tongues and then another one gave the interpretation. . . . Afterwards, the pastor of the church turned to the choir directoress and asked her if she knew the men. When she replied that she did, he asked her if they knew Hebrew. When she replied that they did not, he told her that he knew Hebrew and that the first man had given a message in high Hebrew and that the second man had given an almost literal translation of the message.[23]

There are numerous such stories but most of them cannot be authenticated as well as this one.

Many Catholic Pentecostals contend that all true glossolalics speak in historical human languages. The languages, however, may not be recognizable because they are extinct. Other Pentecostals feel that glossolalia may be gibberish understood by God alone.

Most psychologists are not impressed by glossolalia. There are those who see the phenomenon as akin to schizophrenia and hysteria. Others find that it is not indicative of any kind of abnormality. A small minority maintain that glossolalics are sensitive people, capable of renouncing immediate satisfactions for long range achievements. In a sense, therefore, they are more "normal" than the average.[24] All seem to agree that the experience is explainable by psychological laws.[25]

This last psychological view is greatly to be respected. Yet one wonders whether theologically it makes any difference if tongues can be scientifically explained. That tongues are explainable does not mean they do not have a divine origin, or that they do not constitute a source of grace for the possessor. Stigmata can be psychologically explained. But this does not detract from their genuine religious worth. We Roman Catholics distinguish ordinary happenings from miraculous occurrences, natural phenomena from supernatural. But these distinctions are valid only from a creaturely point of view. All things are "natural" to God. In Eastern Christianity the clear-cut distinction between natural and supernatural order does not exist. The whole of the universe is seen as bathing in divine grace. All things are "supernatural," because all are oriented toward God. All things bespeak the glory of God.

Perhaps it is best not to attempt to pass judgment upon the phenomenon of glossolalia as regards its natural or supernatural nature. When tongue speaking is real, it is a truly Christian action. All truly Christian actions, though human, have the Holy Spirit as their author. They are all *magnalia Dei*.

Evaluating Pentecostalism

No doubt there are Catholics today who cast aside glossolalia simply as nonsense. In fact, they might label the whole Catholic Pentecostal movement as nonsense. Those people would do well to contemplate the following words of St. Paul: "An unspiritual person is one who does not accept anything of the Spirit of God: he sees it as nonsense; it is beyond his understanding because it can only be understood by means of the Spirit" (1 Cor. 2:14).

They might likewise consider the rather positive tone of a report submitted to the Catholic hierarchy of this country by Bishop Alexander Zaleski, of Lansing, Michigan, concerning the Catholic Pentecostal movement. Bishop Zaleski headed an episcopal commission appointed to study Catholic Pentecostalism. The commission submitted its findings to the meeting of American bishops in Washington, D.C., November 10-14, 1969.

Perhaps our most prudent way to judge the validity of the claims of the Pentecostal movement is to observe the effects on those who participate in the prayer meetings. There are many indications that this participation leads to a better understanding of the role the Christian plays in the Church. Many have experienced progress in their spiritual life. They are attracted to the reading of the Scriptures and to a deeper understanding of their faith. They seem to grow in their attachment to certain established devotional patterns such as devotion to the Real Presence and the Rosary.

It is the conclusion of the Committee on Doctrine that the movement should at this point not be inhibited but allowed to develop.[26]

There is great wisdom in the bishop's report. What better way to judge a movement, such as Catholic Pentecostalism, which claims to be of the Spirit, if not by its fruits? What is of the Spirit is Spirit.

A Pharisee by the name of Gamaliel once made a prophetic utterance before the Sanhedrin of Israel concerning the apostles and their message of faith: "Now I say to you. Keep away from these men and let them alone. For if this plan or work is of men, it will be overthrown; but if it is of God, you will not be able to overthrow it. Else perhaps you may find yourselves fighting even against God" (Acts 5:39).

If the Catholic Pentecostal movement is of the Holy Spirit, it will increase and multiply. It is surely wonderful to think that God could have chosen this our age for a new experiential outpouring of his Spirit.

NOTES

1. Fabian Osowski, "Pentecost and Pentecostals: A Happening," *Review for Religious* 2 (1968), 1077-78.

2. This does not mean that isolated cases did not exist. A year ago I had the good fortune of meeting in Washington, D.C., a sixty-year-old blind clarinet player by the name of Caleb Joshua Rowe. After I had explained to him the nature of the Catholic Pentecostal movement, he confided to me that in his youth he had experienced the phenomenon of singing spontaneously in a language he did not know. He mentioned the incident to a priest who admitted the possibility of such an occurrence, but also encouraged him not to broadcast the incident.

3. William J. Whalen, "Catholic Pentecostals," *U.S. Catholic and Jubilee,* 35 (November 1970): 8.

4. Kevin and Dorothy Ranaghan, *Catholic Pentecostals* (New York: Paulist Press, 1969), pp. 155-56.

5. Edward O'Connor "Pentecost and Catholicism," *Ecumenist,* 6 (July-August 1968): 163.

6. *Ibid.* These separated Christians might well be compared to Cornelius who, as recorded in Acts 10, received the fullness of the Spirit with the accompanying gift of tongues even before being baptized.

7. Kilian McDonnell, "The Spirit and Pentecostalism," in *God, Jesus, Spirit,* ed. Daniel Callahan (New York: Herder and Herder, 1969), pp. 290-308.

8. Whalen, *op. cit.,* p. 8.

9. The "Statement of Faith" found in every issue of *The Pentecostal Evangel,* a weekly periodical representing the official voice of the Assemblies of God, attests to the centrality of the Holy Spirit in the lives of Pentecostals.

10. One thing that characterizes the Catholic Pentecostal movement is the competent theological guidance it has received from the very beginning. Cf. Kilian McDonnell, *Catholic Pentecostalism: Problems in Evaluation* (Pecos, New Mexico: Dove Publications, 1970), p. 23.

11. Catholic Pentecostals relate extraordinary happenings taking place in their lives which manifest the presence of God. David Wilkerson is a classical Pentecostal but his experiences typify in a supreme fashion the unusual occurrences I am referring to. Cf. David Wilkerson, *The Cross and the Switchblade* (New York: Pyramid Books, 1964), pp. 30-32; also pp. 111-113.

12. Jim Cavnar, *Prayer Meetings* (Pecos, New Mexico: Dove Publications, 1969), p. 21. Cavnar writes: "The prayer meeting should have a tone of rest, of resting in God, of peacefulness, not of pushiness or anxiety or tension."

13. "Roman Catholic Pentecostal meetings tend to be the height of propriety." McDonnell, *Catholic Pentecostalism,* p. 11.

14. I tend to agree with Christopher Rigby who writes that "some alternative name for the baptism of the Spirit is needed." See Christopher Rigby, "A Personal Report on Catholic Pentecostalism," *Ecumenist,* 7 (July-August 1969): 73-76.

15. Stephen Clark recognizes in the baptism of the Spirit a kind of re-

newal of the sacrament of confirmation. The grace of confirmation which is the presence of the Holy Spirit is suddenly experienced in greater fullness. See Stephen B. Clark, *Confirmation and the Baptism of the Holy Spirit* (Pecos, New Mexico: Dove Publications, 1969), pp. 12-16.

16. Edward O'Connor, "Baptism of the Spirit: Emotional Therapy?" *Ave Maria*, 106 (19 August 1967): 11-14.

17. Edward O'Connor, *The Laying on of Hands* (Pecos, New Mexico, Dove Publications, 1969), pp. 3-10.

18. McDonnell, *Catholic Pentecostalism*, p. 9.

19. O'Connor, *Ecumenist* 6 (July-August 1968): 161. See also James F. Powers, "Catholic Pentecostals," *America*, 119 (20 July 1968): 43-44. He writes: "The Pentecostals seek those gifts of the Spirit whereby they might become more holy in Christ. They strive to deepen their lives of prayer and thus open their hearts more completely to the workings of Christ's Spirit. They also wish to become freer, more supple apostles, instruments of the power of love which is the Spirit of Jesus Christ" (p. 44).

20. Stephen B. Clark, *Spiritual Gifts* (Pecos, New Mexico: Dove Publications, 1969), pp. 9-23. The Council Fathers at Vatican II very much recognized the validity of charismatic gifts distributed among the faithful by the Holy Spirit. In the *Constitution on the Church* (no. 12) we read as follows: "It is not only through the sacraments and Church ministries that the same Holy Spirit sanctifies and leads the people of God and enriches it with virtues. Allotting his gifts 'to everyone according as he will' (1 Cor. 12:11), he distributes special graces among the faithful of every rank. . . . These charismatic gifts, whether they be the most outstanding or the more simple and widely diffused, are to be received with thanksgiving and consolation. . . ." (Walter Abbott, ed., *The Documents of Vatican II* [New York: America Press, 1966], p. 30). By way of comment let us mention that the gifts listed in 1 Corinthians are not meant to be exhaustive. St. Paul lists several others in Romans 12:4ff. He mentions the charismatic gifts of ministry, exhortation, generosity, presiding, and mercy.

21. The interpretation was shorter than the original utterance, which seems strange. But apparently this is possible since it is the essential meaning of the communication that is sought, not a translation. See Kenneth Hagin, *The Gift of Prophecy* (Tulsa, Oklahoma: Private Publication), p. 18.

22. Actually it is considered less important than many of the other gifts. Christopher Rigby writes: "The most noted of the Pentecostal gifts is one of the least significant—namely, speaking in tongues." *Ecumenist*, 7 (July-August 1969): 76.

23. Clark, *Spiritual Gifts*, pp. 22-23.

24. See McDonnell, "The Spirit and Pentecostalism," in *God, Jesus, Spirit*, pp. 299-301. Also Osowski, *Review for Religious* 27, p. 1083.

25. Whalen, *U.S. Catholic and Jubilee* 35 (November 1970): 11. Whalen quotes Dr. E. Mansell Pattison, psychiatrist on the staff of the University of Washington School of Medicine. Dr. Pattison explains that "as a psychological phenomenon, glossolalia is easy to produce and readily understandable." Whalen also quotes George B. Cutten, a recognized authority on glossolalia, who states: "As far as I know there is no case of speaking in strange languages which has been strictly and scientifically investigated that cannot be explained by recognized psychological laws." It is interesting to note that glossolalia is common outside of Christianity. It existed in the an-

cient pagan world and can be found today in Africa. Cf. Rigby, *The Ecumenist* 7 (July-August 1969): 75.

26. McDonnell, *Catholic Pentecostalism*, p. 45.

SUGGESTED READINGS

The Pentecostal Movement in the Catholic Church by Edward O'Conor, C.S.C. (Notre Dame, Indiana: Ave Maria Press, 1971, paperback) is a smooth-reading, reliable introduction. The serviceable, annotated bibliography covers both Catholic and Protestant trends. Besides the books there listed, I would suggest the following: *Glossolalia Tongue Speaking in Biblical, Historical and Psychological Perspective* by Frank Stagg, E. Glenn Hinson and Wayne E. Oates (N.Y.: Abingdon Press, 1967, paperback), and *The Psychology of Speaking in Tongues* by John P. Kildahl (N.Y.: Harper and Row, 1972). Both are written from a religious perspective and portray a depth of psychological discernment and caution. While tongue speaking is a phenomena of secondary importance in Pentecostalism, the remarks in these works add a psychological depth often missed from the more general works. From a psychological point of view speaking in tongues may be autistic, egocentric, exhibitionistic, or it may be an internally satisfying linkage of feeling with belief and an attempt at socialization, either or both, depending on the person's level of maturity. Again, tongue speaking and interpretation may be a mutual monologue involving projection and an avoidance of respect for true otherness, or it may be a language symbol around which constellates genuine caring. Two special criteria for evaluation are: (a) the level of maturity of the person(s) involved (b) the degree to which it helps to build community, as Paul ruled in I Corinthians 14:5. (Cf. especially Oates and Kildahl.)

J. Massingberd Ford's *Baptism of the Spirit* (Techny, Ill.: Divine Word Publications, 1971, paperback) gives a fine summary of the scriptural background, and surveys the opinions of scriptural exegetes on the meaning of speaking in tongues. Dove Publications, Pecos, New Mexico, specializes in publishing inexpensive booklets on Pentecostalism. In particular, I suggest *Baptized in the Spirit* by Stephen B. Clark (1970), and *Catholic Pentecostalism: Problems in Evaluation* by Kilian McDonnell, O.S.B. (1970).

Within the wider context of the theology of the spirit, Lindsay Dewar's *The Holy Spirit and Modern Thought* (N.Y.: Harper and Brothers, 1959) offers a scholarly study which utilizes Jung's concept of the unconscious in working out a theology of the Holy Spirit. This approach is criticized by Orville S. Walters in "Psychodynamics and the Holy Spirit," *Journal of Religion and Health,* July 1971, pp. 246-255. Walters claims that in asking the question—"Does the Holy Spirit influence the unconscious?"—one illegitimately joins a theological model, the Holy Spirit, with a scientific model, the unconscious. Many ideas in the articles are provocative, whether or not one agrees with its general thrust.

For a brief historical survey of charismatic movements beginning with Montanism, see the first chapter in *Pentecostalism* (N.Y.: Paulist Press, 1971) by Donald Gelpi, S.J. The remainder of this work is not for beginners. The classic study, of course, is Ronald Knox's *Enthusiasm* (N.Y.: Galaxy, 1961).

14 Parapsychology: Survival after Death

H. Richard Neff

To place an article on parapsychology after a discussion on Pentecostalism in no way is meant to suggest an implicit equation between the two. However, a consideration of glossolalia and of spiritual and physical healing which sometimes occur at Pentecostal sessions quite naturally turns our interest in this direction.

Parapsychology—this, if anywhere, is an area where the gullible gather. And as the controversial George Tyrrell said at the beginning of this century, gullibility in the listener breeds untruthfulness in the speaker. The market is now flooded with pop writing in the area of parapsychology and the occult. But there is a small hard core of quality work in the field, and the results of this work will not disappear with a wave of the hand, whether the hand belongs to a psychologist or to a theologian.

I have chosen for the following reading an excerpt on personal survival from H. Richard Neff's *Psychic Phenomena and Religion: ESP, Prayer, Healing and Survival.** Neff defines parapsychology as "the application of scientific method to the study of psychic phenomena." Extrasensory perception, psychokinesis (PK), prayer power, unexplainable healing occurrences—all of these are clearly related to the fields of psychology and religion. It is quite difficult, if not impossible, to deny the reality of some operative

* From *Psychic Phenomena and Religion,* by H. Richard Neff. Copyright © MCMLXXI, The Westminster Press, pp. 114-131. Used by permission.

power in these experiences, the source of which we do not as yet understand. The believer may no more attribute these experiences to an immediate divine power than the person who does not believe in God. Thus we are faced with a dimly lit terrain which arouses our fascination and curiosity. Curiosity may have killed the cat but it helps to keep a man alive.

I have deliberately chosen an excerpt which discusses one of the most "far out" aspects of parapsychology. I have done this because I believe that a frequently met attitude among Christian theologians deserves to be challenged, namely, that to be concerned with personal survival is selfish and unethical. This can be true only if we are speaking of childish self-interest and aggrandizement, or if genuine self-love (in Fromm's sense) is unethical, or if the self is totally an illusion. (One wonders whether Freud's principle of wish-fulfillment is at all applicable to the descriptions of existence beyond death, often presented in parapsychological literature, with its demands for an extremely lengthy period of often painful growth.)

The reader may, with the editor, retain a certain reserve about conclusions on personal survival drawn from seance sittings. Still, the psychology of discovery cannot be divorced from genuine faith. H. Richard Neff himself is cautious, sober and balanced throughout his book. Neff is pastor of the Christian Community Presbyterian Church, Bowie, Maryland.

I know that some readers who have been interested in the material in the previous chapters will have trouble with some subjects in this one. For a variety of reasons people find it very difficult to consider mediums, séances, and subjects such as reincarnation from an objective point of view. But if a person is to look at the subject matter of parapsychology, he must at some time give serious consideration to the theory of personal survival after death and the phenomena that suggest this possibility. Furthermore, there is a practical reason for considering this. A friend sent me a newspaper clipping that reported that a young man who had been murdered led his father to the person who had committed the crime. According to the father, the dead youth spoke to him and guided him to the man who eventually was apprehended and charged with murder. When you read such a news article, how do you interpret it? If you seek an explanation for such a phenomenon, you must consider the possibility of psychic events that involve discarnate personalities. Then, too, occasionally what is represented as communication with the dead through a medium breaks into the news. The supposed communication of Bishop Pike with his deceased son is an example of this. How do you evaluate such a report when you receive it? You have no basis for evaluating it objectively unless you are willing to look seriously at such a phenomenon. The major questions, then, in this chapter are these: Does the human personality survive death? and, Is communication possible between those who survive death and those who still live as human beings?

When a person's brain ceases to function at death, consciousness lapses. The empirical evidence seems to indicate that at that time life terminates. The logical, reasonable conclusion is that after the body and the brain die, nothing remains alive. But in the face of this materialistic conclusion, many persons of differing persuasions have made a faith affirmation—man survives death. Is this affirmation reasonable, or is it simply a product of man's desire for immortality? What evidence is there from psychic experience that may lend credence to the faith affirmation that man survives death?

Mediumistic Communications

Trance mediumship is an unusual phenomenon; very few people possess the ability to practice it. Furthermore, it is a phenomenon that is suspect because many persons who claim to be adept at it have been exposed as fraudulent. Yet a few have exhibited abilities that seem to be authentic. Arthur Ford, whose name was publicized as one of the persons Bishop Pike used to contact his son, was such a medium.

Arthur Ford reports that he discovered his psychic abilities during World War I when he was a young army officer. He began to visualize on waking from sleep in the morning the list of men who had died the previous night from influenza. Invariably the envisioned list matched the real roster Lieut. Ford picked up from the adjutant's office.[1] At first he was puzzled by these experiences, but eventually he understood and developed his gift. Through the years until his recent death he had displayed unusual ability as a trance medium.

What happens at a séance with a trance medium? The medium seems to be talking in his sleep. What apparently has happened is that he has placed himself in a hypnotic trance. A discarnate personality supposedly speaks through the medium, bringing messages from other persons who have died to the "sitters" seated with the medium.[2] In a séance, then, communication purports to involve at least four people, two discarnate personalities and two carnate persons. On the "other side" are the discarnate originator of the message and the discarnate control who speaks through the medium. From this side of death are the medium and the sitter. When Arthur Ford, the medium, went into trance, a discarnate personality named Fletcher, who was his control, by some means used the medium's vocal cords to convey messages from discarnate personalities to the sitters.

In October, 1968, my wife and I had a sitting with Arthur Ford in his Philadelphia apartment. A number of persons communicated with us. The conversation was recorded on tape, and an accurate record was transcribed from the tape.

The sitting that we had began with the pleasantries one expects when people meet for the first time. We said, "Hello," and Fletcher, the control, responded. Then, through the medium, Fletcher began to tell us some things about ourselves. He mentioned that someone where he was said she was the one after whom Trudy had been named. This could have been her aunt or grandmother. He correctly identified a spot where scar tissue had formed from a minor surgical procedure. And he gave me some advice about my ministry. Then he told about an older man who had had a brief contact with me in college. He described the nature of this contact, and he correctly identified the place of this man's death. He was incorrect when he said this man knew my father. He said next that my grandfather was there and correctly identified him as a member of a Pennsylvania Dutch plain sect. He spoke about the sale of some land in which our family would be involved. He said the land would be sold, which turned out to be accurate, but said, too, that a portion of the land would be retained, which was inaccurate. Then he said that one of us had a brother who had died in infancy. This was incorrect. He talked about my mother-in-law and identified her final illness, but he said she was in a coma before her death and this was not true. Then he spoke of a good friend of hers who had preceded her in death. After this he said to Trudy: "I guess your father is still living, isn't he?" Trudy told him that her father had died a year before, but there was no further mention of her father.

The control then began to talk about a friend who had died a short time before the sitting. He mentioned the nationality of her name but not the name itself, and said a few things about the circumstances of her death. At this point we responded with too much information, but later, without our prompting, he did supply some other details about her that were correct. Then he talked about the wife of an acquaintance who had died accidentally. He correctly identified my contact with this man, and he accurately gave a detailed account of the accident. He was incorrect when he said I had met the wife.

The control then began to talk about a doctor from the era of the Revolutionary War who was supposedly an ancestor of Trudy's and through whom Trudy was related to a minister in Philadelphia. This is the one piece of evidence in the sitting we have been unable to research. We know that the minister is a descendant of this man, but we have not been able to establish a relationship from this doctor to Trudy. The sitting closed with some comments about the future of the church and my future in the church.

In our sitting, there were seven discarnate personalities who communicated with us. Four were relatives, although one of these would have to be termed an ancestor, since the relationship, if it does exist, spans five or six generations. One was a friend who had died just a year before the sitting. The other two were persons who at one time in my life had had a contact with me. My wife and I were able to investigate all the information given in the sitting with the exception of one very important piece of evidence. This was the statement that Trudy is related to a minister in Philadelphia through a doctor who lived at the time of the Revolutionary War. With the exception of this information, everything else in the sitting has been carefully checked. Of the wealth of detailed information given, only five minor points proved not to be true—he said the man who had a contact with me in college knew my father, and this proved to be false; he said I had met the woman who was killed accidentally, and I had not; he said a part of some property to be sold would be retained by the seller, and it was not; he said my wife or I had a brother who had died as an infant, and this is not true; and he said my mother-in-law was in a coma before she died, and she was not. Everything else said to us in the sitting proved to be accurate.

But, in evaluating the material given in a sitting with a trance medium and offering it as evidence for the personal survival of death, one must go beyond the question of whether or not the information is true. Could this information have been secured in ways other than through communication with discarnate spirits? There are six theories that may explain this phenomenon, and they will be considered in order: conscious fraud—investigation, conscious fraud—guesswork, subconscious thought, extrasensory perception, comic consciousness, and genuine communication with discarnate spirits.

1. Fraud—Investigation

This theory is simply that the medium investigates the background of the sitters, and in a feigned trance, that is, in a conscious state, the supposed medium reports the results of his investigations. Arthur Ford knew for approximately six weeks that we would be coming for a sitting. Did he in that time gather facts that he then used in the sitting?

We must admit that all the evidence we have verified could have been obtained through investigation. But could the necessary investigative work be done? If Arthur Ford had contacted a person who knew us and our families quite intimately, he could have obtained much of the information, but such a person probably would have spoken to us about the contact. With no single contact, Mr. Ford would have had to conduct investigations in Philadelphia, Lancaster, and Harrisburg, Pennsylvania. Certain facts would have been very difficult to discover, as we learned when we tried to follow leads to the sources of information. He correctly identified the place of death of one person in a small Pennsylvania town when the obituary for this man and his ecclesiastical record, both of which I saw, listed a larger nearby city as the place of death. Only because I knew the locale was I able to verify where the nursing home was in which he died. Mr. Ford also identified a friend of my mother-in-law, who was remembered by only one member of my wife's family. On another occasion I contacted a person for verification concerning facts about his family, and he suggested that since all the information Mr. Ford gave was in the newspaper reports of a tragic event, the medium had simply secured his information from this source and recited it in our sitting. However, it is worth noting that Mr. Ford not only gave correct information concerning names and events that were in the newspaper, but also correctly identified my contact with this man in an organization in which our memberships overlapped for about a year some seven years prior to the sitting. This fact would have been rather difficult to research.

In addition, if Arthur Ford had conducted an investigation into our past, he would certainly have learned that neither of us had brothers and that Trudy's father was deceased, facts he seemed not to know. In fact, if he had simply been reciting facts discovered by investigation, it is difficult to imagine why he would not use any information about Trudy's father, who had died only eighteen months before the sitting. He could easily have obtained information from many sources about him, and this information would have been very satisfying to Trudy. Yet no such information was offered.

Although the theory of fraud through investigation cannot be completely ruled out, there is substantial evidence that suggests that it is an improbable explanation for at least some of the information offered in this sitting.

2. Fraud—Guesswork

This theory is that the medium simulates a trance, and then by educated guesses and ambiguous statements leads the sitter into a conversation in which the sitter offers much of the significant information. There was one point in the transcript of this sitting where we did provide the significant information. In this sequence Mr. Ford suggested the nationality of the person's name and some things about the circumstances of her death. Without thinking, we gave him the name, her relationship to us, as well as a full description of the incident that caused her death and events that followed her death.

However, in most of the other parts of the transcript, information was given in an unambiguous way, and we did not contribute significant information. This theory, then, can hardly be used to explain the entire sitting.

3. *Subconscious Thought*

This theory is that the medium's trance is genuine, but that in this trance he recites information from his own subconscious mind, as does a hypnotized subject, and not information from the mind of a discarnate spirit. There are several places where this theory possibly may be applied in the record of this sitting. Arthur Ford in the sitting made some comments about the church and the ministry, and he admitted that these comments coincided with his own ideas about the future of the church. Was this information simply offered from Arthur Ford's subconscious mind or did his ideas come through his relationship with his control, Fletcher? Either is a possibility.

Another point where this theory may apply is in the reference to the death of Trudy's mother. Arthur Ford subconsciously may have assumed that because she had cancer she was in a coma, drug induced or natural, before she died. However, the actual cause of death was not cancer, and she was not in a comatose state when she died.

In addition, this theory may apply to the section mentioned before concerning the doctor from Revolutionary times who is supposedly my wife's ancestor. The doctor's name was Dr. Harvey. Just before Dr. Harvey was introduced, Arthur Ford asked Trudy her father's name. She responded first by giving his common name, Harvey, then his first and second names, Alfred Harvey. Then after a second query from the medium, she gave his full name, Alfred

Harvey Simmons. We learned later that the information linking Dr. Harvey to a minister in Philadelphia had been given in a sitting some years before. It is possible that subconsciously my father-in-law's name, Harvey, was associated with information about Dr. Harvey from the Revolutionary War era that had been given in a previous sitting. If there proves to be no genealogical link between Trudy and Dr. Harvey, this would be the most logical explanation for this information. However, this theory could not be used to explain most of the information given in the sitting. Arthur Ford could not have had all the information about our families stored in his subconscious mind unless he had previously conducted an extensive investigation.

Some psychic investigators say that even in the best sittings the medium's subconscious mind runs along with the conversation and at points interjects information. This may account for some of the inaccurate or trivial information given in sittings.[3] But it cannot possibly account for all the information that came in this sitting.

4. *Extrasensory Perception*

This theory is that the medium in trance can, through extrasensory perception, gather information from the conscious and subconscious parts of the sitters' minds. This information, then, is given back in the sitting. The ESP theory has been confirmed in some investigations. S. G. Soal tells of a series of sittings with a particular medium that he entered with certain fragmentary information about a person. The medium confirmed this information, and the story became more definite and more detailed in his mind. The story developed through several sittings until independent investigation proved that the account was completely false. Then in a subsequent sitting no further information on this was given. It is apparent that in those sittings there was an unconscious telepathic fabrication between the medium's and the sitter's minds. Soal's conclusion as a psychic investigator is that in 90 percent of the cases mediums "read" the sitters' minds, and only rarely do they tell them anything that is not in their conscious or subconscious memories.[4]

Can this theory account for the information given in our sitting? Or, were facts given that were unknown to the sitters? There were several facts that were not in the memories of the sitters: the place of death for the man who knew me in college, the details of a fatal accident that took the life of an acquaintance's wife, and all the information about Dr. Harvey.

I learned, too, from friends who had had sittings with Arthur Ford that through the medium they received communications from persons they did not know had died. Extrasensory perception could hardly account for this, for they thought these persons were still alive. Bishop Pike in his sitting with Arthur Ford had the same experience.[5] It is significant, too, that in Bishop Pike's second sitting with Arthur Ford details concerning his son's death were given and later verified that could not have come to the medium through a telepathic link with the sitters' minds.[6] This ESP theory may account for some of the information given in a good sitting, but it cannot account for all of it.

A corollary to the ESP theory is that the medium "reads" not only the sitters' minds but the minds of other persons as well. Of course, it is possible that in a sitting Arthur Ford could reach out telepathically to other minds. Certainly, all the information given in a sitting is stored in someone's mind somewhere. The problem with this corollary is a practical one. How would the sitter choose which mind to contact and what information to extract from that person's memory?

The extrasensory perception theory, then, may apply to some information given in a sitting, but this theory seems inadequate to explain the entire phenomenon.

5. Cosmic Consciousness

Some persons have suggested a theory that every event leaves some kind of psychic tracing on a cosmic mind or consciousness. The medium in a sitting, according to this theory, is able to pick out relevant information from this cosmic mind to report to the sitters. There are no surviving personalities on the "other side," this theory says; there is only a cosmic consciousness.

This formulation can hardly be proved or disproved. Certainly such a theory could account for everything communicated in a sitting. The problem with the theory is that it is more difficult to conceptualize than the theory that the communication is genuine. How, for example, can the medium sift through the information accumulated in a cosmic consciousness to pick out what is relevant for a certain sitter? And is it not more difficult to conceptualize such a cosmic consciousness than it is to believe that what happens in a sitting is authentic communication between the spirit of a person who has survived death and the sitter? This theory cannot be ruled out as impossible, but it is an improbable theory.

6. Communication with Surviving Personalities

The one theory remaining is that in a sitting one communicates with personalities who have survived death. It has been shown that each of the other theories is inadequate as an explanation for what happened in our sitting with Arthur Ford. But could a combination of two or more theories account for all the information? It is improbable that as many as four theories, the first four, would all be operating in a sitting. But even if they were, there is one bit of verified information that could not be accounted for, that is, the place of death mentioned previously for one who communicated with us. However, proof of survival after death cannot be built on this one fact, for Arthur Ford may have secured this information from a person in a previous sitting.

The unverified information linking Trudy to Dr. Harvey, if and when it is verified, would be substantial evidence for survival. This information could hardly have been secured in any other way than communication with discarnate personalities. But one cannot build a conclusion on this information until the facts are verified.

The conclusion I have reached after carefully investigating this sitting is that it does offer a significant evidence that supports the theory of survival after death. I cannot believe that Arthur Ford deliberately deceived us. The necessary investigations would have been very difficult to make. Furthermore, what motive would he have for doing this? His reputation was well established, and we gave him no money for our sitting. It seems to me that three forces could possibly have been active in the sitting. Some of the information may have come from the medium's subconscious mind; some of it may have come through ESP from the sitters' memories; but some of it, I believe, came from discarnate personalities through the control named Fletcher. These personalities have survived death. I realize that my conclusion cannot be offered as proof of survival, but I believe there is sufficient evidence here to point toward that conclusion.

What kind of evidence from a medium would prove survival? Some suggest that the phenomenon known as cross correspondence is proof. This is described with an example by S. Ralph Harlow in his book *A Life After Death*. The discarnate spirit was a man named Walter Stinson. The medium was Walter's sister, Margery Crandon.

In this spectacular phenomenon (cross correspondence), . . . a so-called "spirit" communicates simultaneously with several mediums separated by long distances, sometimes hundreds of miles. He chops his message into as many parts as there are receivers or mediums, and sends one part to each of them. When the portions are joined they make the complete message. In essence this is thought transference, but instead of being between humans it is between a spirit and several humans.

The particular case of cross correspondence that I witnessed involved three groups—those of us with Margery in Boston; a group 400 miles away in Niagara Falls, New York, with the medium Dr. Henry Hardwicke; and a group 175 miles away in New York City with George Valentine, a man of remarkable psychic powers. . . .

We saw Margery go into trance about 9:30 and Walter chatted with us for a few minutes, greeting those who were in the circle and commenting, "Well, I'm going to have to move like lightning tonight. I've got to watch over you people here even while I go to Niagara Falls and New York. Now here's what I'm going to do. I'll give Margery an arithmetic problem and part of a sentence. The answer to the problem and the words necessary for the completion of the sentence will be deposited in New York and Niagara Falls. You have your arrangements made for getting the other parts back here to you."

We nodded in the séance room, and almost immediately—at 9:52 P.M., according to the official transcript of the sitting—Margery picked up a pencil and wrote, "11 x 2." Beneath it she wrote "kick a dead"—then stopped writing. That was all, and Walter was no longer with us at 10 Lime Street. All members of the group signed this sheet to validate the experiment and Dr. Crandon telephoned the Valentine group in New York City.

There Dr. T. H. Pearson . . . reported that at exactly 9:50 Valentine had written, "equals 2," and "no one ever stops to." The message was signed, "Walter."

Not much later a telegram from the Hardwicke group in Niagara Falls reported to us. At precisely 9:50 Dr. Hardwicke had gone into trance. With his right hand still in contact with the left hand of his neighbor, he picked up a pencil and wrote rapidly and accurately on two sheets of paper in the center of the table. One sheet read, "2." On the other was the word "horse."

We assembled the three parts. It was not difficult, for not a word was missing or confused. The arithmetic problem read, "11 x 2 equals 22." The sentence, which Margery later told us was one of Walter's favorite sayings when he was alive, was, "no one ever stops to kick a dead horse." [7]

Some critics, however, point out that, remarkable as cross correspondence is, it cannot be used as proof of survival. Dr. Harlow ventures the opinion that cross correspondence involves thought transference between a spirit and several humans. However, it is possible that a person in trance could, through thought transference, convey the parts of a message to others in trance without the aid of a discarnate personality. Cross correspondence, then, constitutes additional evidence for survival but not proof that man survives death.

Is there any evidence from mediumistic communications that would verify the fact of survival after death? Gardner Murphy, in *Three Papers on the Survival Problem,* says that the most cogent type of survival evidence is that which takes the form of postmortem interaction of two or more communicators. He writes:

Some years ago I tried to contrive a plan for survival evidence based on this principle: let us say that Paul Kempton, of Tulsa, Oklahoma, Pierre Leclerc, of Pawtucket, Rhode Island, Angus MacGregor, of Sterling, Scotland, and Leslie Durand, of the Isle of Wright, meet on the "other side." They wish to give evidence to their families. Checking over their various life activities they discover they all had one thing in common: they all had made collections of rare old Wedgwood china. No living human being ever knew they had this *in common;* it is the kind of fact that could be ascertained post-mortem, but not before. It is true that the method would be laborious, and that the practical difficulties of carrying out the plan would be great; indeed, an attempt to give just such a test through Mrs. Leonard did not meet with a notable success. But if such a plan did succeed it would be worth almost any amount of labor.[8]

There is one communication called the "Ear of Dionysius" case reported by Dr. Murphy that does seem to involve coopera- tion between discarnate personalities.[9] This communication re- ported in the *Proceedings* of the Society for Psychical Research, Vol. XXIX, came through the mediumship of Mrs. Willett. It involves a story that developed from elements of classical literature and was communicated in sittings over a period of more than a year. The postmortem cooperation was between A. W. Verrall and Professor Henry Butcher. The whole story is filled with classical elements very familiar to Mr. Verrall, but interwoven with these items there appeared appropriate references to Aristotle's *Poetics,* and to other Aristotelian associations characteristic of Professor Butcher. All the facts given were unknown to Mrs. Willett. Even Mrs. Verrall and the other scholars studying the scripts failed to understand the allusions until the final clue was given. This con- stitutes very strong evidence for survival.

Mediumistic communications provide substantial evidence for personal survival after death. So far, however, nothing can be reported from this source that would constitute proof strong enough to convince a determined skeptic. But there is good evi- dence that makes the theory that in some form the personality of a man does survive death credible to those who are willing to con- sider the phenomenon with an open mind.

But how open-minded should a person be? Anyone who pub- licizes the fact that he has visited a medium will sooner or later meet a person who reminds him about the Biblical admonitions not to visit mediums and wizards. When I first confronted this atti- tude, I was ready to discount it, but the more experiences I have in this field, the more I realize there is some wisdom in this admoni- tion. I do not accept the reasoning of some people who class all of parapsychology as the "work of the devil." Nor can I accept the careful distinction some people make between legitimate practices —spiritual healing, prayer, ESP experiments—and evil practices —telling the future (precognition) and visiting mediums. But there are possible dangers in consulting mediums. One peril is that not everything the medium says is true. Of course, many persons who claim to be mediums are fraudulent, and their word cannot be trusted. Even those who are not fraudulent are not infallible. A person may approach a sitting with the feeling that since the communication is coming from those who are freed from the limitations of an earthly perspective, what they say will be completely accurate. This is not true, and anyone who does not attempt to verify everything before accepting it is exposing himself unnecessarily to danger. Another peril in visiting mediums exists for people who have recently had a close relative die. Through the medium the bereaved tries to maintain a contact with his deceased relative. This may prevent him from working through his grief and so moving beyond his loss to live a productive life.

The reason that Biblical writers warned the people not to visit mediums was that what they said could not be trusted. I believe that one should heed this warning and not accept uncritically what a medium reports from the "other side." I do, however, think that some things that are said in sittings lend some support to the belief that man survives death, and it is this evidence which warrants the serious investigation of this phenomenon.

In addition, because some people "play" with instruments that are supposed to provide a means of communication with spirits, I feel compelled to say a word about ouija boards and such objects. From my limited experience with ouija boards, I have concluded that for the most part they work through autosuggestion. In other words, I believe that in most cases our subconscious minds make the planchette move across the board. Buried in everyone's subconscious mind are thoughts and feelings he finds unacceptable. Sometimes in ouija sessions these thoughts and feelings have come out. A sufficient number of people have got into serious psychological difficulty through the use of a ouija board to warn us that these instruments may not be "innocent toys." Most serious students of parapsychology strongly advise people not to use ouija boards and such instruments. Some believe, as I do, that the danger is psychological. Others believe "mischievous spirits" influence the results and purposely mislead people, taking them into difficult situations. Whichever is true, it is not a good practice to "play" with such "toys."

NOTES

1. Arthur Ford, with Marguerite Bro, *Nothing So Strange* (Paperback Library, Inc., 1968), pp. 10-11.

2. Arthur Ford, *Unknown But Known: My Adventure into the Meditative Dimension* (Harper & Row, 1968), p. 58.

3. Hereward Carrington, *Mysterious Psychic Phenomenon* (Christopher Publishing House, 1954), p. 142.

4. Samuel G. Soal and Frederick Bateman, *Modern Experiments in Telepathy* (Yale University Press, 1954), pp. 263-265.

5. James A. Pike, *The Other Side* (Dell Publishing Co., Inc., 1968), pp. 221-222.

6. *Ibid.*, pp. 277-278.

7. S. Ralph Harlow, *A Life After Death* (MacFadden-Bertell Corp., 1968), pp. 60-62.

8. Gardner Murphy, *Three Papers on the Survival Problem* (The American Society for Psychical Research, Inc., 1945), p. 208.

9. *Ibid.*

SUGGESTED READINGS

Perhaps one would best begin by reading the entire work from which the excerpt is taken, *Psychic Phenomena and Religion —ESP, Prayer, Healing, Survival* (Phila.: Westminster Press, 1971, paperback). In the book, Neff also studies apparitions, out-of-body experiences and reincarnation. In place of the theory of reincarnation, he leans to the theory that a person may unconsciously tune in on another person's existence. Also worth reading is the work of the respected psychic, Arthur Ford, *The Life Beyond Death,* as told to Jerome Ellison (N.Y.: Medallion Books, 1971, paperback). Chapter V, "The Revelations of Frederic Meyers," even if it is not given credence, has a way of getting to a person who on other grounds may believe in life after death. Ford's *Nothing So Strange* (N.Y.: Paperback Library, 1968), and James A. Pike's *The Other Side* (N.Y.: Dell Publishing Co., 1968, paperback) give a good sense of the psychics' approaches. Stuart Edward White's *The Unobstructed Universe* (N.Y.: E. P. Dutton, 1940, paperback) is perhaps the most metaphysical and philosophically challenging.

Semi-popular treatments of the survival question, which also cover psychic research in general, are *The Imprisoned Splendour* by Raynor C. Johnson (Wheaton, Ill.: Quest Books, 1953, paperback), and Colin Wilson's *The Occult* (N.Y.: Random House, 1971).

Nat Freedland's sweeping, popular survey, *The Occult Explosion* (N.Y.: Berkley-Medallion Books, 1972), quotes a letter from Freud to the psychic investigator, H. Carrington, "If I had my life to live over again I should devote myself to psychical research rather than psychoanalysis" (p. 38)! For the work of three major psychologists cited in this book, see Freud's *Studies in Parapsychology* (N.Y.: Collier Books, 1963, paperback); Jung's *Memories, Dreams, Reflections, op. cit.,* on the archetype of immortality, pp. 299 ff.; *William James on Psychical Research,* compiled and edited by Gardner Murphy and Robert O. Ballou (N.Y.: The Viking Press, 1960). *Psychology and Extrasensory Perception,* edited and with an introduction by Raymond Van Over (N.Y.: New American Library, 1972, paperback), presents the views of major psychologists on ESP.

For critical and theoretical approaches, see C. J. Ducasse's *A Critical Examination of Belief in Life After Death* (N.Y.: Charles C. Thomas, 1961), a short excerpt of which is found in *Body, Mind and Death,* edited by A. Flew (N.Y.: Macmillan, 1964, paperback), pp. 221-230; G. M. Tyrrell's *Apparitions* (N.Y.: Collier Books, 1963, paperback); Gardner Murphy's *Three Papers on the Survival Problem* (N.Y.: American Society for Psychical Research, 1945). As we have limited ourselves to one problem in the field of parapsychology, I have omitted mention of works which cover many other topics, such as the work of Edgar Cayce, etc.

For a fluent, popular overview, see Jess Stearn's *Adventures into the Psychic* (N.Y.: Coward-McCann, Inc., 1969, paperback), and *The Miracle Workers—America's Psychic Consultants* (Garden City, N.Y.: Doubleday & Co. Inc., 1972, paperback). For a more theoretical but still popular synthesis, see Kenneth Walker's *The Extra-Sensory Mind* (N.Y.: Harper & Row, 1972, paperback edition).

N.B. The forthcoming *Arthur Ford: The Man Who Talked with the Dead* (N.Y.: W. W. Norton & Co., 1973) by Allen Spraggett and William V. Rauscher indicates some covert information-gathering by Ford, though the authors still consider him a gifted psychic.

II

SELF-TRANSCENDENCE AND ULTIMATE MEANING

15 Man's Search for Meaning

VIKTOR FRANKL

Viktor Frankl may be considered a member of the "third force" in psychology, that is, he is neither a behaviorist nor an orthodox Freudian. He has reacted against what he believes to be an excessive emphasis on instincts in Freud and an excessive emphasis on the unconscious in Jung. He proposes a new "height psychology" to supplement depth psychology. Many neuroses, he believes, arise from an existential vacuum, a loss of sense of value or meaning. In his best known work, *Man's Search for Meaning,* Frankl considered the problem of meaning as it manifested itself in his concentration camp experience at Auschwitz and Dachau. As a result of that experience a phrase from Nietzsche took on new light for him: "He who has a *why* to live can bear almost any *how.*"

Frankl might be read in conjunction with Part I of this book. I have included him in Part II which approaches the problem of meaning in a wider philosophical and theological sense.* This is not to suggest that Frankl is to be considered a philosopher or a theologian, which he is not, although his work has philosophical tendencies. Reading Frankl, however, opens one to a consideration of meaning from a philosophical and theological viewpoint. Thus he can be seen as a bridge between the within and the beyond.

* From *Psychotherapy and Existentialism—Papers on Logotherapy,* pp. 5-9, 11-15, 32-34, 35. Copyright © 1967 by Viktor E. Frankl. Reprinted by permission of Washington Square Press, Inc., division of Simon & Schuster, Inc.

Frankl compared psychoanalysis with his system of "logotherapy." The latter, he said, is less introspective and less retrospective than psychoanalysis. "Logotherapy focuses rather on the future, that is to say, on the assignments and meanings to be fulfilled. . . " It may help us to pause for a moment and consider the concept of "meaning." If the reader consults, for example, the Encyclopedia *Sacramentum Mundi,* under the word "meaning" he will find many diverse applications. Meaning may be found in moments of truth, when one rests in the solution of a mathematical or theoretical problem. It is found in the relationship of love, whether for a person or for a cause. Meaning has its epiphany also in works of art and beauty. Meaning is found in political institutions insofar as they further the life of fellowship. Lastly, meaning is found in an overarching sense in aesthetics, in philosophy and in religious belief and worship, that is, in God.

When Frankl speaks of meaning, he refers not to meaning and purpose of the world as a whole, but to individual, specifically personal, meaning. For example, a person may find meaning in simply having a task to perform, work to do. Nevertheless, he sees a connection between individual meaning and ultimate or "super-meaning." With regard to the latter, he supports "the Kantian postulate of reason: our minds require its existence at the same time that it is to our minds unfathomable" (*Ibid.* p. 25). For Frankl, religion may be an asset to a person in his quest for meaning and health but its presence is not essential to logotherapy.

If one studies the uses of the word "meaning" found in *Psychotherapy and Existentialism,* the work from which the following excerpt is taken, a certain pattern can be discerned: meaning implies or demands self-transcendence; it involves values or goals beyond the self; it has an eternal value; it is not grasped intellec-

tually but by an act of commitment; it includes a
basic and unconditional trust in being.

Frankl suggests that meaning can be found especially
in three experiences: responsibleness to values, love
and suffering. His famous therapeutic method of
"paradoxical intention" aims at a self-transcendence
through the liberating and self-distancing power of
humor.

For didactic reasons the will to meaning has
been counterposed by way of a heuristic
oversimplification both to the pleasure principle, which is so pervasive in psychoanalytic motivational theories, and to the will to
power, the concept which plays such a decisive role in Adlerian
psychology. I do not weary of contending that the will to pleasure
is really a self-defeating principle inasmuch as the more a man
would actually set out to strive for pleasure the less he would gain
it. This is due to the fundamental fact that pleasure is a by-product,
or side effect, of the fulfillment of our strivings, but is destroyed and
spoiled to the extent to which it is made a goal or target. The more
a man aims at pleasure by way of a direct intention, the more he
misses his aim. And this, I venture to say, is a mechanism etiologi-
cally underlying most cases of sexual neurosis. Accordingly, a
logotherapeutic technique based on this theory of the self-thwarting
quality of pleasure intention yields remarkable short-term results,
and this technique has been used effectively even by psychodynamically oriented therapists on my staff. One of them, to whom I have
assigned the responsibility for treatment of all sexually neurotic
patients, has used this technique exclusively—in terms of a short-
term procedure which has been the only one indicated in the given
setting.

In the last analysis, it turns out that both the will to pleasure
and the will to power are derivatives of the original will to meaning. Pleasure, as we have said above, is an effect of meaning fulfillment; power is a means to an end. A certain amount of power,
such as economic or financial power, is generally a prerequisite
for meaning fulfillment. Thus we could say that while the will to

pleasure mistakes the effect for the end, the will to power mistakes the means to an end for the end itself.

We are not really justified, however, in speaking of a *will* to pleasure or power in connection with psychodynamically oriented schools of thought; they assume that man aims for the goals of his behavior unwillingly and unwittingly and that his conscious motivations are not his actual motivations. Erich Fromm, for instance, only recently spoke of "the motivating forces which make man act in certain ways, the drives which propel him to strive in certain directions." [1] As for myself, however, it is not conceivable that man be really driven to strivings; I would say either that he is striving or that he is driven. *Tertium non datur.* Ignoring this difference or, rather, sacrificing one phenomenon to another, is a procedure unworthy of a scientist. To do so is to allow one's adherence to hypotheses to blind one to facts. One such distortion is the assumption that man "is lived by" his instincts. Since the man quoted here is Sigmund Freud, for the sake of justice, another of Freud's statements which is not so well known must be added. In a book review he wrote for the *Wiener Medizinische Wochenschrift* in 1889, he says: "Reverence before the greatness of a genius is certainly a great thing. But our reverence before facts should exceed it."

Freud, and consequently his epigones, have taught us always to see something behind, or beneath, human volitions: unconscious motivations, underlying dynamics. Freud never took a human phenomenon at its face value; or, to adopt the formulation used by Gordon W. Allport, "Freud was a specialist in precisely those motives that cannot be taken at their face value." [2] Does this, however, imply that there are no motives at all which should be taken at their face value? Such an assumption is comparable to the attitude of the man who, when he was shown a stork, said, "Oh, I thought the stork didn't exist!" Does the fact that the stork has been used to hide the facts of life from children in any way deny that bird's reality?

The reality principle is, according to Freud's own words, a mere extension of the pleasure principle; one which serves the pleasure principle's purpose. One could just as well say that the pleasure principle itself is a mere extension working in the service of a wider concept called the homeostasis principle and serves *its* purposes. Ultimately, the psychodynamic concept of man presents him as a being basically concerned with maintaining or restoring his inner equilibrium, and in order to do so, he is trying to gratify his drives and satisfy his instincts. Even in the perspective in which man has been portrayed by Jungian psychology, human motivation is interpreted along this line. Just think of archetypes. They, too, are mythical beings (as Freud called the instincts). Again man is seen as bent on getting rid of tensions, be they aroused by drives and instincts claiming their gratification and satisfaction, or by archetypes urging their materialization. In either case, reality, the world of beings and meanings, is debased and degraded to a pool of more or less workable instruments to be used to get rid of various stimuli such as irritating superegos or archetypes. What has been sacrificed, however, and hence totally eliminated in this view of man, is the fundamental fact which lends itself to a phenomeno-logical analysis—namely, that man is a being encountering other beings and reaching out for meanings to fulfill.

And this is precisely the reason why I speak of a will to mean-ing rather than a need for meaning or a drive to meaning. If man were really driven to meaning he would embark on meaning ful-fillment solely for the sake of getting rid of this drive, in order to restore homeostasis within himself. At the same time, however, he would no longer be really concerned with meaning itself but rather with his own equilibrium and thus, in the final analysis, with himself.

It may now have become clear that a concept such as self-actualization, or self-realization, is not a sufficient ground for a motivational theory. This is mainly due to the fact that self-actuali-zation, like power and pleasure, also belongs to the class of phe-nomena which can only be obtained as a side effect and are thwarted precisely to the degree to which they are made a matter of direct intention. Self-actualization is a good thing; however, I maintain that man can only actualize himself to the extent to which he fulfills meaning. Then self-actualization occurs spontaneously; it is contravened when it is made an end in itself.

When I was lecturing at Melbourne University some years ago, I was given as a souvenir an Australian boomerang. While contemplating this unusual gift, it occurred to me that in a sense it was a symbol of human existence. Generally, one assumes that a boomerang returns to the hunter; but actually, I have been told in Australia, a boomerang only comes back to the hunter when it has missed its target, the prey. Well, man also only returns to himself, to being concerned with his self, after he has missed his mission, has failed to find a meaning in his life.

Ernest Keen, one of my assistants during a teaching period at the Harvard Summer Session, devoted his doctoral dissertation to demonstrating that the shortcomings of Freudian psychoanalysis have been compensated for by Heinz Hartmann's ego psychology, and the deficiencies of ego psychology, in turn, by Erikson's identity concept. However, Keen contends, a last link was still missing, and this link is logotherapy. In fact, it is my conviction that man should not, indeed cannot, struggle for identity in a direct way; he rather finds identity to the extent to which he commits himself to something beyond himself, to a cause greater than himself. No one has put it as cogently as Karl Jaspers did when he said: "What man is, he ultimately becomes through the cause which he has made his own." . . .

The otherness of the other being should not be blurred in existential thinking, as Erwin Straus has so rightly stressed; and this also holds true for meaning. The meaning which a being has to fulfill is something beyond himself, it is never just himself. Only if this otherness is retained by meaning, can meaning exert upon a being that demand quality which yields itself to a phenomenological analysis of our experience of existence. Only a meaning which is not just an expression of the being itself represents a true challenge. You remember the story in the Bible: When the Israelites wandered through the desert God's glory went before in the form of a cloud; only in this way was it possible for the Israelites to be guided by God. Imagine, on the other hand, what would have happened if God's presence, the cloud, had dwelled in the midst of Israelites; rather than leading them the right way, this cloud would have clouded everything, and the Israelites would have gone astray.

In other words, meaning must not coincide with being; meaning must be ahead of being. Meaning sets the pace for being. Existence falters unless it is lived in terms of transcendence toward something beyond itself. Viewed from this angle, we might distinguish between people who are pacemakers and those who are peacemakers: the former confront us with meanings and values, thus supporting our meaning orientation; the latter alleviate the burden of meaning confrontation. In this sense Moses was a pacemaker; he did not soothe man's conscience but rather stirred it up. Moses confronted his people with the Ten Commandments and did not spare them confrontation with ideals and values. Peacemakers, on the other hand, appease people; they try to reconcile them with themselves. "Let's face facts," they say. "Why worry about your shortcomings? Only a minority live up to ideals. So let's forget them; let's care for peace of mind, or soul, rather than those existential meanings which just arouse tensions in human beings."

What the peacemakers overlook is the wisdom laid down in Goethe's warning: "If we take man as he is, we make him worse; if we take him as he ought to be, we help him become it."

Once meaning orientation turns into meaning confrontation, that stage of maturation and development is reached in which freedom—that concept so much emphasized by existentialist philosophy—becomes responsibleness. Man is responsible for the fulfillment of the specific meaning of his personal life. But he is also responsible *before* something, or *to* something, be it society, or humanity, or mankind, or his own conscience. However, there is a significant number of people who interpret their own existence not just in terms of being responsible to something but rather to someone, namely, to God.[3]

Logotherapy, as a secular theory and medical practice, must restrict itself to factual statements, leaving to the patient the decision as to how to understand his own being-responsible: whether along the lines of religious beliefs or agnostic convictions. Logotherapy must remain available for everyone; I would be obliged to adhere to this by my Hippocratic oath, if for no other reason. Logotherapy is applicable in cases of atheistic patients and usable in the hands of atheistic doctors. In any case, logotherapy sees in responsibleness the very essence of human existence. Capitalizing on responsibleness to this extent, a logotherapist cannot spare his patient the decision for what, and to what, or to whom, he feels responsible.

A logotherapist is not entitled consciously to influence the patient's decision as to how to interpret his own responsibleness, or as to what to embrace as his personal meaning. Anyone's conscience, as anything human, is subject to error; but this does not release man from his obligation to obey it—existence involves the risk of error. Man must risk committing himself to a cause not worthy of his commitment. Perhaps my commitment to the cause of logotherapy is erroneous. But I prefer to live in a world in which man has the right to make choices, even if they are wrong choices, rather than a world in which no choice at all is left to him. In other words, I prefer a world in which, on the one hand, a phenomenon such as Adolf Hitler can occur, and on the other hand, phenomena such as the many saints who have lived can occur also. I prefer this world to a world of total, or totalitarian, conformism and collectivism in which man is debased and degraded to a mere functionary of a party or the state.

The Meaning of Life

We have now reached the point of the third basic assumption: After discussing freedom of will and will to meaning, meaning itself becomes the topic.

While no logotherapist *prescribes* a meaning he may well *describe* it. By this I mean describing what is going on in a man when he experiences something as meaningful, without applying to such experiences any preconceived pattern of interpretation. In short, our task is to resort to a phenomenological investigation of the immediate data of actual life experience. In a phenomenological way, the logotherapist might widen and broaden the visual field of his patient in terms of meanings and values, making them loom large, as it were. In the course of a growing awareness, it might then finally turn out that life never ceases to hold and retain a meaning up to its very last moment. This is due to the fact that, as a phenomenological analysis can show us, man not only finds his life meaningful through his deeds, his works, his creativity, but also through his experiences, his encounters with what is true, good, and beautiful in the world, and last but not least, his encounter with others, with fellow human beings and their unique qualities. To grasp another person in his uniqueness means to love him. But even in a situation in which man is deprived of both creativity and receptivity, he can still fulfill a meaning in his life.

It is precisely when facing such a fate, when being confronted with a hopeless situation, that man is given a last opportunity to fulfill a meaning—to realize even the highest value, to fulfill even the deepest meaning—and that is the meaning of suffering.[4]

Let me summarize. Life can be made meaningful in a three-fold way: first, through *what we give* to life (in terms of our creative works); second, by *what we take* from the world (in terms of our experiencing values); and third, through *the stand we take* toward a fate we no longer can change (an incurable disease, an inoperable cancer, or the like). However, even apart from this, man is not spared facing his human condition which includes what I call the tragic triad of human existence; namely, pain, death, and guilt. By pain, I mean suffering; by the two other constituents of the tragic triad, I mean the twofold fact of man's mortality and fallibility.

Stressing these tragic aspects of man's life is not as superfluous as it may seem to be at first sight. In particular, the fear of aging and dying is pervasive in the present culture, and Edith Weisskopf-Joelson, professor of psychology at Duke University, has claimed that logotherapy might help counteract these particularly widespread American anxieties. As a matter of fact, it is my contention, and a tenet of logotherapy, that life's transitoriness does not in the least detract from its meaningfulness. The same holds for man's fallibility. So there is no need to reinforce our patients' escapism in the face of the tragic triad of existence. . . .

It is not the least task of psychotherapy to bring about reconciliation and to bring consolation: Man has to be reconciled to his finiteness, and he also has to be enabled to face the transitoriness of his life. With these efforts psychotherapy indeed touches the realm of religion. There is common ground enough to warrant mutual rapprochement. Bridging, however, does not mean merging. There still remains the essential difference between the respective aims of psychotherapy and religion. The goal of psychotherapy, of psychiatry and, quite generally, of medicine, is health. The goal of religion, however, is something essentially different: salvation. So much for the difference of goals. The results achieved, however, are another matter. Although religion may not aim at mental health it might result in it. Psychotherapy, in turn, often results in an analogous by-product; while the doctor is not, and must not be, concerned with helping the patient to regain his belief in God, time and again this is just what occurs, unintended and unexpected as it is.

How, then, does this occur in the actual situation? Let me return to the logotherapeutic group session, or logodrama, which I mentioned before. During the discussion of the meaning of suffering I asked the whole group whether an ape which is punctured many times in order to develop poliomyelitis serum is able to grasp the meaning of its suffering. Unanimously the group replied, "Of course it would not! For with its limited intelligence it cannot enter the world of man, i.e., that world in which its suffering would be understandable." I then pressed on with the following: "And what about man? Are you sure that the human world is the terminal point in the evolution of the cosmos? Is it not conceivable that there is still another dimension, a world beyond man's world; a world in which the question of an ultimate meaning to man's suffering is answered?"

By its very nature this ultimate meaning exceeds man's limited intellectual capacity. In contrast to those existential writers who declare that man has to stand the ultimate absurdity of being human, it is my contention that man has to stand only his incapacity to grasp the ultimate meaning on intellectual grounds. Man is only called upon to decide between the alternatives of "ultimate absurdity or ultimate meaning" on existential grounds, through the mode of existence which he chooses. In the "How" of existence, I would say, lies the answer to the question for its "Why."

Thus, the ultimate meaning is no longer a matter of intellectual cognition but of existential commitment. One might as well say that a meaning can be understood but that the ultimate meaning must be interpreted. An interpretation, however, involves a decision. . . .

Man cannot avoid decisions. Reality inescapably forces man to decide. Man makes decisions in every moment, even unwittingly and against his will. Through these decisions man decides upon himself. Continually and incessantly he shapes and reshapes himself. Thomas Aquinas' *"agere sequitur esse"* is but half the truth: Man not only behaves according to what he is, he also becomes what he is according to how he behaves. Man is not a thing among others —things determine each other—but man is ultimately self-determining. What he becomes—within the limits of endowment and environment—he has made himself. In the living laboratories of the concentration camps we watched comrades behaving like swine while others behaved like saints. Man has both these potentialities within himself. Which one he actualizes depends on decision, not on conditions. It is time that this decision quality of human existence be included in our definition of man. Our generation has come to know man as he really is: the being that has invented the gas chambers of Auschwitz, and also the being who entered those gas chambers upright, the Lord's Prayer or the *Shema Yisrael* on his lips.

NOTES

1. *Beyond the Chains of Illusion* (New York: Simon & Schuster, Inc., 1962), p. 38.
2. *Personality and Social Encounter* (Boston: Beacon Press, 1960), p. 103.
3. I personally doubt whether, within religion, truth can ever be distinguished from untruth by evidence which is universally acceptable to man. It seems to me that the various religious denominations are something like different languages. It is not possible, either, to declare that any one of them is superior to the others. Similarly, no language can justifiably be called "true" or "false," but through each of them truth—the one truth—may be approached as if from different sides, and through each language it is also possible to err, and even to lie.
4. It goes without saying that suffering can be meaningful only if the situation cannot be changed—otherwise we would not be dealing with heroism but rather masochism.

SUGGESTED READINGS

Frankl's *Man's Search for Meaning—An Introduction to Logotherapy* (N.Y.: Washington Square Press, 1963) combines a description of his concentration camp experience with the principles of logotherapy. More extensive treatment of the theory as well as bibliographical material are found in *Psychotherapy and Exis-*

tentialism—Selected Papers on Logotherapy, with contributions by James C. Crumbaugh, Hans O. Gerz, Leonard T. Maholick (N.Y.: Simon and Schuster, a Clarion Book paperback, 1967); *The Will to Meaning: Foundations and Applications of Logotherapy* (N.Y.: New American Library, paperback, 1969); *The Doctor and the Soul* (N.Y.: Bantam Books, 1967, paperback). Joseph B. Fabry's *The Pursuit of Meaning: Logotherapy Applied to Life,* preface by V. Frankl (Boston: Beacon Press, 1968, paperback), and A. J. Ungersma's *The Search for Meaning—A New Approach in Psychotherapy,* foreword by V. Frankl (Phila.: Westminster Press, 1961, paperback) are two helpful overviews. Criticism of Frankl's approach in comparison with that of his onetime teacher, Alfred Adler, is presented by Walter E. O'Connell in "Frankl, Adler, and Spirituality," *Journal of Religion and Health,* Vol. 11, no. 2, April 1972, pp. 134-138. O'Connell says Frankl misinterprets the will to power, is "existential-philosophical" rather than "existential-psychological," and tends to become an "orthodox tutor."

(For an excellent approach to the question of transcendence in general, see *Transcendence,* edited by Herbert W. Richardson and Donald R. Cutler [Boston: Beacon Press, 1969, paperback].)

16 Meaning and Experience

WILLIAM JAMES

The Varieties of Religious Experience by William James (1842-1910) was the most important and influential pioneer work in American religious psychology. James' pragmatism is too subtle to be handled at length here, and the reader would be well advised to fit the following excerpt * from the conclusion of *The Varieties of Religious Experience* into the wider context of his general principles (cf. suggested readings). For James, pragmatism is the attitude of looking away from first principles and roots and of looking toward fruits, conduct and consequences. An idea without any perceivable experiential consequences is empty. But one should move toward an understanding of the *sum total* of the consequences of an idea because: "What immediately feels most 'good' is not always most 'true,' when measured by the verdict of the rest of experience" (*Varieties,* p. 25).

James does not use pragmatism to discover truth which can be deduced with certainty from evidence through intellectual process. Rather he applies it to options where the intellect is not coerced by the evidence and to options which are live, momentous and necessary. In these cases James recurs to what he calls one's "passional nature" or "the sentiment of rationality." In this regard he held that whatever conception of the universe blocked the zest for life and the will to action cannot be "true," that is true in the pragmatic sense. But he added: ". . . the

---

* From *The Varieties of Religious Experience* by William James, pp. 454-464. Reprinted by permission of Doubleday & Company, Inc.

existence of the object, whenever the idea asserts itself "truly," is the only reason, in innumerable cases, why the idea does work successfully, if it works at all" (*Pragmatism and Other Essays*, p. 139). James believed that the word "rational" had been used in a too restrictive, intellectual sense. Whatever is rational "must appeal not only to our theoretical but also to our practical and affective side." In this sense the existence of God is "rational" for James, a position which is the opposite of Freud's. James' God, however, is not infinite. Only God as finite, it seemed to James, would allow for an intimate relationship with each human being.

We must next pass beyond the point of view of merely subjective utility, and make inquiry into the intellectual content itself.

First, is there, under all the discrepancies of the creeds, a common nucleus to which they bear their testimony unanimously?

And second, ought we to consider the testimony true?

I will take up the first question first, and answer it immediately in the affirmative. The warring gods and formulas of the various religions do indeed cancel each other, but there is a certain uniform deliverance in which religions all appear to meet. It consists of two parts:—

1. An uneasiness; and
2. Its solution.

1. The uneasiness, reduced to its simplest terms, is a sense that there is *something wrong about us* as we naturally stand.

2. The solution is a sense that *we are saved from the wrongness* by making proper connection with the higher powers.

In those more developed minds which alone we are studying, the wrongness takes a moral character, and the salvation takes a mystical tinge. I think we shall keep well within the limits of what is common to all such minds if we formulate the essence of their religious experience in terms like these:—

The individual, so far as he suffers from his wrongness and criticises it, is to that extent consciously beyond it, and in at least possible touch with something higher, if anything higher exist. Along with the wrong part there is thus a better part of him, even though it may be but a most helpless germ. With which part he should identify his real being is by no means obvious at this stage; but when stage 2 (the stage of solution or salvation) arrives,[1] the man identifies his real being with the germinal higher part of himself; and does so in the following way. *He becomes conscious that this higher part is conterminous and continuous with a* MORE *of the same quality, which is operative in the universe outside of him, and which he can keep in working touch with, and in a fashion get on board of and save himself when all his lower being has gone to pieces in the wreck.*

It seems to me that all the phenomena are accurately describable in these very simple general terms.[2] They allow for the divided self and the struggle; they involve the change of personal centre and the surrender of the lower self; they express the appearance of exteriority of the helping power and yet account for our sense of union with it,[3] and they fully justify our feelings of security and joy. There is probably no autobiographic document, among all those which I have quoted, to which the description will not well apply. One need only add such specific details as will adapt it to various theologies and various personal temperaments, and one will then have the various experiences reconstructed in their individual forms.

So far, however, as this analysis goes, the experiences are only psychological phenomena. They possess, it is true, enormous biological worth. Spiritual strength really increases in the subject when he has them, a new life opens for him, and they seem to him a place of conflux where the forces of two universes meet; and yet this may be nothing but his subjective way of feeling things, a mood of his own fancy, in spite of the effects produced. I now turn to my second question: What is the objective "truth" of their content? [4]

The part of the content concerning which the question of truth most pertinently arises is that "MORE of the same quality" with which our own higher self appears in the experience to come into harmonious working relation. Is such a "more" merely our own notion, or does it really exist? If so, in what shape does it exist?

Does it act, as well as exist? And in what form should we conceive of that "union" with it of which religious geniuses are so convinced?

It is in answering these questions that the various theologies perform their theoretic work, and that their divergencies most come to light. They all agree that the "more" really exists; though some of them hold it to exist in the shape of a personal god or gods, while others are satisfied to conceive it as a stream of ideal tendency embedded in the eternal structure of the world. They all agree, moreover, that it acts as well as exists, and that something really is effected for the better when you throw your life into its hands. It is when they treat of the experience of "union" with it that their speculative differences appear most clearly. Over this point pantheism and theism, nature and second birth, works and grace and karma, immortality and reincarnation, rationalism and mysticism, carry on inveterate disputes.

At the end of my lecture on Philosophy [5] I held out the notion that an impartial science of religions might sift out from the midst of their discrepancies a common body of doctrine which she might also formulate in terms to which physical science need not object. This, I said, she might adopt as her own reconciling hypothesis, and recommend it for general belief. I also said that in my last lecture I should have to try my own hand at framing such an hypothesis.

The time has now come for this attempt. Who says "hypothesis" renounces the ambition to be coercive in his arguments. The most I can do is, accordingly, to offer something that may fit the facts so easily that your scientific logic will find no plausible pretext for vetoing your impulse to welcome it as true.

The "more," as we called it, and the meaning of our "union" with it, form the nucleus of our inquiry. Into what definite description can these words be translated, and for what definite facts do they stand? It would never do for us to place ourselves offhand at the position of a particular theology, the Christian theology, for example, and proceed immediately to define the "more" as Jehovah, and the "union" as his imputation to us of the righteousness of Christ. That would be unfair to other religions, and, from our present standpoint at least, would be an over-belief.

We must begin by using less particularized terms; and, since one of the duties of the science of religions is to keep religion in connection with the rest of science, we shall do well to seek first of all a way of describing the "more," which psychologists may also recognize as real. The *subconscious self* is nowadays a well-accredited psychological entity; and I believe that in it we have exactly the mediating term required. Apart from all religious considerations, there is actually and literally more life in our total soul than we are at any time aware of. The exploration of the transmarginal field has hardly yet been seriously undertaken, but what Mr. Myers said in 1892 in his essay on the Subliminal Consciousness [6] is as true as when it was first written: "Each of us is in reality an abiding psychical entity far more extensive than he knows—an individuality which can never express itself completely through any corporeal manifestation. The Self manifests through the organism; but there is always some part of the Self unmanifested; and always, as it seems, some power of organic expression in abeyance or reserve." [7] Much of the content of this larger background against which our conscious being stands out in relief is insignificant. Imperfect memories, silly jingles, inhibitive timidities, "dissolutive" phenomena of various sorts, as Myers calls them, enters into it for a large part. But in it many of the performances of genius seem also to have their origin; and in our study of conversion, of mystical experiences, and of prayer, we have seen how striking a part invasions from this region play in the religious life.

Let me then propose, as an hypothesis, that whatever it may be on its *farther* side, the "more" with which in religious experience we feel ourselves connected is on its *hither* side the subconscious continuation of our conscious life. Starting thus with a recognized psychological fact as our basis, we seem to preserve a contact with "science" which the ordinary theologian lacks. At the same time the theologian's contention that the religious man is moved by an external power is vindicated, for it is one of the peculiarities of invasions from the subconscious region to take on objective appearances, and to suggest to the Subject an external control. In the religious life the control is felt as "higher"; but since on our hypothesis it is primarily the higher faculties of our own hidden mind which are controlling, the sense of union with the power beyond us is a sense of something, not merely apparently, but literally true.

This doorway into the subject seems to me the best one for

a science of religions, for it mediates between a number of different points of view. Yet it is only a doorway, and difficulties present themselves as soon as we step through it, and ask how far our transmarginal consciousness carries us if we follow it on its remoter side. Here the over-beliefs begin: here mysticism and the conversion-rapture and Vedantism and transcendental idealism bring in their monistic interpretations [8] and tell us that the finite self rejoins the absolute self, for it was always one with God and identical with the soul of the world.[9] Here the prophets of all the different religions come with their visions, voices, raptures, and other openings, supposed by each to authenticate his own peculiar faith.

Those of us who are not personally favored with such specific revelations must stand outside of them altogether and, for the present at least, decide that, since they corroborate incompatible theological doctrines, they neutralize one another and leave no fixed results. If we follow any one of them, or if we follow philosophical theory and embrace monistic pantheism on non-mystical grounds, we do so in the exercise of our individual freedom, and build out our religion in the way most congruous with our personal susceptibilities. Among these susceptibilities intellectual ones play a decisive part. Although the religious question is primarily a question of life, of living or not living in the higher union which opens itself to us as a gift, yet the spiritual excitement in which the gift appears a real one will often fail to be aroused in an individual until certain particular intellectual beliefs or ideas which, as we say, come home to him, are touched.[10] These ideas will thus be essential to that individual's religion;—which is as much as to say that over-beliefs in various directions are absolutely indispensable, and that we should treat them with tenderness and tolerance so long as they are not intolerant themselves. As I have elsewhere written, the most interesting and valuable things about a man are usually his over-beliefs.

Disregarding the over-beliefs, and confining ourselves to what is common and generic, we have in *the fact that the conscious person is continuous with a wider self through which saving experiences come,*[11] a positive content of religious experience, which, it seems to me, *is literally and objectively true as far as it goes.* If I now proceed to state my own hypothesis about the farther limits of this extension of our personality, I shall be offering my own over-belief—though I know it will appear a sorry under-belief to some of you—for which I can only bespeak the same indulgence which in a converse case I should accord to yours.

The further limits of our being plunge, it seems to me, into an altogether other dimension of existence from the sensible and merely "understandable" world. Name it the mystical region, or the supernatural region, whichever you choose. So far as our ideal impulses originate in this region (and most of them do originate in it, for we find them possessing us in a way for which we cannot articulately account), we belong to it in a more intimate sense than that in which we belong to the visible world, for we belong in the most intimate sense wherever our ideals belong. Yet the unseen region in question is not merely ideal, for it produces effects in this world. When we commune with it, work is actually done upon our finite personality, for we are turned into new men, and consequences in the way of conduct follow in the natural world upon our regenerative change.[12] But that which produces effects within another reality must be termed a reality itself, so I feel as if we had no philosophic excuse for calling the unseen or mystical world unreal.

God is the natural appellation, for us Christians at least, for the supreme reality, so I will call this higher part of the universe by the name of God.[13] We and God have business with each other; and in opening ourselves to his influence our deepest destiny is fulfilled. The universe, at those parts of it which our personal being constitutes, takes a turn genuinely for the worse or for the better in proportion as each one of us fulfills or evades God's demands. As far as this goes I probably have you with me, for I only translate into schematic language what I may call the instinctive belief of mankind: God is real since he produces real effects.

The real effects in question, so far as I have as yet admitted them, are exerted on the personal centres of energy of the various subjects, but the spontaneous faith of most of the subjects is that they embrace a wider sphere than this. Most religious men believe (or "know," if they be mystical) that not only they themselves, but the whole universe of beings to whom the God is present, are secure in his parental hands. There is a sense, a dimension, they are sure, in which we are *all* saved, in spite of the gates of hell and all adverse terrestrial appearances. God's existence is the guarantee of an ideal order that shall be permanently preserved. This world may indeed, as science assures us, some day burn up or freeze; but if it is part of his order, the old ideals are sure to be brought elsewhere to fruition, so that where God is, tragedy is only provisional and partial, and shipwreck and dissolution are not the absolutely final things. Only when this farther step of faith concerning God is taken, and remote objective consequences are predicted, does religion, as it seems to me, get wholly free from the first immediate subjective experience, and bring a *real hypothesis* into play. A good hypothesis in science must have other properties than those of the phenomenon it is immediately invoked to explain, otherwise it is not prolific enough. God, meaning only what enters into the religious man's experience of union, falls short of being an hypothesis of this more useful order. He needs to enter into wider cosmic relations in order to justify the subject's absolute confidence and peace.

That the God with whom, starting from the hither side of our own extra-marginal self, we come at its remoter margin into commerce should be the absolute world-ruler, is of course a very considerable over-belief. Over-belief as it is, though, it is an article of almost every one's religion. Most of us pretend in some way to prop it upon our philosophy, but the philosophy itself is really propped upon this faith. What is this but to say that Religion, in her fullest exercise of function, is not a mere illumination of facts already elsewhere given, not a mere passion, like love, which views things in a rosier light. It is indeed that, as we have seen abundantly. But it is something more, namely, a postulator of new *facts* as well. The world interpreted religiously is not the materialistic world over again, with an altered expression; it must have, over and above the altered expression, *a natural constitution* different at some point from that which a materialistic world would have. It must be such that different events can be expected in it, different conduct must be required.

This thoroughly "pragmatic" view of religion has usually been taken as a matter of course by common men. They have interpolated divine miracles into the field of nature, they have built a heaven out beyond the grave. It is only transcendentalist metaphysicians who think that, without adding any concrete details to Nature, or subtracting any, but by simply calling it the expression of absolute spirit, you make it more divine just as it stands. I believe the pragmatic way of taking religion to be the deeper way. It gives it body as well as soul, it makes it claim, as everything real must claim, some characteristic realm of fact as its very own. What the more characteristically divine facts are, apart from the actual inflow of energy in the faith-state and the prayer-state, I know not. But the over-belief on which I am ready to make my personal venture is that they exist. The whole drift of my education goes to persuade me that the world of our present consciousness is only one out of many worlds of consciousness that exist, and that those other worlds must contain experiences which have a meaning for our life also; and that although in the main their experiences and those of this world keep discrete, yet the two become continuous at certain points, and higher energies filter in. By being faithful in my poor measure to this over-belief, I seem to myself to keep more sane and true. I *can,* of course, put myself into the sectarian scientist's attitude, and imagine vividly that the world of sensations and of scientific laws and objects may be all. But whenever I do this, I hear that inward monitor of which W. K. Clifford once wrote, whispering the word "bosh!" Humbug is humbug, even though it bear the scientific name, and the total expression of human experience, as I view it objectively, invincibly urges me beyond the narrow "scientific" bounds. Assuredly, the real world is of a different temperament—more intricately built than physical science allows. So my objective and my subjective conscience both hold me to the over-belief which I express. Who knows whether the faithfulness of individuals here below to their own poor over-beliefs may not actually help God in turn to be more effectively faithful to his own greater tasks?

NOTES

1. Remember that for some men it arrives suddenly, for others gradually, whilst others again practically enjoy it all their life.

2. The practical difficulties are: 1, to "realize the reality" of one's higher part; 2, to identify one's self with it exclusively; and 3, to identify it with all the rest of ideal being.

3. "When mystical activity is at its height, we find consciousness possessed by the sense of a being at once *excessive* and *identical* with the self: great enough to be God; interior enough to be *me*. The "objectivity" of it ought in that case to be called *excessivity,* rather, or exceedingness." RÉCÉJAC: Essai sur les fondements de la conscience mystique, 1897, p. 46.

4. The word "truth" is here taken to mean something additional to bare value for life, although the natural propensity of man is to believe that whatever has great value for life is thereby certified as true.

5. Above, p. 409.

6. Proceedings of the Society for Psychical Research, vol. vii, p. 305. For a full statement of Mr. Myers's views, I may refer to his posthumous work, "Human Personality in the Light of Recent Research," which is already announced by Messrs. Longmans, Green & Co. as being in press. Mr. Myers for the first time proposed as a general psychological problem the exploration of the subliminal region of consciousness throughout its whole extent, and made the first methical steps in its topography by treating as a natural series a mass of subliminal facts hitherto considered only as curious isolated facts, and subjecting them to a systematized nomenclature. How important this exploration will prove, future work upon the path which Myers has opened can alone show. Compare my paper: "Frederic Myers's Services to Psychology," in the said Proceedings, part xlii., May, 1901.

7. Compare the inventory given above on pp. 433-435, and also what is said of the subconscious self on pp. 215-217, 221-222.

8. Compare above, pp. 379ff.

9. One more expression of this belief, to increase the reader's familiarity with the notion of it:—

"If this room is full of darkness for thousands of years, and you come in and begin to weep and wail, 'Oh, the darkness,' will the darkness vanish? Bring the light in, strike a match, and light comes in a moment. So what good will it do you to think all your lives, 'Oh, I have done evil, I have made many mistakes'? It requires no ghost to tell us that. Bring in the light, and the evil goes in a moment. Strengthen the real nature, build up yourselves, the effulgent, the resplendent, the ever pure, call that up in every one whom you see. I wish that every one of us had come to such a state that even when we see the vilest of human beings we can see the God within, and instead of condemning, say, 'Rise, thou effulgent One, rise thou who art always pure, rise thou birthless and deathless, rise almighty, and manifest your nature.' . . . This is the highest prayer that the Advaita teaches. This is the one prayer: remembering our nature." . . . "Why does man go out to look for a God? . . . It is your own heart beating, and you did not know, you were mistaking it for something external. He, nearest of the near, my own self, the reality of my own life, my body and my soul.—I am Thee and Thou art Me. That is your own nature. Assert it, manifest it. Not to become pure, you are pure already. You are not to be perfect, you are that already. Every good thought which you think or act upon is simply tearing the veil, as it were, and the purity, the Infinity, the God behind, manifests itself—the eternal Subject of everything, the eternal Witness in this universe, your own Self. Knowledge is, as it were, a lower step, a degradation. We are It already; how to know It?" SWAMI VIVEKANANDA: Addresses, No. XII., Practical Vedanta, part iv. pp. 172, 174, London, 1897; and Lectures, The Real and the Apparent Man, p. 24, abridged.

10. For instance, here is a case where a person exposed from her birth to Christian ideas had to wait till they came to her clad in spiritistic formulas before the saving experience set in:—

"For myself I can say that spiritualism has saved me. It was revealed to me at a critical moment of my life, and without it I don't know what I should have done. It has taught me to detach myself from worldly things and to place my hope in things to come. Through it I have learned to see in all men, even in those most criminal, even in those from whom I have most suffered, undeveloped brothers to whom I owed assistance, love, and forgiveness. I have learned that I must lose my temper over nothing, despise no one, and pray for all. Most of all I have learned to pray! And although I have still much to learn in this domain, prayer ever brings me more strength, consolation, and comfort. I feel more than ever that I have only made a few steps on the long road of progress; but I look at its length without dismay, for I have confidence that the day will come when all my efforts shall be rewarded. So Spiritualism has a great place in my life, indeed it holds the first place there." Flournoy Collection.

11. "The influence of the Holy Spirit, exquisitely called the Comforter, is a matter of actual experience, as solid a reality as that of electro-magnetism." W. C. BROWNELL, Scribner's Magazine, vol. xxx, p. 112.

12. That the transaction of opening ourselves, otherwise called prayer, is a perfectly definite one for certain persons, appears abundantly in the preceding lectures. I append another concrete example to reinforce the impression on the reader's mind:—

"Man can learn to transcend these limitations [of finite thought] and draw power and wisdom at will. . . . The divine presence is known through experience. The turning to a higher plane is a distinct act of consciousness. It is not a vague, twilight or semi-conscious experience. It is not an ecstasy; it is not a trance. It is not super-consciousness in the Vedantic sense. It is not due to self-hypnotization. It is a perfectly calm, sane, sound, rational common-sense shifting of consciousness from the phenomena of sense-perception to the phenomena of seership, from the thought of self to a distinctively higher realm. . . . For example, if the lower self be nervous, anxious, tense, one can in a few moments compel it to be calm. This is not done by a word simply. Again I say, it is not hypnotism. It is by the exercise of power. One feels the spirit of peace as definitely as heat is perceived on a hot summer day. The power can be as surely used as the sun's rays can be focused and made to do work, to set fire to wood." The Higher Law, vol. iv, pp. 4, 6, Boston, August, 1901.

13. Transcendentalists are fond of the term "Over-soul," but as a rule they use it in an intellectualist sense, as meaning only a medium of communion. "God" is a causal agent as well as a medium of communion, and that is the aspect which I wish to emphasize.

SUGGESTED READINGS

The Varieties of Religious Experience (New York: Doubleday and Company, Inc., a Dolphin Books paperback, the 1901-1902

Gifford Lectures) is a classic which retains its freshness with its wealth of case material, the memorable phrase, and religious insight. *Pragmatism and Other Essays* (N.Y.: Washington Square Press, 1963) presents the theoretical basis for James' religious thought. Perhaps the most famous essay here is "The Will to Believe." See also *Essays in Radical Empiricism and a Pluralistic Universe,* edited by Ralph Barton Perry, introduction by Richard J. Bernstein (N.Y.: E. P. Dutton and Co., Inc., 1971, paperback, especially pp. 265-278); John J. McDermott's *The Writings of William James: A Comprehensive Edition* (N.Y.: The Modern Library, 1968), with full bibliography and illuminating introduction. *American Religious Philosophy* by Robert J. Roth, S.J. (N.Y.: Harcourt, Brace and World, Inc., 1967, paperback) contains a sympathetic but critical introduction (pp. 27-62), together with a bibliography. Likewise see John E. Smith's *The Spirit of American Philosophy* (N.Y.: Oxford University Press, Galaxy paperback, 1963) pp. 38-79. Smith suggests that one should pay more attention to James' "radical empiricism" than to the pragmatism as found, for example, in "The Will to Believe," a phrase which connotes arbitrariness. Later in life, James wished he had phrased it "the right to believe." The story of James' life, his struggle with a depressive temperament, his wide circle of friends and the development of his thought, makes absorbing reading. Two good biographies are *Thought and Character of William James* by Ralph Barton Perry, 2 Vols. (Boston: Little, Brown and Company, 1935) and *William James—A Biography* by Gay Wilson Allen (N.Y.: The Viking Press, 1967).

17 Meaning and Action: The Blondellian Spirit

JOHN J. HEANEY

Maurice Blondel (1861-1949) is not well known in the U.S., in part because only a small portion of his work has been translated into English. Blondel's reputation was established with the publication of a major philosophical work in 1893, *L'Action, essai d'une critique de la vie et d'une science de la pratique*. He entered into theological debate with Alfred Loisy during the Roman Catholic Modernist crisis at the beginning of this century. He was also a close friend of Teilhard de Chardin and influenced his concept of the universe as an organism in action. Furthermore, he was one of the main inspirations for the modern Catholic intellectual movement which is called Transcendental Thomism. However, Blondel was not a Thomist but a rather original philosopher in his own right, and in his early days he was rather antipathetic to neo-scholastic Thomism. But Blondel had a profound influence on Joseph Marechal, S.J., who developed the original structure of Transcendental Thomist thought. Karl Rahner, S.J., in turn, was deeply indebted to Marechal's insights, though he did not read Blondel until he had already developed his metaphysical system.

A main point of departure for the Transcendental Thomists as well as for Blondel was Emmanuel Kant. When Kant concluded that the noumenal world, the thing in itself, could not be reached through theoretical reason and that the *a priori* category of causality, for example, could not be legitimately extended beyond the finite world, this seemed to mark the demise of "natural theology" or a metaphysics about God. One would thus be confined to a study of practical reason or the postulates of moral consciousness. God perhaps "ought to be" but one cannot say that He "is."

Many modern religious psychologists have been inspired by Kant. We have already noted this in the chapter on Viktor Frankl. Jung too said that he restricted himself to the "psychically experienced" and rejected the metaphysical: "what I intend to say is approximately the same thing Kant meant when he called 'the thing in itself' a 'merely negative boundary concept.' Every statement about the transcendental is to be avoided because it is invariably a laughable presumption on the part of the human mind, which is unconscious of its limitations" (*Psyche and Symbol,* p. 350).

Blondel and the Transcendental Thomists believed that Kant's theory of knowledge began from too restricted a base, the *a priori* categories as the conditions for the possibility of theoretical knowledge. Blondel believed that if philosophy sought for the meaning of life, it should not begin from the study of ideas or concepts, but from a study of action. He believed that everyone carried within him meaning inscribed in action. After investigating the various dynamic tendencies and explanations of human action, he concluded that beyond the *a priori* categories of Kant there was something deeper. The very possession of the Personal Transcendent within a man was the pre-condition for the possibility, not just of knowledge, but of experience and action. Thus, one does not face the problem of the transcendental barrier. Rather, if one cannot act without the inner presence of the Personal Absolute, the problem is not so much to reach God as to show that man is not part of God himself, a point which Blondel also developed.

In the title of this chapter I have inserted the words

"The Blondellian Spirit" rather than the name of Maurice Blondel. I have done this because the following article, which is a revision of "The Beyond Within" (*New Catholic World,* May-June 1972, pp. 130-134) is a rather free handling of Blondel's thought. It does not treat some of Blondel's more complicated but important metaphysical insights. The limits of space and the purposes of this book seemed to preclude such an endeavor. I have also added many metaphors and images not used by Blondel; however, I believe the essay remains faithful to the main thrust of Blondel's thought.

"Yes or no, has human life a meaning? Has man a destiny? I act, yet without realizing what action is, without having desired to live and without knowing exactly who I am or whether I am." [1] Thus began Maurice Blondel's monumental work *L'Action.* Blondel believed that the meaning of life lay inscribed in human action and not exclusively in thought. Philosophy then should begin from a study of human action.

Several excellent introductions to Blondel's thought have now been published in English and there are a number of insightful articles which survey the movement of his system. But Blondel's theory does not yield itself to excerpting and the published articles presume some prior acquaintance with Blondel. Therefore, in this essay I will attempt to catch the main lines of Blondel's thought as found in *L'Action.* However, I will present his thought in a somewhat more contemporary setting, introduce new images, and thus run the risk of oversimplification. This risk, I believe, is worth taking if it results in whetting the reader's appetite for a deeper understanding of a great mind.

The philosophy of action begins from an analysis of what man *does* and not simply from what he says or thinks. Action includes everything that man does, whether it be walking, talking, thinking, achieving, desiring, loving. Action, then, means all of this. But the philosophy of action in the final analysis is principally concerned with desiring and willing, the mainspring of action. We could not even know without desiring or aspiring to knowledge. On the other hand, we must not rank Blondel among the voluntarists. He never accepted an either-or choice between the intellect and the will, between knowing and loving. After all, knowing is one of the highest forms of action. As James Somerville, one of Blondel's best commentators said: "When faced with the dilemma of choosing between the two, between theory and practice, Blondel refused the option." [2] I will divide the discussion of the philosophy of action into three successive steps: first, an analysis of the phenomenon of action; second, a reflection on the necessary emergence of the *idea* of God and revelation; third, an analysis of man's option.

First, let us make a brief analysis of *the phenomenon of action*. I suggest that we begin with an analogy which Blondel never used. Man's existence is like a rock cast into a vast lake. His action is like the concentric ripples which move out to the edge of that lake, an edge which is still beyond the horizon. In man's case what or where is the edge? Toward what border is he moving?

The infant begins acting in a world which is confined almost exclusively within the sense area. Gradually it determines itself as a separated sense-center of consciousness. It learns that the crib is not the self. It hurts to strike against the crib's side. The crib is not the self. The mother's breast, the bottle—both disappear and arrive. They are not the self. Pleasure objects come and go. One is more desirable than another. Gradually the pleasure of crawling and of semi-independence surpasses the pleasure of total, passive security. Walking succeeds crawling and the child moves upward and outward.

Discovery and exploration begin. With the years, the question "why" is formed. A primitive power of abstraction and judgment is actualized and the child finds itself in a new circle of existence. Relationship dawns, not to objects now but to persons as persons. Love enters as a bud and the child is drawn to a new sphere, that of values. Bit by bit, the previously automatically internalized superego is transformed into autonomous conscience. Thus begins an ever continuing process, never fully completed.

The adolescent often falls back to the almost exclusively sense level in personal relationships. The young boy or the young girl may treat the other as a "sense object." Then he or she must later, with some pain, journey back into the circle of love. Something within insistently calls man beyond the place where he is.

Step by step man feels called toward the sphere of love. This love may be for a person or for a cause championed by a group of persons. A scientist or a consecrated religious may follow the call and dedicate self to the cause of truth or to the service of mankind. Usually man's impulse carries him beyond the self to the other in marriage and love. The circle enlarges to two. Blondel said the mysticism of love is a trap only for the egotist.

The two find that they cannot stand still in endless mutual adoration. Life takes care of that. If an "égoisme a deux," a kind of mutual egotism, were to persist, growth would halt and disaster threaten because of what we might call the Elvira Madigan syndrome. The call of friendship and other interests perdures and isolation is surmounted, for health and life call lovers outward. Usually the couple moves out to a new circle. Generally this occurs in the altruistic call arising from a new birth, a child. Or else the couple develop new interests which transcend themselves. New friendships form; old friendships deepen or change.

As man builds his family, he is caught in an ever widening circle of interests, joys and problems. Jobs, the competition of companies, the problems of others, their celebrations—wider and wider concerns call man out of himself. Can he totally ignore a people suffering from starvation, the problems of his environment, the vote to be cast? In some area of our lives we all halt in the movement toward the wider circle. Some halt early and almost completely, but all feel the pull. We might take the glass facade structure of the United Nations building as the symbol of an advanced stage of the ever widening circle of man's horizon. Man has moved, or feels the call to move, from the tribal circle of exclusiveness found in the totem object to the building and contemplation of a universal human symbol.

However, checkmates arise which make man wonder toward what he is moving. Sometimes he is sick, sometimes tired, and failure induces a puzzlement about the direction of his action. Yet we all know of some people who never seem to be discontented or restless. An analysis of human action should avoid pretending that all men are explicitly and consciously restless. It is true that St. Augustine said, "Our hearts are restless for Thee, O God, and they will not rest until they rest in Thee." Blondel's theory of action would not understand this statement as a description of an experience which all are consciously aware of. He would, at the end of his analysis, consider it as a metaphysical description. That is, many people are not reflexively aware of any restlessness. It is only the "science of action," a metaphysical process, which reveals the true state. No matter what a man says, there is no one who does not in action move toward new depths in some area of his life or of his desires. Utter apathy would be the result otherwise, and that would be the death of action.

Is there no bourne for our desires? Is there no overarching goal or final meaning to our action? The question necessarily arises at sometime to all.

Blondel traced down the "determinism" or goal of action through many labyrinthian ways in science and life to see if he could find there the answer to the great question of meaning. Here we will look at a few of his probings. Various answers to the great question arise and they tend to become movements or "isms." Dilettantism refuses the great question as illegitimate. "Gather ye rosebuds while ye may," it says, and where you can. The philosophy of action, however, analyzes the dilettante's action and not his verbal philosophy. Dilettantism is the continual changing of will objects, or objects of interest. Desire flits, butterfly-like, from object to object, from person to person. But the very changing of objects implies an unsatisfied desire, a will which is not sated, or else there would be no such changing. The philosophy or "logic of action" finds that dilettantism supports the idea of a deeper will in us (a "primordial will") which our actual desires and our specific will acts cannot catch up with. Much of literature is filled with this idea as, for example, Browning's line: "Ah, but a man's reach should exceed his grasp, or what's a heaven for." Dilettantism implies an aspiration beyond our actual grasp and is not a self-sufficing philosophy.

Philosophical pessimism arises as another answer to the great question. Philosophical pessimism may admit to a local, day-to-day meaning, as found in fostering a love or completing a task. But it denies the existence of any ultimate or final meaning. But if we are to will what is true, the logical outcome would be a "will to nothingness." This is a step which pessimism ordinarily does not take, for it trips over the great "rock of scandal," as Blondel called it—there *is* something. Furthermore, while pessimism says there is no meaning to life, still it seems to imply some pre-conceptual, ineffable experience of meaning. The very sense of its lack implies some pre-conceptual or para-conceptual experience of its existence.

The fascination arising out of a play by Beckett, for example, seems to the present writer to be explained precisely by the experiential dialectic treated by Blondel. Similarly we might today apply Blondel's insight to Camus, though I would not rank that great humanist as truly a pessimist. Shubert Ogden in *The Reality of God* very succinctly makes the point which I wish to convey:

According to Camus the whole character of human life is determined by its essential absurdity by the unclosable gap between our demand for rationality, practical as well as theoretical and the 'unreasonable silence of the world.' Thus we may live without any guarantee that our own actions or the human enterprise as such are finally worthwhile. Nevertheless Camus insists that the only fitting response to this absurdity is heroic resistance against it, which includes an absolute lucidity about our condition together with an affirmation of our life in spite of its ultimate meaninglessness . . . (and he) comes to embrace a profoundly humanistic ethic of love . . . But intriguing as this notion of the absurd hero doubtless is, it can hardly define a real possibility, whether for thought or for existential choice. If all our actions are in principle absurd, the act of heroically resisting their absurdity must also be absurd. It too is *ex hypotesi,* a totally meaningless response and can be supposed not a bit more fitting than the various attempts to flee absurdity that Camus so unsparingly condemns. Or if the resistance is somehow meaningful, the absurdity of existence cannot be so unrelieved as was alleged.[3]

This citation is in perfect alignment with the thrust of Blondel's thought, although he did not write about Camus. He did, however, have some illuminating things to say about what Westerners have sometimes called "Oriental religious pessimism." Blondel said that many Oriental "pessimists" only *seem* to the superficial observer to be taking a stand against being or meaning. What they are really experiencing is the insufficiency (maya) of phenomena, a state which is possible only because man is "initially penetrated with the grandeur of being." All pessimism affirms being and meaning "before denying it and in order to deny it." [4]

Sometimes the answer to the great question of life is proposed by a philosophy which makes pure liberty into the goal of life (e.g., Sartre).[5] This type of philosophy insists that there is no meaning or goal beyond man. The only goal is self-determination in pure liberty. Blondel said that this is partly true in the sense that there is always more to love, more to will, more to know. Life is an endless growth toward liberty. But, Blondel pointed out, this goal as an absolute is chimerical. It can never be reached and it simply tantalizes man. Man is not able freely to determine his own being because no matter what progress he makes, no matter to what degree he actualizes the world according to his desires, he is always brought up short by this checkmate: there is something in us which is not from our autonomous self-determination—*man wills but he has not willed to will*. That "benign tyrant," the primordial will or aspiration, persists apart from our conscious will. We have never freely willed at this source our basic aspirations. Are we then condemned to absurdity, to search for that which we cannot reach? If the philosophy of absolute liberty as man's only goal in a closed absurd world were true, this philosophy itself becomes no less absurd, no more true or false than all else in an "absurd" world.

At this point, let us pause to draw a principle out of the data which emerge from our inventory of human action. There are, as it were, two wills in man. Let us call the deepest will the "primordial will" or the aspiration or the élan (eros in the widest sense). The other will is the will act, the time-bound decision. The principle then is this: *the dynamic of human action is constituted by an effort to put an equal sign between the time-bound will act, the decision, and the primordial will or aspiration*. We are never able to insert that equal sign within a naturalistic humanism.

We will now move on to the second step in our analysis and consider the necessary emergence of the *idea* of God and of a *possible* revelation. In action man begins to be aware of the failure of his desires and of his will acts to equal the primordial will. Blondel wrote: "I would not be conscious of this failure if there were not within me a will superior to the contradictions of life." Many men catch this insight reflectively; others have only a primitive awareness of it. But there is present to every mature person some awareness that what he strives for and what is necessary for the fullness of human action is simultaneously inaccessible to him in a closed human system where man would be alone in the universe. This is how the *idea* of God arises. That is why every philosopher ultimately treats of the question of God, even if only to deny his existence. Similarly, the person who is indifferent to the question or its solution has at some time faced the idea as a hypothetical possibility. Blondel, as a typical early twentieth century man, mainly saw the question as it arises in the West, about the existence of a personal God. In some parts of the East the question arises as the question about Brahman or Nirvana. We will not here try to bridge this apparent dichotomy (cf. chapter XII).

As the *idea* of God arises, there also arises a wonder about his purpose. Would this God not have entered into communication with man? Would he not have made a gesture of initiative? "And Thou are silent whilst the world contends about its many creeds. Speak! Whisper to my watching heart one word." Any man who reads these words from Gerard Manley Hopkins' poem *Nondum* understands its meaning. But it is not always recognized that the eternal silence of space astounds us only because we would have expected some "word." There is in us all at least a dim awareness of a possible revelation which would speak of a proffered intimacy with the Absolute. Also, we live in an historical world where the various religions insist that a word has come. Christianity sees Christ as the Word. (Blondel touches only briefly on the Absolute of far-Eastern religion, but we might recall here that Hinduism speaks of Brahman and Atman, and Buddhism of Nirvana and Karma.) Thus far we have been discussing only an *idea*. Yet man lives in a world of action and as Blondel said, "Is it not true that action alone can define the idea?" [6] Thus the philosophy of action takes us to our last point, the option.

Surrounded by warring creeds, many men simply say, "I do not know what the answer to the great question is." But the philosophy of action says, "Look first for the solution not in words but in action." Many who do not open out to the Personal Absolute in words do so in action. Consciously the option comes to us in words. "Yes or no, does life have an ultimate meaning?" Or, "Yes or no, is there a God?" which for Blondel is equivalently the same question, related as the implicit is to the explicit.

"Meaning" signifies to intend. Intend or intention comes from the Latin *intendo,* to stretch toward a goal. Intend means to have a direction with a goal. When something has a meaning, it has a solution, an explanation, a goal. "Absurd" means contrary to reason which seeks goals. To say life is absurd means there is no ultimate meaning. Sartre said: "Man is a useless passion. To get drunk by yourself in a bar or to be a leader of nations is equally pointless."

If we answer "yes" to the great option, then life has a meaning. Action becomes intelligible because it is reaching toward what *is*. Many answer "perhaps" to the great question. But in the world of action, there is no "perhaps." In the ocean of life into which we have been thrown, it is either sink or swim. Whether "perhaps" means "yes" or "no" can be determined only from its embodiment in *action*. Some say "no," there is no meaning. But then they become a living contradiction. While they say "no" in word, in action they go on affirming meaning or seeking it. Sartre seems to say "no" to our question. Yet he goes on working feverishly, writing, communicating, engaging in politics. One says, "No, there is no ultimate meaning," yet goes on energetically communicating the message with the meaning, "There is no meaning." "Meaning," especially as incarnated in action, reminds one of Francis Thompson's "hound of heaven." We simply can't avoid it. All action betrays him who betrays it. The "no" turns out to be a "no" only in words.

But doesn't this seem to be a strange option? No matter what one does, one embodies meaning. Even suicide can often be seen as an act brought about by disgust with the found lack of meaning.

In one sense this is what the philosophy of action leads to. We cannot escape the embodiment of the Absolute in our action. However, there *is* a *real* option in favor of "no" which is open to us. But the really decisive "no" is found in action, not in words. "No" is embodied in action when we refuse to open up or open out. When we enclose ourself in self, when we absolutely refuse charity, this is a "no" embodied in act. This is the real atheism, in action. This is the very meaning of the parable of the sheep and goats at the last judgment as told by Jesus. Jesus did not here demand explicit belief. What he demanded was belief in action, the opening out to the needy and the lonely. The sheep embodied in act a "yes" in giving food to the hungry even though they said "but we never knew You." As Blondel said: "Nor is there any need to be able to name the presence whose abode is prepared when man empties himself of himself." [7]

To return to the great option about the meaning of life: there is a paradox in that those who say it does not have a meaning go on trying to equal act with aspiration as if their action had a meaning. This would be an ultimate meaning because in the interrelations of man's life the everyday cannot be separated from the whole.

They write books, make plays, etc., seeking to communicate. But their very writing belies their statement. That is they seek to communicate when really they should say nothing. Only the silence of action negates meaning. And no one is able to take no action.

What the philosophy of action makes explicit often goes on without much reflection whatever upon it. The philosophy of action brings to reflex consciousness the Presence which we always implicitly affirm in action. However, while action implicitly affirms the Presence *in* us, it may deny the Presence *for* us. The murderer who engineers the perfect criminal act is caught up in the dynamism of meaning-affirming action but he refuses the Presence for himself. To refuse to bear sacrifice and to affirm love is to deny God. As Blondel put it, the world can be called the body of the action of God and our dilemma is either to incarnate God without God and against God, or for God and with God. Blondel, of course, was interested in bringing man to an explicit affirmation of God's presence, for otherwise one exploits the Presence without acknowledging it. Still, even without this explicit affirmation, man can have ultimate meaning, he can coincide with himself, i.e., adequate his two wills. This is done not by knowing all that God knows but by willing all that he wills. Implicitly, this is found in an absolute affirmation of and trust in existence. Blondel said, in a sense we do not know anything if we do not love. Being is reached through knowledge but also and moreso by love. Absolute Being, then, must be love and thus Personal because love alone can be the full object of love.[8]

Somerville points out what might seem to be a begging of the question in Blondel. One interprets the will's perpetual restlessness and self-transcendence as a demonstration of the reality of the infinite but this is precisely what is in question. He well shows how Blondel answers this. "We cannot escape the urgency of what we will and of what wills in us. . . . The reality of the Uniquely Necessary (Blondel's term for God) . . . is not an ideal projection of man's wishful desire, but the very ground in us which makes the desire possible . . . It is real before it is ideal."[9]

But let us return to the movement of the philosophy of action. God is seen as the goal. But God cannot be seen only as the goal. If one goes back along the line of our thought, it is seen that the primordial desire or aspiration was there from the beginning, from the first moments of our life as an infant. It is the fingerprint within us of the Absolute. It precedes conceptual thought and rationalizing. Therefore from the very beginning, the Face of the Absolute was imprinted within my desire, my will, my action. God is not the "God of the gaps." Nor is he found simply at the end of the quest. He is present always as the Eternal lure of action. He is the Beyond within. It is precisely in immanence that transcendence is found. Thus Kant's *a priori* categories are not the fundamental "conditions of possibility" for man. They presuppose the prior "condition of possibility" for experiencing anything, the presence of the Absolute within us.

The philosophy of action concludes that in all desiring there is a co-desired: in all loving, there is a co-loved; in all knowing, there is a co-known. In sum it ends with the mystical statement: in all action, there is a co-actor. Life is a human and trans-human partnership. God is more intimate to me than I am to myself. We are all mystics, in the sense that we are all pilgrims of the Absolute. Our pilgrimage is one of discovering what we already possess.

> We shall not cease from exploration
> And the end of all our exploring
> Will be to arrive where we started
> And know the place for the first time.[10]

If we seek the face of God, then, look for his Face first in human action. Man is certainly a wonder. He is the *symbol-in-action* of transcendence. He embodies the Beyond Within, always beyond, yet always within. No image fits him. In action we are thrown beyond images to the God who acts in the man who acts.

The man who knows God in this way knows experientially within himself what he is looking for when he looks for God's word. He has a pre-understanding of it to some degree. And when the great religions ask him to "Take up and read" or "Look and see what I have," he is open to them because he has a sense of what he is seeking. The Christian is the one who says, yes, I have seen the face of God in the *Act* of Christ.[11] The philosophy of action cannot lead a man into the visions proposed by the various great religions. It can lead him only to the threshold. And all the great religions know that one must "Come and see." Yet it does lead a man to "see" the Face in human action. But it is still to a degree that of a stranger. How do we overcome estrangement? For Christianity the overcoming is in Christ. "It is the same God that said, 'Let there be light shining out of darkness,' who has shone in our minds to radiate the light of the knowledge of God's glory, the glory on the face of Christ" (2 Cor. 4:6).

I wish to conclude with a brief reference to the first authors treated in this book. I think Blondel would have sincerely appreciated Freud's discoveries but that his philosophy would have led him to the conclusion that Freud misinterpreted the data. For Blondel, God is not the substitute for the father, but, as Victor White, O.P., put it, the father (or the mother) is the first substitute for God. Man has a tendency to try to embody or incarnate the Absolute by projecting the Absolute into the people he is drawn to. This is one reason for disillusionment with parents, friends, loves or causes. To a degree this is necessary, for man seeks more than he can find. Blondel cautioned the pilgrim of the Absolute against reacting to his frustration with the finite by using people as means for the mystic flight or movement. There can be no genuine movement unless finite ends are fully savored and exhausted. Persons must be treated as ends in themselves, he said, and the meaning of a person can never be fully savored or exhausted.

Blondel was disturbed by naturalistic humanism as represented, for example, by Freud. Since man tends to be an idol-making organism, even after burning his other idols, he will begin to set up a new ritualism which he "prepares for his own apotheosis. . . ." [12] The necessary consequence, according to Blondel's theory, is disillusionment and perhaps destruction, for man seeks more than he can find.

Jung's thought is much more congenial to Blondel's system. Action, Blondel said, cannot be imagined. It itself creates symbols. These arise from the unconscious for, as Blondel puts it, "all gestation takes place in the dark." But the motive force "is more than the expression of the energies of the unconscious; it dominates them and exploits their power in order to realize new ends, always adding an increase of force and creative energy that could never be found in the sum of its antecedents." [13] Once again Blondel demands a Beyond within. The esotericism and what some have called the gnosticism in Jung are absent from

Blondel's philosophy. For Blondel, there is no secret knowledge, no special lore to be assimilated. There is only the secret knowledge hidden in the mystery of action.

NOTES

1. Translation by James Somerville, "The Theory and Practice of Action, *Cross Currents,* Spring-Summer, 1954, p. 251.

2. "Action and the Silence of Being," found in *A Modern Introduction to Metaphysics,* edited by D. A. Drennen (N.Y.: Macmillan, The Free Press of Glencoe, 1962), p. 421.

3. *The Reality of God and Other Essays* (N.Y.: Harper and Row, 1966), p. 11.

4. James Somerville, *Total Commitment: Blondel's L'Action* (Washington, D.C.: Corpus Books, 1968), p. 67. I am greatly indebted to this work for my own presentation.

5. Two years before his death and still writing although blind, Blondel published "The Inconsistency of J.-P. Sartre's Logic," *The Thomist* 10 (1947), pp. 393-397. What I have written in the body of this article goes back rather to what Blondel wrote in *L'Action,* before Sartre was born.

6. Cited in Somerville, *Total Commitment,* op. cit., p. 7.

7. *Ibid.,* p. 245.

8. Only love can reach the wholeness of reality. The mind through analysis can reach only part. Parenthetically we might mention here that Blondel claimed the system which he offered was not pragmatism or pure voluntarism. As he saw it, pragmatism led only to the threshold of metaphysics or being and expressed only the subjective needs of the will. "The logic of action" by reflexive analysis makes what is immanent to the will immanent to thought (Somerville, p. 288). Kant's moral imperative is both rational and practical. Here is where being, knowing and willing join hands. Action is the bond between being and knowing, as being is the bond between action and knowing. However, there *is* a metaphysical option and this requires a "kind of trust in the rationality of human experience" (Somerville, p. 291). But this is not a blind leap. It is our mind which sees what is necessarily voluntary and what falls short of this in daily decision. It is our mind which moves toward the Absolute of the will as its own object. However, we are never coerced. Being becomes *for us* in the last resort only when we opt *for it.*

9. *Ibid.,* p. 362. I have only touched upon Blondel's intricate metaphysical development of this point. I suggest that the reader turn to the last chapter in this book together with its introduction. There it will be seen why the Infinite in man cannot be simply man's unconscious in action.

10. T. S. Eliot, "Little Gidding," from *Four Quartets* (London: Faber and Faber, 1959), p. 240.

11. Blondel made further philosophical exploration into the notion of Christian dogma. We omit that discussion in the present article.

12. Somerville, *op. cit.*, p. 196.
13. *Ibid.*, pp. 110, 263.

SUGGESTED READINGS

Blondel's *L'Action* has not been translated. James Somerville's *Total Commitment: Blondel's L'Action* (Washington, D.C.: Corpus Books, 1968) is a demanding, paraphrastic interpretation which marvelously clarifies and captures the moving inspiration of *L'Action*, (with full bibliography). His article "Maurice Blondel: 1861-1949," *Thought* 36 (1961), pp. 371-410, and the entry on Blondel in the *New Catholic Encyclopedia* are useful introductions. Henri Bouillard, S.J., also offers an introduction in *The Logic of Faith* (Dublin: Gill, 1967), part III, Chapter 2, and presents a solid but also demanding overview in *Blondel and Christianity* (Washington, D.C.: Corpus Books, 1969). A very fine literate and manageable introduction which is both historical and philosophical is offered by Alexander Dru and Illtyd Trethowan in *Maurice Blondel—The Letter on Apologetics and History and Dogma* (N.Y.: Holt, Rinehart and Winston, 1964), pp. 11-116. Jean Lacroix's *Maurice Blondel: An Introduction to the Man and His Philosophy* (N.Y.: Sheed and Ward, 1968, paperback) is a solid presentation by an expert, but the style is somewhat dense for the beginner. The second half of the book consists of large excerpts from Blondel. *Correspondence: Pierre Teilhard de Chardin—Maurice Blondel*, with notes and commentary by Henri de Lubac (N.Y.: Herder and Herder, 1967) shows the two great minds in dialogue. The essential spirit of the discussion is captured by Christopher Mooney, S.J., in "Blondel and Teilhard de Chardin: An Exchange of Letters," *Thought*, Winter 1962, pp. 543-562. For Blondel's role in the Modernist crisis, the reader might refer to Alec Vidler's *The Modernist Movement in the Roman Church* (N.Y.: Cambridge University Press, 1934), or to the editor's own work, *The Modernist Crisis: von Hugel* (Washington, D.C.: Corpus Books, 1968) pp. 83-107. The relationship of Blondel to pragmatism is discussed in *H. S. Thayer, Meaning and Action: A Critical History of Pragmatism* (N.Y.: Bobbs-Merrill Co., Inc.), pp. 315-319.

18 God and the Dynamism of the Mind: Karl Rahner

JOSEPH DONCEEL, S.J.

The philosophy of religion and theology has been immensely enriched through the discoveries of psychology as it was applied to the religious area. On the other hand, the philosophy of religion and theology has made its own contributions in this dialogue. Not the least of these contributions is a reasoned insistence on a Real Otherness, a Personal Transcendent, lying at the heart of man's psyche. The philosophy of religion is an autonomous discipline. However, theology itself must have a philosophy, and when theology enlists in its service a certain philosophy of religion, the resultant specialty is called, especially in Catholic circles, fundamental theology, that is, a reasoned analysis of the presuppositions of theology itself. Karl Rahner, S.J., calls his famous *Hearers of the Word* "fundamental-theological anthropology" (p. viii). The following article on Rahner by Joseph Donceel, S.J.,* may be read, I believe, either as a work in the philosophy of religion or as an aspect of fundamental theology.

Rahner's main accent falls upon the study of the dynamism of the intellect. The reader should be cautioned, however, against slipping into the oversimplification that Rahner studies the mind while Blondel studied the will, or that Rahner's work centers on truth-seeking, Blondel's on good-seeking. It is true that neo-scholasticism not only distinguished knowing from willing and loving (and it distinguished both from feeling), but it also tended to separate

* From *America*, October 31, 1970. © 1970, America Press, Inc. Reprinted with permission.

these powers into watertight categories. Both Blondel and Rahner rejected this tendency in the older scholastic "faculty psychology." Both emphasize the mutual reciprocity between knowing, willing, loving and depth-feeling. Rahner, for example, wrote: "At the heart of knowledge is love" and "love is . . . the condition of the knowledge of God" (*Hearers of the Word*, pp. 102, 105). Similarly, Blondel maintained that love and will presuppose knowledge, however obscure or implicit it may be.

The author of the following article, Joseph Donceel, S.J., of Fordham University, is an expert on transcendental Thomism, the editor of *A Maréchal Reader*, and author of *Natural Theology*, among other works.

Is it still possible to demonstrate God's existence despite the objections of Hume and of Kant? Karl Rahner holds that it is, but his argument differs considerably from the traditional approach of the Five Ways. Or rather, in order to escape modern objections, Rahner felt obliged to dig deeper, all the way down to the underlying argument, the theme which the five famous ways of St. Thomas are but variations of. He speaks of affirmation more than of causality; he pays attention to the human intellect more than to the things out there; he relies on the metaphysics of our knowledge of being more than on the metaphysics of being. He does not say: things exist only if God exists; he says: we know that things exist only because we affirm the existence of God.

This approach avoids a basic difficulty that may be raised against most traditional arguments. If we claim that we know God as the cause of all that exists, we may be hard put to answer the following objection: why do finite and contingent effects demand an infinite and necessary cause? From finite and contingent effects we may conclude only to a finite and contingent cause.

Rahner would admit this. But he inquires at once: how do we know that the objects of our experience are finite and contingent? This is certainly not given to us in sense experience, nor do we know it from reasoning. Rahner claims that we are aware of these features because, as soon as we grasp any reality at all, our intellect surges beyond it and refers it to the infinite and necessary reality. Of everything we get to know we affirm implicitly that it is. Yet no object of our experience simply is. It is *this* or *that*. The predicate we always use (*is*) is too wide for all the subjects we apply it to. Our intellect keeps looking for a reality to which we may apply our basic predicate in its fullest amplitude, of which we can say in all truth: this reality *is*. No restrictions, no specification. This reality simply *is*. The reality which simply *is*, without being *this* or *that*, is the fullness of being, is God.

In other words, we are aware at once that everything we know is finite. Even the universe as a whole is finite, if not in space, at least in perfection. But it is impossible to be aware of a limit as limit unless one is already beyond this limit, either in fact, or at least in desire. Hence our intellect keeps striving beyond anything it knows or can know, toward the Illimited, the Infinitely Perfect, toward God.

Thus, Rahner holds that in every act of intellectual knowledge we implicitly affirm the existence of God. God is known by us as the "whereunto" of the dynamism of our intellect. We know Him in a way that differs radically from the way we know all other realities. We know Him by intending Him, pointing towards Him, striving towards Him. We know Him through what Rahner calls a *Vorgriff*, a pre-apprehension, an anticipating grasp. God is not an object of our knowledge, but the always co-affirmed condition of the possibility of all knowledge. He is the illimited horizon against which we project all that we know.

This affirmation of the infinite "whereunto" of our intellect's dynamism is so central to our existence that man might be defined as "an embodied affirmation of the Absolute," or as the being who is "always already beyond." Beyond what? Beyond everything, beyond finite truth, finite goodness, finite beauty, finite happiness. Man knows God somewhat in the way in which the Hudson River would know the ocean, if the river were aware of its own flow, which carries it irresistibly towards the Atlantic.

Rahner's views entail important consequences. Thus, we understand better why we know God only analogically, that is, by adding negations of our every affirmation about Him. When we think or speak of God, we make Him into an object of our thought or of our speech. But God is not such an object; He is the condition of the possibility of every object. What we think or say of Him is, therefore, not quite true, and we know that it is not quite true, even while we are thinking or saying it, because we are aware of the dynamism of our intellect, which carries us beyond anything we can put in concepts or express in words.

The famous objection that, if we start from the finite, we can never reach the infinite, consequently loses its punch. We do not really "reach" God; we are with Him from the start. We do not begin with finite realities, but with God, affirmed *unconsciously* in our knowledge of finite realities, from God co-affirmed as the condition of the possibility of all knowledge. All "demonstrations" of the existence of God consist simply in making us aware of what we already know.

What about the principle of causality, which is supposed to have been shown up as invalid by Hume and by Kant? Rahner does not use the principle of efficient causality, but the principle of final causality. God is known to us at once not as the efficient cause of the universe (which He is) but as the final cause of our thinking. Man does not reach God as maker of his universe but as the final horizon of his thinking and feeling. Should the principle of final causality not be demonstrated before we use it in this way? Rahner would say that it cannot be demonstrated in the strict sense of the word, since the demonstration itself would take it for granted. It can only be vindicated against all objections by showing that the one who objects uses the principle in his very objection. This vindication coincides practically with the vindication of our right of affirming God's existence. The *Vorgriff,* the pre-apprehension, *is* the principle of causality in action, as we "live" it in our every affirmation.

Let us return to our previous comparison. We know God somewhat as the Hudson River would know the ocean if it were aware of its own flow. Now, every bit of water that trickles into the Hudson is carried by the river to the ocean. In the same way, everything that enters our mind is referred by its dynamism to the ultimate end of this dynamism, to the ocean of being, to God. And this is the principle of final causality in action.

Rahner's natural theology influences his attitude towards atheism. There are, according to him, many kinds of atheism. There is conscious and unconscious atheism; there is guilty and innocent atheism; there is the atheism of the unbeliever and the atheism of the believer. As he puts it: "Only when we admit that atheism is a perpetual temptation of the theist, a 'situation' of our faith, can we honestly, lovingly and humbly speak of the atheists who are outside."

Rahner frequently insists upon the distinction between our transcendental and our categorical affirmation of God. The transcendental affirmation is the one that results from the dynamism of our intellect, from the *Vorgriff*. It is present in all human beings; it is that which makes them into human beings. It is unconscious and not free. If we consider it alone, in its mere givenness, we may bluntly state that there are no atheists.

But this transcendental affirmation must become categorical, that is, conscious and free. It must be translated not only into thought but also into action. Man translates it into thought when, having become aware of it, he tries to express it conceptually, when he consciously and freely affirms God as the ultimate end of the movement of his mind. He translates it into action when he lives up to the tremendous implications of the reality of the Being he keeps affirming. Practically, this means: when he obeys the voice of his conscience, when he sincerely acts according to his lights.

Some people acknowledge God transcendentally and categorically, both in words and in deeds. Such are the believers who are aware of the utter "otherness" of God and who live up to the knowledge they profess of Him. There are other believers who acknowledge God transcendentally, who translate this belief into actions through a good and honest life, but who fail, more or less, to express it correctly in their thinking. The God they consciously profess is an idol, he does not exist. Many good and simple Christians may belong to this class. Their moral goodness corrects their doctrinal deficiencies. Although the God of their mind may be an idol, the God of their heart is not. There are other believers, or so-called believers, who may or may not have an adequate conception of God, but who do not live up to what God really is. They consciously profess theism, but, in reality, they are atheists. Their atheism is, to some extent at least, of the guilty kind.

Next we have the professed atheists. Some of them are atheists to the fullest extent. They freely reject the transcendental affirmation of God which they are; they reject it not only in thought but also in action. They deny the existence of the real God and make themselves the center of their universe, in pride, greed and selfishness.

But there are other atheists—and Rahner holds that their number keeps increasing—who, in fact, pay allegiance to the true God. They affirm God's existence transcendentally, as all human beings do; they deny it categorically, in their thinking, but they profess and admit it through their moral activity, by being "men of good will." These are good and decent people who cannot accept the existence of God *as they understand Him*. This God is generally not the real God; he is an idol who does not exist. They feel unable, mostly on account of their education or their environment, to proceed intellectually beyond this pseudo-God, to the mysterious "whereunto" of their intellect and will. But they keep groping for Him, unconsciously and unfreely on the transcendental level, unconsciously but freely on the categorical level of their moral life. Rahner calls these people "anonymous theists."

Rahner's conception of the way in which man knows God— a conception he took over from his Belgian fellow Jesuit Joseph Maréchal—has allowed him to open up wide new avenues of thought in theology. We can only briefly refer to them here.

Man is a finite being endowed with an infinite capacity. He feels made for something that he is unable to reach by his own means. He is capable of receiving the Infinite, but he is unable to grasp Him by himself. Therefore, if he is to satisfy the deepest yearnings of his mind and of his heart, man must listen to a possible communication coming from the Infinite (revelation); he must welcome the additional light that may help him grasp God to some extent (faith).

Man will be totally himself only by becoming more than himself, which he does by letting God, who is his maker, become as it were his very life with sanctifying grace. All this, however, does not yet totally fill the capacity of human nature, its "obediential potency." When God deigns to fill it to its utmost capacity, then the human being who receives this unique divine invitation, who is rendered capable of yielding to it totally by God Himself, in whom God's invitation and man's loving response fully coincide, is himself God (Incarnation).

Summarizing a few of Rahner's ideas, as I have tried to do here, is like summarizing a Shakespearean play. It makes sense only as an invitation to the reader to study by himself the greatest theologian of our time.

SUGGESTED READINGS

For our purpose, Rahner's *Hearers of the Word* (N.Y.: Herder and Herder, 1969) is the basic work, although to some extent this presupposes the prior work *Spirit in the World* (N.Y.: Herder and Herder, 1968). Both offer rather formidable reading for the beginner. Perhaps Joseph Donceel's *Natural Theology* (N.Y.: Sheed and Ward, 1962), pp. 48-92, provides the simplest accurate introduction.

Brief, helpful sections are found in *Interpreting the Doctrine of God* by Charles Bent, S.J. (Paramus, N.J.: Paulist Press, 1968, paperback), which has a good bibliography; Louis Roberts' *The Achievement of Karl Rahner* (N.Y.: Herder and Herder, 1967); *Life and Light—A Guide to the Theology of Karl Rahner* by Donald Gelpi, S.J. (N.Y.: Sheed and Ward, 1966); *The Theology of Karl Rahner* by Gerald McCool, S.J. (Albany: Magi Books, Inc., 1969, paperback). Michael Novak's *Belief and Unbelief* (N.Y.: The New American Library, 1967, a Mentor-Omega paperback) develops out of the insight of Bernard Lonergan, S.J. But it also initiates in the reader a feeling for the thought-dynamics of kindred spirits, such as Rahner, and it does so in an interesting and semi-popular fashion. See especially chapter 5.

With regard to the Kantian problematic, I would suggest George F. Thomas' *Philosophy and Religious Belief* (N.Y.: Charles Scribner's Sons, 1970), pp. 135ff., and A. Boyce Gibson's *Theism and Empiricism* (N.Y.: Schocken Books, 1970), pp. 132ff. For the problematic in relating an approach like Rahner's to the modern world see Langdon Gilkey's *Naming the Whirlwind* (Indianapolis: Bobbs-Merrill, 1969, paperback) pp. 223ff. A fine presentation of Blondel's notion of conscience and freedom by John J. McNeill, S.J., "Freedom of Conscience in Theological Perspective," is found in *Conscience: Its Freedom and Limitations,* edited by William C. Bier, S.J. (N.Y.: Fordham University Press, 1971), pp. 107-124.

19 The Theological Significance of Existentialism and Psychoanalysis

PAUL TILLICH

In the following essay * from *Theology of Culture,* Paul Tillich presents a synoptic view of a number of issues which have been discussed in our previous chapters.

Tillich believed that the philosophy of religion should take as its point of departure the Platonic-Augustinian-Franciscan approach as opposed to the Aristotelian-Thomistic approach. The first he called the ontological approach (which is not the same as "the ontological argument"); the second he called the cosmological approach. The latter concludes to the existence of God from argumentative inference. The cosmological approach without the ontological as its basis led, he felt, to a destructive cleavage between philosophy and religion. Many Thomists insist that Tillich misunderstood St. Thomas. At any rate, he was not directing his criticism at the later transcendental thinking described in the two preceding chapters. But Tillich denied the possibility of an argumentative knowledge of God. Immediate knowledge is the only knowledge possible, for God is the answer implied in finitude. Tillich said it is "senseless to ask whether there is an unconditional meaning; for the very question presupposes an ultimate meaning" (James Luther Adams, *Paul Tillich's Philosophy of*

* From *The Theology of Culture,* edited by Robert C. Kimball (N.Y.: Oxford University Press, 1964), pp. 112-126; originally printed in *Faith and Freedom* (Autumn 1955, No. 25), Manchester College, Oxford, and reprinted by permission.

Culture, Science, and Religion, N.Y.: Schocken Books, 1950, paperback, p. 41).

In this essay Tillich speaks of essence and existence. Man's essence is his potential self which is united with "the ground of being" or God. Existence means man's actual life in which man is estranged from what he essentially is, and this is precisely the human predicament. "Whenever the ideal is held against the real, truth against error, good against evil, a distortion of essential being is presupposed" (*Systematic Theology,* Chicago: University of Chicago Press, 1951, Vol. I, pp. 202).

We shall be using the two words psychoanalysis and theology. By their very nature they pose semantic problems for us. Psychoanalysis can be a special term, and it is often usurped by the Freudian school, which declares that no other school has a right to use the term. A recent conversation with a representative of this school moved cordially up to the moment when people like Horney, Fromm, Jung, and Rank were called psychoanalysts. At this moment the Freudian broke in and said, "They are dishonest in calling themselves psychoanalysts. They shouldn't do it. They do it only for purposes of profit."

This situation shows that we have to do something about this term. It is not used here as this psychoanalyst used it, but rather in the meaning into which this term has been transformed and enlarged during the last half-century. These developments surely are dependent on the basic Freudian discovery, namely, the role of the unconscious. However, there are two other words which indicate something about the matter itself and could be used here: "therapeutic psychology" is one term often used, and another is "depth psychology."

About the term theology, perhaps many of you know that in our theological seminaries and divinity schools, the word theology often is used exclusively for systematic theology, and that historical and practical theology are not considered theology at all. We will enlarge the concept of theology for our discussion of its relationship to depth psychology and include in it past religious movements and great religious figures, and also the New Testament writings. Also, we want to include practical theology, where the relationship to psychoanalysis has become most conspicuous, namely, in the function of the counsellor who gives counsel in religious and in psychoanalytic terms at the same time.

Then we must also discuss the gap that has developed in the relation of existentialism to psychoanalysis. This is a real gap, because existentialism is now taken in a much broader sense than it was a few years after the Second World War. At that time existentialism was identified with the philosophy of Sartre. But existentialism appears in decisive forms early in the 17th and in the 19th centuries, and it is incorporated in almost all great creations in all areas of life in the 20th century. If you understand existentialism in this broader sense, it suggests very definitely a relationship between existentialism and psychoanalysis. A basic assertion to be made about the relationship of theology and psychoanalysis is that psychoanalysis belongs fundamentally to the whole existentialist movement of the 20th century, and that as a part of this movement it must be understood in its relationship to theology in the same way in which the relationship of existentialism generally must be understood.

This factor reveals something about the philosophical implications of depth psychology, and also about the interdependence between this movement and the existentialist movement of the 19th and 20th centuries. It is a fact that psychoanalysis and existentialism have been connected with each other from the very beginning; they have mutually influenced each other in the most radical and profound ways. Everybody who has looked into the works of existentialist writers from Dostoyevsky on to the present will immediately agree that there is much depth-psychological material in the novels, the dramas, and the poems, as well as in the visual arts—modern art being the existentialist form of visual art. All this is understandable only if we see that there is a common root and intention in existentialism and psychoanalysis.

If these common roots are found, the question of the relationship of psychoanalysis and theology is brought into a larger and more fundamental framework. Then it is possible to reject the attempts of some theologians and some psychologists to divide these two realms carefully and give to each of them a special sphere. It is then possible to disregard those people who tell us to stay in this or that field: here a system of theological doctrines and there congeries of psychological insights. This is not so. The relationship is not one of existing alongside each other; it is a relationship of mutual interpenetration.

The common root of existentialism and psychoanalysis is the protest against the increasing power of the philosophy of consciousness in modern industrial society. This conflict between the philosophy of consciousness and the protest against it is of course much older than modern industrial society. It appeared in the 13th century in the famous conflict between the primacy of the intellect in Thomas Aquinas and the primacy of the irrational will in Duns Scotus. Both of these men were theologians, and I mention them mainly in order to show how untenable theological positions are which want to exclude philosophical and psychological problems from theology. The struggle between these two basic attitudes towards not only the nature of man but also the nature of God and the world has continued ever since.

In the Renaissance, we have philosophers of consciousness, for instance, humanists of the type of Erasmus of Rotterdam or scientists of the type of Galileo. But against them stood others, as for instance, Paracelsus in the realm of medical philosophy who fought against the anatomical mechanization of medicine and against the separation of body and mind, or Jacob Boehme, who influenced the subsequent period very much, particularly by his description in mythological terms of the unconscious elements in the ground of the divine life itself and therefore of all life. We find the same conflict in the Reformation: on the one hand the victory of consciousness in reformers like Melanchthon, Zwingli, and Calvin, all of them dependent on humanists of the Erasmus type, while the irrational will was emphasized by Luther, on whom Jacob Boehme was largely dependent.

The history of industrial society, the end of which we are experiencing, represents the history of the victory of the philosophy of consciousness over the philosophy of the unconscious, irrational will. The symbolic name for the complete victory of the philosophy of consciousness is René Descartes; and the victory became complete, even in religion, at the moment when Protestant theology became the ally of the Cartesian emphasis on man as pure consciousness on the one hand, and a mechanical process called body on the other hand. In Lutheranism it was especially the cognitive side of man's consciousness which overwhelmed the early Luther's understanding of the irrational will. In Calvin it was the moral consciousness, the moral self-controlling center of consciousness that predominated. We have in America, which is mostly dependent on Calvinism and related outlooks, the moralistic and oppressive types of Protestantism which are the result of the complete victory of the philosophy of consciousness in modern Protestantism. But in spite of this victory, the protest was not silenced.

Pascal in the 17th century stood in conscious opposition to Descartes. His was the first existentialist analysis of the human situation, and he described it in ways very similar to those of later existentialist and non-existentialist philosophers, that is, in terms of anxiety, of finitude, of doubt, of guilt, of meaninglessness, of a world in which Newtonian atoms and cosmic bodies move according to mechanical laws; and as we know from many utterances, man decentralized, deprived of the earth as center, felt completely lost in this mechanized universe, in anxiety and meaninglessness. There were others in the 18th century; for example, Hamann, who is very little known outside of Germany, a kind of prophetic spirit anticipating many of the existentialist ideas. But the most radical protest came at the moment when the philosophy of consciousness reached its peak in the philosophy of Hegel. Against this victorious philosophy of consciousness Schelling arose, giving to Kierkegaard and many others the basic concepts of existentialism; then Schopenhauer's irrational will, Hartmann's philosophy of the unconscious, Nietzsche's analysis which anticipated most of the results of later depth-psychological inquiries. The protest appeared also in Kierkegaard's and Marx's description of the human predicament, in finitude, estrangement, and loss of subjectivity. And in Dostoyevsky we find the description of the demonic subconscious in man; we find it also in French poetry of the type of Rimbaud and Baudelaire. This was the preparation of the ground for what was to follow in the 20th century.

All the things which in these men were ontological intuition or theological analysis now through Freud became methodological scientific words. Freud, in his discovery of the unconscious, rediscovered something that was known long before, and had been used for many decades and even centuries to fight the victorious philosophy of consciousness. What Freud did was to give to this protest a scientific methodological foundation. In him we must see the old protest against the philosophy of consciousness. Especially in men like Heidegger and Sartre, and in the whole literature and art of the 20th century, the existentialist point of view became aware of itself. It now was expressed intentionally and directly, and not only as a suppressed element of protest.

This short survey shows the inseparability of depth psychology from philosophy, and of both of them from theology. It is also clear that they cannot be separated if we now compare depth psychology and existentialist philosophy in their differences and in their similarities. The basic point is that both existentialism and depth psychology are interested in the description of man's existential predicament—in time and space, in finitude and estrangement—in contrast to man's essential nature, for if you speak of man's existential predicament as opposite to his essential nature, you must in some way presuppose an idea of his essential nature. But this is not the purpose to which all existentialist literature is directed. Instead, the focus in both existentialism and depth psychology is man's estranged existence, the characteristics and symptoms of this estrangement, and the conditions of existence in time and space. The term "therapeutic psychology" shows clearly that here something that contradicts the norm, that must be healed, is expressed. It shows the relation between disease—mental, bodily, or psychosomatic—and man's existential predicament.

It is also clear that all existential utterances deal with the boundary line between healthy and sick and ask one question—you can reduce it to this—how is it possible that a being has a structure that produces psychosomatic diseases? Existentialism in order to answer these questions points to the possible experience of meaninglessness, to the continuous experience of loneliness, to the widespread feeling of emptiness. It derives them from finitude, from the awareness of finitude which is anxiety; it derives them from estrangement from oneself and one's world. It points to the possibility and the danger of freedom, and to the threat of nonbeing in all respects—from death to guilt. All these are characteristic of man's existential predicament, and in this, depth psychology and existentialism agree.

However, there is a basic difference between them. Existentialism as philosophy speaks of the universal human situation, which refers to everybody, healthy or sick. Depth psychology points to the ways in which people try to escape the situation by fleeing into neurosis and falling into psychosis. In existentialist literature, not only in novels and poems and dramas but even in philosophy, it is difficult to distinguish clearly the boundary line between man's universal existential situation based on finitude and estrangement on the one hand, and man's psychosomatic disease which is considered an attempt to escape from this situation and its anxieties by fleeing into a mental fortress.

Now how are theological judgments applied to depth psychology and existentialism (which are in reality one thing). The relation between man's essential nature and his existential predicament is the first and basic question that theology has asked whenever it encounters existentialist analyses and psychoanalytic material. In the Christian tradition, there are three fundamental concepts. First: *Esse qua esse bonum est.* This Latin phrase is a basic dogma of Christianity. It means "Being as being is good," or in the biblical mythological form: God saw everything that he had created, and behold, it was good. The second statement is the universal fall—fall meaning the transition from this essential goodness into existential estrangement from oneself, which happens in every living being and in every time. The third statement refers to the possibility of salvation. We should remember that salvation is derived from *salvus* or *salus* in Latin, which means "healed" or "whole," as opposed to disruptiveness.

These three considerations of human nature are present in all genuine theological thinking: essential goodness, existential estrangement, and the possibility of something, a "third," beyond essence and existence, through which the cleavage is overcome and healed. Now, in philosophical terms, this means that man's essential and existential nature points to his teleological nature (derived from *telos,* aim, that for which and towards which his life drives).

If you do not distinguish these three elements, which are always present in man, you will fall into innumerable confusions. Every criticism of existentialism and psychoanalysis on the basis of this tripartite view of human nature is directed against the confusion of these three fundamental elements, which always must be distinguished although they always are together in all of us. Freud, in this respect, was unclear, namely, he was not able to distinguish man's essential and existential nature. This is a basic theological criticism, not of any special result of his thinking, but of his doctrine of man and the central intuition he has of man. His thought about libido makes this deficiency very obvious.

Man, according to him, has infinite libido which never can be satisfied and which therefore produces the desire to get rid of oneself, the desire he has called the death instinct. And this is not only true of the individual, it is also true of man's relation to culture as a whole. His dismay about culture shows that he is very consistent in his negative judgments about man as existentially distorted. Now if you see man only from the point of view of existence and not from the point of view of essence, only from the point of view of estrangement and not from the point of view of essential goodness, then this consequence is unavoidable. And it is true for Freud in this respect.

Let us make this clear by means of a theological concept which is very old, the classical concept of concupiscence. This concept is used in Christian theology exactly as libido is used by Freud, but it is used for man under the conditions of existence; it is the indefinite striving beyond any given satisfaction, to induce satisfaction beyond the given one. But according to theological doctrine, man in his essential goodness is not in the state of concupiscence or indefinite libido. Rather he is directed to a definite special subject, to content, to somebody, to something with which he is connected in love, or *eros,* or *agape,* whatever it may be. If this is the case, then the situation is quite different. Then you can have libido, but the fulfilled libido is real fulfillment, and you are not driven beyond this indefinitely. This means that Freud's description of libido is to be viewed theologically as the description of man in his existential self-estrangement. But Freud does not know any other man, and this is the basic criticism that theology would weigh against him on this point.

Now, fortunately, Freud, like most great men, was not consistent. With respect to the healing process, he knew something about the healed man, man in the third form, teleological man. And in so far as he was thus convinced of the possibility of healing, this contradicted profoundly his fundamental restriction to existential man. In popular terms, his pessimism about the nature of man and his optimism about the possibilities of healing were never reconciled in him or in his followers.

But some of his followers have done something else. They have rejected the profound insight of Freud about existential libido and the death instinct, and in so doing they have reduced and cut off from Freud what made him and still makes him the most profound of all the depth psychologists. This can be said even in relation to Jung, who is much more religiously interested than was Freud. But Freud, theologically speaking, saw more about human nature than all his followers who, when they lost the existentialist element in Freud, went more to an essentialist and optimistic view of man.

We can make the same criticism of Sartre's pure existentialism and his sensitive psychological analysis. The greatness of this man is that he is the psychological interpreter of Heidegger. He is perhaps misinterpreted on many points, but nevertheless his psychological insights are profound. But here we have the same thing that we have found before: Sartre says man's essence is his existence. In saying this he makes it impossible for man to be saved or to be healed. Sartre knows this, and every one of his plays shows this too. But here also we have a happy inconsistency. He calls his existentialism humanism. But if he calls it humanism, that means he has an idea of what man essentially is, and he must consider the possibility that the essential being of man, his freedom, might be lost. And if this is a possibility, then he makes, against his own will, a distinction between man as he essentially is and man as he can be lost: man is to be free and to create himself.

We have the same problem in Heidegger. Heidegger talks also as if there were no norms whatsoever, no essential man, as if man makes himself. On the other hand, he speaks of the difference between authentic existence and unauthentic existence, falling into the average existence of conventional thought and nonsense—into an existence where he has lost himself. This is very interesting, because it shows that even the most radical existentialist, if he wants to say something, necessarily falls back to some essentialist statements because without them he cannot even speak.

Other psychoanalysts have described the human situation

as correctible and amendable, as a weakness only. But we can ask: is man essentially healthy? If he is, only his basic anxiety has to be taken away; for example, if you save him from the evil influences of society, of competition and things like that, everything will be all right. Men like Fromm speak of the possibility of becoming an autonomous non-authoritarian personality who develops himself according to reason. And even Jung, who knows so much about the depths of the human soul and about the religious symbols, thinks that there are essential structures in the human soul and that it is possible (and one may be successful) to search for personality.

In all these representatives of contemporary depth psychology we miss the depths of Freud. We miss the feeling for the irrational element that we have in Freud and in much of the existentialist literature. Dostoyevsky has already been mentioned. We could also mention Kafka and many others.

Now we come to the third element, namely, the teleological, the element of fulfillment, the question of healing. Here we have the difference between the healing of an acute illness and the healing of the existential presuppositions of every disease and of every healthy existence. This is the basis for the healing of special acute illnesses; on this all groups agree. There are acute illnesses that produce psychosomatic irregularities and destruction. There are compulsive restrictions of man's potentialities which lead to neurosis and eventually to psychosis. But beyond this there are the existential presuppositions. Neither Freudianism nor any purely existentialist consideration can heal these fundamental presuppositions. Many psychoanalysts try to do it. They try with their methods to overcome existential negativity, anxiety, estrangement, meaninglessness, or guilt. They deny that they are universal, that they are existential in this sense. They call all anxiety, all guilt, all emptiness, illnesses which can be overcome as any illness can be, and they try to remove them. But this is impossible. The existential structures cannot be healed by the most refined techniques. They are objects of salvation. The analyst can be an instrument of salvation as every friend, every parent, every child can be an instrument of salvation. But as analyst he cannot bring salvation by means of his medical methods, for this requires the healing of the center of the personality. So much for the criticism.

Now how can theology deal with depth psychology? Certainly the growth of the two movements, existentialism and depth psychology, is of infinite value for theology. Both of them brought to theology something which it always should have known but which it had forgotten and covered up. They helped to rediscover the immense depth psychological material which we find in the religious literature of the last two thousand years and even beyond that. Almost every insight concerning the movement of the soul can be found in this literature, and the most classical example of all is perhaps Dante's *Divine Comedy,* especially in the description of hell and purgatory, and of the inner self-destructiveness of man in his estrangement from his essential being.

Second, it was a rediscovery of the meaning of the word "sin" which had become entirely unintelligible by the identification of sin with sins, and by the identification of sins with certain acts that are not conventional or not approvable. Sin is something quite different. It is universal, tragic estrangement, based on freedom and destiny in all human beings, and should never be used in the plural. Sin is separation, estrangement from one's essential being. That is what it means; and if this is the result of depth psychological work, then this of course is a great gift that depth psychology and existentialism have offered to theology.

Thirdly, depth psychology has helped theology to rediscover the demonic structures that determine our consciousness and our decisions. Again, this is very important. It means that if we believe we are free in terms of conscious decision, we can find that something has happened to us which directed these decisions before we made them. The illusion of freedom in the absolute sense in which it was used is included in this rediscovery. This is not determinism. Existentialism is certainly not determinism. But existentialism and especially psychoanalysis and the whole philosophy of the unconscious have rediscovered the totality of the personality in which not only the conscious elements are decisive.

The fourth point, connected with the previous one, is that moralism can be conquered to a great extent in Christian theology. The call for moralism was one of the great forms of self-estrangement of theology from its whole being. And it is indeed important to know that theology had to learn from the psychoanalytic method the meaning of grace, the meaning of forgiveness as acceptance of those who are unacceptable and not of those who are the good people. On the contrary, the non-good people are those who are accepted, or in religious language, forgiven, justified, whatever you wish to call it. The word grace, which had lost any meaning, has gained a new meaning by the way in which the analyst deals with his patient. He accepts him. He does not say, "You are acceptable," but he accepts him. And that is the way in which, according to religious symbolism, God deals with us; and it is the way every minister and every Christian should deal with the other person.

Before the rediscovery of confession and counselling (which were completely lost in Protestantism), everybody was asked to do something, and if he didn't do it he was reproached. Now he can go to somebody, can talk to him, and in talking he can objectify what is in him and get rid of it. If the counsellor or confessor is somebody who knows the human situation, he can be a medium of grace for him who comes to him, a medium for the feeling of overcoming the cleavage between essence and existence.

Finally, what is the influence of psychoanalysis on systematic theology? The interpretation of man's predicament by psychoanalysis raises the question that is implied in man's very existence. Systematic theology has to show that the religious symbols are answers to this question. Now, if you understand the relation of theology and depth psychology in this way, you have grasped the fundamental importance, the final and decisive importance, of all this for theology. There is no theistic and non-theistic existentialism or psychoanalysis. They analyze the human situation. Whenever the analysts or the philosophers give an answer, they do it not as existentialists. They do it from other traditions, whether it be Catholic, Protestant, Lutheran, humanist, or socialist. Traditions come from everywhere, but they do not come from the *question*.

In a long talk in London with T. S. Eliot, who is really considered to be an existentialist, we talked about just this problem. I told him, "I believe that you cannot answer the question you develop in your plays and your poems on the basis of your plays and poems, because they only develop the question—they describe human existence. But if there is an answer, it comes from somewhere else." He replied, "That is exactly what I am fighting for all the time. I am, as you know, an Episcopalian." And he is really a faithful Episcopalian; he answers as an Episcopalian but not as an existentialist. This means that the existentialist raises the question and analyzes the human situation to which the theologian can then give the answer, an answer given not from the question but from somewhere else, and not from the human situation itself.

Theology has received tremendous gifts from existentialism and psychoanalysis, gifts not dreamed of fifty years ago or even thirty years ago. We have these gifts. Existentialists and analysts themselves do not need to know that they have given to theology these great things. But the theologians should know it.

SUGGESTED READINGS

Tillich returns to psychology and religion in "The Meaning of Health," *Religion and Medicine,* David Belgum, editor (Ames, Iowa: Iowa State University Press, 1967) pp. 3-12. There is a brief, incisive critique of Freud as compared with Feuerbach in *Perspectives on 19th and 20th Century Protestant Theology* (N.Y.: Harper and Row, 1967), pp. 139-141. "Only if there is an awareness of something unconditional or infinite within us can we understand why the projected images have to be divine figures or symbols." Projection theories must explain not only projection but projection to the infinite. A brief, penetrating analysis of Jung is found in *Carl Gustav Jung 1875-1961—A Memorial Meeting, Dec. 1, 1961* (N.Y.: The Analytical Psychology Club, 1962). Tillich, who wrote chapter V, pages 28-32, says that Jung, despite his fear of metaphysics, reached deeply into a doctrine of being through his theory of the archetypes which involve a transtemporal and universal structure. For Tillich's evaluation of Buber, see "An Evaluation of Martin Buber: Protestant and Jewish Thought," *Theology of Culture,* edited by Robert Kimball (N.Y.: Oxford University Press, 1964, paperback), pp. 188-199. Especially valuable is "Paul Tillich Converses with Psychotherapists," by Rev. James B. Ashbrook, Ph.D., *Journal of Religion and Health,* January 1972, Vol. II, I, pp. 40-72. Tillich compares the compassion of Buddhism with love in Christianity, and finds that the latter retains the element of criticism. He also discusses the experience of guilt, the cross of Christ, and the need for acceptance beyond self-acceptance. Tillich's *The Courage To Be* (New Haven: Yale University Press, 1952, paperback) and *Dynamics of Faith* (N.Y.: Harper and Row, 1957, paperback) are closely related to the psychology-religion area. Some good introductions to Tillich's thought are *The Theology of Paul Tillich,* edited by Charles W. Kegley and Robert W. Bretall (N.Y.: the Macmillan Company, 1952, paperback); *The Vision of Paul Tillich* by Carl Armbruster, S.J. (N.Y.: Sheed and Ward, 1967); *The Power of Self-Transcendence* by Guyton B. Hammond (St. Louis: The Bethany Press, 1966, paperback). With regard to Tillich's insistence on the rejection of argumentative constructs as the basis of an approach to God, see William J. Wainwright's "Paul Tillich and Arguments for the Existence of God," *Journal of the American Academy of Religion,* June 1971, 39, 2, pp. 171-185, and Clark M. Williamson's "Tillich's Two Types of Philosophy of Religion: A Reconstruction," *The Journal of Religion,* July 1972, 53, 3, pp. 205-222.

For a popularization of Tillich's notion of acceptance related to aspects of Freud's thought, see Thomas A. Harris, *I'm OK, You're OK. A Practical Guide to Transactional Analysis* (N.Y.: Harper & Row, Publishers, 1973, paperback edition), esp. pp. 213ff.

20 Meaning, Purpose and the Universe

L. CHARLES BIRCH

The concluding essay * is by L. Charles Birch, a biologist from the University of Sydney, Australia. I have included this essay for two reasons. First, the school of process theology has not yet been touched upon in this book. Process theology distinguishes two aspects in the nature of God, the primordial nature and the consequent nature, and it sees God himself as in process in his consequent nature. Process theology has deep implications for the psychology of religion, because the God of process can in no way be seen as unrelated to man and his world. Dr. Birch relies on process thinkers for the development of his own thought.

Secondly, if one consistently reads works in the psychology of religion, often enough the reader is imbued with a *vague feeling* that, when one speaks of God, one means either the collective unconscious or simply man's immanent highest ideal. This is the basis of "psychologism." Nothing forces psychologism to open out from its self-enclosure more readily than the realization that there was a time before the existence of either a collective unconscious or a human ideal. Yet during this period before man existed, the universe operated like a gigantic organism "in action."

In the past, we have separated mind and matter, spirit and energy, much too drastically. Physics and biology seemed to have little connection with human-

* From *Zygon,* March 1971, vol. 6, no. 1, pp. 4-27, The University of Chicago Press. Reprinted with permission.

istic psychology or mysticism. But for some time now, voices have been raised which proclaim the discernment of a faintly glimpsed convergence. Jung, for example, spoke of "an unexpected parallelism of psychic and physical events." He wrote: "Sooner or later nuclear physics and the psychology of the unconscious will draw closer together as both of them, independently of one another and from opposite directions, push forward into transcendental territory, the one with the concept of the atom, the other with that of the archetype" (from his *Aion,* cited by Aniela Jaffe, *From the Life and Work of C. G. Jung,* N.Y.: Harper and Row, 1971, paperback, p. 43). Similarly Teilhard de Chardin demonstrated an intimate relationship between evolution, as seen by physics and biology, and psychological-cultural evolution. He wrote: ". . . a natural connection is drawn between the two worlds of physics and psychology, hitherto supposed irreconcilable. Matter and consciousness are bound together: not in the sense that consciousness becomes directly measurable, but in the sense that it becomes organically and physically rooted in the same cosmic process with which physics is concerned" (from *The Vision of the Past,* N.Y.: Harper and Row, 1966, p. 227). One can take numberless statements made by theoretical physicists and place them side by side with quotations from the psychologists of old, the mystics, and find them indistinguishable, as Philip Le Shan has done ("The Quotation Game," *Intellectual Digest,* Feb. 1972, pp. 47-49). See also Arthur Koestler's *The Roots of Coincidence* (N.Y.: Random House, 1972).

Fundamentalist concordism and premature simplification, of course, are the great dangers here, and the preceding remarks have been made merely to provide a backdrop for Dr. Birch's essay.

"Of course, it may be said that the impulsion to 'make sense of existence' is just the beginning of wish fantasy, a desperate subterfuge to conceal the unbearable truth that existence is indeed absurd. This may be the case. But at least let us give the matter a hearing before we make up our minds to dismiss it." [1]

There is a formlessness or yawning in much of modern life that has four obvious aspects:

1. Our inner chaos: the inability to live in harmony with oneself, to accept oneself, to discover one's identity, and to let body, feelings, and thought dwell together in friendship.
2. Our social chaos: the lack of relatedness to others, the inability to live in harmony with others, the generation gap, the problems of the old, polarization within society, and failure to find common national and international goals.
3. Our environmental chaos: the green and varied landscape in which man evolved is swiftly being replaced by a polluted wilderness of concrete and steel; not only has this man-created environment produced physical ills but it seems also to be accentuating psychological disease and lack of rapport with our surroundings. Man himself has become the chief earth pest.
4. Our metaphysical chaos: the sense of separation from the "whole scheme of things" because we have no conviction that there is any scheme of things or value in the universe. Sartre contends that man must give himself meaning in a universe itself devoid of value, but, as Hartshorne [2] affirms, "if we have no value for the cosmos, we have no value—period." The question then arises, if we have no value for the cosmos, can there be any value or meaning within human life, in human relationships, and in our relationship to our environment?

Estrangement and Integrity

Our lack of a sense of oneness with self, with others, with the world, and with the whole scheme of things has many names: disintegration, separation, alienation, disengagement, noninvolvement, apathy, and, perhaps most descriptive of all, estrangement. Increasingly, the vocabulary of social commentary is dominated by these terms.

But there is a happier state of man that some men know some

of the time, and perhaps some know all the time. It is an opening of the heart for the beauty of the world and humanity. It is the state of being at one with self, with others, with the world, and with the "whole scheme of things." This is a dynamic, not a static, state, for contentedness in this sense can never really endure for a period without swinging to a discontentedness with all that is incomplete and unfinished. To be sensitive is to be aware of much that is potentially possible but which is not yet concretely real in this world. A state of hippie bliss may endure for a season, but it will leave the world unchanged if it is not balanced by a deep sense of discontentedness which is a spring of action for change. The same could be said of what Northrop [3] calls "the satisfied Left Bank Parisian boredom, which the Existentialists call *Sorge*" and which leaves the world unchanged.

There are words that give a name to this state of contentedness and discontentedness; integrity, which comes from integer, meaning undivided, at-one-ment, wholeness, health, and holiness —they all mean the one thing and the opposite of estrangement.

Secular man is said to accept provisional answers to limited questions. Yet there is a groping in modern man for an all-inclusive coherence and integrity. Man wants to know if what he does has a value extending beyond his own experience and that of others to some sort of ultimate worthwhileness. We set our sights on lesser goals which let us down. There is a sense in which the passion of our involvement depends upon the extent to which we feel a value more ultimate than ourselves or even the human race, and it is this aspect of purpose and value that finds us more at sea than any other. The old metaphysical structures have broken down, and many know of nothing to replace them. There are many who will be content to live without an overall view. Life is enjoyed as it is lived in relation to near goals and immediate purposes. I wonder, however, if this is not in part an adaptation to survive psychologically against the fear of ultimate meaninglessness. If there is an overall view that makes sense and has some validity, are we not missing out on life by not seeking it more deliberately and passionately? There must be a difference in life lived for its moments and life lived as a part of a greater whole in which what is achieved is achieved not just for one person or one species, but is more enduring than either. Is it perhaps the difference between listening to a symphony bar by bar or in the way suggested in Mozart's supposed letter to a friend: "The whole composition, though it be long, arrives in my head almost complete, so that I can survey it, like a lovely picture or a beautiful person, at a glance. In my imagination I do not hear the parts successively, but I hear them, as it were, all at once. . . . And to hear them thus, all together, is much the best way!" [4]

Man's groping for an integrity in modern life is indicated by worldwide movements in each of the four main areas of man's relatedness. Sensitivity and encounter groups speak to man's inner chaos and need of interior oneness. Activist movements have, for many, brought a sense of relatedness to others. The ecology movement, which began in the United States, has spread to most of the rest of the world, finding eager support from youth. The relation of man's future to science and technology and its effects has produced an array of concerned groups. The groping for a metaphysic finds its expression in mysticism, Zen, and a renewed interest in process philosophy.

In each of the areas where man needs to find integrity there are at least three conditions for achieving it. The goal or purpose must be clearly seen. It must be evaluated as being of great worth and embraced with passionate involvement. The means for achieving the initial steps must be known. A vision, its evaluation, and knowledge of the way seem to characterize those people who stand out as committed to a purpose and its achievement. But this is all stated too baldly. Those persons who have discovered an integrity that is all-inclusive and transforming feel not that they have invented something but that they are claimed by something. They feel called forward from the present state of things to much greater possibilities often only vaguely perceived. In Matthew Arnold's phrase, we sense "a power beyond ourselves that makes for righteousness." [5] Cobb speaks of "that which calls" or even "one who calls" as a distinct aspect of experience; that human behavior is explained not just in terms of antecedent conditions but by confrontation with possibilities of the future. [6] Overreaching all our commitments and discoveries of integrity is the question of whether we are responding to some actuality in the universe that is itself one. Parallel to this is the question of whether there is any ultimate significance in what we do and what happens. That is the metaphysical aspect of purpose; man "seeking," says Whitehead, "amid the dim recesses of his ape-like consciousness and beyond the reach of dictionary language, for the premises implicit in all reasoning." [7] He suggests that the zest for human adventure presupposes for its material a scheme of things with a worth beyond any single occasion, a deep feeling of an aim in the universe. For Teilhard de Chardin it was based on "that aspect of life which most stirs my soul, . . . the ability to share in an undertaking, in a reality, more enduring than myself." [8] And for John B. Cobb, "What happens really matters only if it matters ultimately, and it matters ultimately only if it matters everlastingly." [9] In what follows I suggest some propositions which I find persuasive to this view. Much of it is speculative, but, as Charles Hartshorne said to me on one occasion, "You have to be imaginative to see the issues." It is the sort of imagination of the tapestry worker who works behind the design he creates.

Inner Chaos versus Inner Integrity

My starting point for a sense of purpose and integrity is man's need for a sense of oneness within his own life. I may not feel at one with myself at all, like the adolescent who knows he behaves differently toward his parents, his peer group, and his teachers, and who asks in all seriousness, "Who is the real me?" He feels he is not one person but many. His own behavior baffles him. Erikson expresses this experience in his concept of "identity confusion" with its opposite, the discovery of one's identity.[10] He argues for the psychological need a man has to discover his identity and with it a sense of self-fulfillment. Man then discovers an integrating influence in his emotional and intellectual life. He has discovered something, someone, particular values to identity himself with and which he feels are worthwhile. A moving account of such a discovery is given by Keniston's analysis of what happened to a group of young radicals in their commitment to a cause in the "Vietnam summer" of 1967.[11] The biblical story of the Gadarene demoniac is a dramatic symbol of identity confusion being replaced by discovery of an identity that was integrating. Rejected by society as a disintegrated personality, he was bound to a tombstone in a graveyard. When asked by Jesus to speak for himself, he made his own diagnosis: "My name is legion for we are many." In the final scene he is at the feet of his newfound friend, "clothed, and in his right mind." I take "clothed" to mean clothed in a new integrity and a new value commitment, just as Kenneth Keniston's radicals found themselves becoming committed to a set of values—"justice, decency, equality, responsibility, non-violence and fairness." The operational factor for both was commitment to a cause beyond themselves which had a transforming influence. They had discovered a purpose, and it became an effective cause of change. I find myself much more sympathetic toward this idealistic approach to human behavior than to the popular-front thinking of Ardrey [12] and Lorenz,[13] who seem to have invented a biological basis of original sin in equipping man with "territorial" and "aggressive" "instincts" because they find these in nonhuman animals. There is a lot we can learn about our animal nature from biology. But it is a one-sided view which has little place for the transforming effect of ideals.

Pascal had man more in balance when he wrote, "It is dangerous to show man too clearly, how much he resembles the animal, unless we show him his greatness at the same time. But it is also dangerous to show him his greatness, without showing him his baseness. The greatest danger is to leave him in ignorance about one and the other. However, it is most useful to show him both." [14]

Social Chaos versus Social Integrity

My alienation or estrangement may be from other people, and that can be deeply disintegrating. I have both a need for some degree of acceptance by others and a need to accept them into my world of experience. We worry, at least when we are young, about what others may think of us. A student said to me that he felt other people were looking at him all the time as he traveled to the university by train. He said he felt sure that they were thinking odd things about him, and perhaps they were right. This was just one symptom of a more general sense of separation from humanity that included his parents. His parents had certainly eaten sour grapes, and the son's teeth were set on edge. He longed to feel unembarrassed in the company of others. Human loneliness is a traumatic experience which is common in our urban civilization. A lad has come down to the city from military camp on weekend leave. Sunday night finds him glued to that electronic companion—television. It bores him, so he wanders out into the empty street. He keeps on wandering until he reaches the city, hopefully catching any glimpse of a group folk singing or otherwise getting together. He gets to Kings Cross in the heart of Sydney. It is late Sunday night. Most places are closed, but there is noise coming from a little place called the Wayside Chapel. It is not a religious noise, so he goes in. It is what they call "question time." The questions people there are asking have to do with drugs, promiscuity, war, and the sort of society youth would like to see in place of what is here. He finds he is not alone in his thoughts. He is accepted and at a level that matters. He says he wants to come back. Or there is the student who, instead of going to bed at that late hour, goes out from his college room into the darkness and wanders, he knows not where, until he comes to a part of Sydney Harbour down by the docks. He looks in the water and sees his face reflected back at him. He could end it all there by jumping in, but then he remembers that he did not go out to do that at all—he went out in search of someone, anyone who would talk with him, talk with him about that private diary he had been writing in such detail and with such urgency all these last months. I do not know how it all started, but, importantly, along the way was the trauma of rejection by his schoolfellows in a boarding school. They found him in the basement secretly painting when the rest of them were bashing each other at football. That was enough to cast him out. When I last saw him, he was discovering an acceptance in a college community which was prepared to ignore some oddities of behavior for the sake of the person he really was. The story of Zacchaeus, the tax collector, is a classic one of such an estrangement from others which becomes replaced by an integrity which was completely transforming. He found a purpose in a new relationship to people. It is my experience that people who reject people and are unwilling to be accepted have themselves been rejected. The totally alienated youth cannot accept love as easily as that. He suspects altruistic behavior in others because he has been hurt too many times by exploiters in the past. What do you expect to get out of me this time? is his response to loving concern. The breakthrough sometimes occurs with the persistent and selfless concern of another, but the road may be long and rough. The big cities of our day are singularly lacking in centers where lost souls can find companionship and where the lonely urban dweller can find others to relate to at more than superficial levels. The "family of man" is no longer a family in the urbanized mobile Western world, and this is a loss which has profound psychological effects.

Environmental Chaos versus Environmental Integrity

Man needs rapport not only with himself and his fellows, but with the physical and biological world around him. The urban environment is now vastly different from the world of green landscapes in which man evolved. It is possible that man is genetically conditioned to need a responsiveness to the world of nature and that his own constructions can become alien to him. Perhaps we have a psychological need for grass and trees and varied patterns of landscape. To regard plants and nonhuman animals as being there primarily for man to use is not only inimical to conserving a natural world but is a devaluation of the natural world. "Behold the lilies of the field" expresses another valuation of nature altogether. It does not mean "Look at those lilies," but, as Sittler points out, "The word 'behold' lies upon that which is beheld with a kind of tenderness which suggests that things in themselves leave their own wondrous authenticity and integrity. . . . 'To behold' means to stand among things with a kind of reverence for life which does not walk through the world of the nonself with one's arrogant hat on." [15] Some primitive societies have been far more sensitive to nature in this way than is our Western culture. Dorothy Lee gives some impressive accounts of this: "They do not set out to control, or master, or exploit. Their ceremonials are often periods of intensified communion, even social affairs, in a broad sense. In their relationships with nature, the people may see themselves as the offspring of a cherished mother, or the guests of a generous hostess. . . . So, when the Baiga in India were urged to change over to the use of an iron plow, they replied with horror that they could not tear the flesh of their mother with knives." [16] Dorothy Lee gives examples of American Indians who used every portion of the carcass of a hunted animal, not for economic thrift, but through courtesy and respect; of others who lived on land so heavily timbered that it was difficult to find sites for houses, but who nevertheless used dead wood only for fuel "out of respect for nature." These people do not so much seek communion with nature as find themselves in communion with it. For them there is no dichotomy between man and nature; man is in nature.

People in the "developed world" have lost this valuation of nature. We are in the world but not of the world. Because of our prevailing values we are prepared to stand by and destroy the earth for a mess of pottage. "Show me a man-oriented society," writes landscape architect McHarg, "in which it is believed that reality exists only because man can perceive it, that the cosmos is a structure erected to support man on its pinnacle, that man exclusively is divine and given dominion over all things, indeed that God is made in the image of man, and I will predict the nature of its cities and their landscapes. I need not look far for we have seen them—the hot-dog stands, the neon shill, the ticky-tacky houses, dysgenic city and mined landscapes. This is the image of the anthropomorphic anthropocentric man; he seeks not unity with nature but conquest." [17]

Lynn White, Jr.,[18] blames our Western attitude of exploitation and rape of the earth on that part of the Judeo-Christian tradition that conceives man as superior to all the rest of creation, which exists merely for his use and exploitation. That there is such a strong tradition within Christendom cannot be denied. Furthermore, the traditional Christian churches have feared an evaluation of nature for its own sake because of a peculiar antipathy to anything that is suggestive of pantheism. It is true, as White says, that "human ecology is deeply conditioned by beliefs about our nature and destiny—that is, by religion." [19] However, Moncrief [20] is nearer the mark when he says that to argue that religion is the primary conditioner of human behavior toward the environment is much more than the data that White cites will bear. No culture, he claims, has been able to screen out completely the egocentric tendencies of human beings. Technology has multiplied the productive capacity of every worker many times what it was prior to the technological revolution. With increased wealth came the increased demand for goods and services. And in the process the environment has taken a terrible beating. The Western world is without any dominant ethic of the environment. It has little moral direction in the use of the world's nonrenewable resources, and it tends to have an undying faith in the capacity of technology to produce a technological rabbit of salvation from the hat when the environment can no longer give of its riches. Six percent of the world's population (in the United States) is consuming 40 percent of the world's nonrenewable resources. If the United States and the rest of the Western world continue their present human growth and industrial development, the world faces, sooner or later, ecological disaster. The only responsible attitude is to reduce economic growth and work for a stable human population and stable ecological system for the world. Only then can man say that he has avoided environmental chaos and found an integrity with his environment. In this connection my own country, Australia, is on the same path of exploitation of the environment and massive urbanization as the rest of the Western world. There is, however, a small group who are working toward a model for Australia in which population and development might be brought into balance with conservation of the quality of the environment. Man cannot save himself without saving his world at the same time. That means establishing right relations with the world. Never before in history has the possibility existed that man could destroy his world. The possibility also exists that man can save the world. Lake Michigan, with the whole of creation, "groans in travail, waiting to be set free from its bondage of decay," as Paul says in the eighth chapter of the book of Romans.

There is now a growing number of groups throughout the world seeking a new integrity of man with that part of his environment we call science and technology. A major cause of man's bewilderment is his inability to cope with the overwhelming nemesis of technology and the new possibilities for the future opened up by science. Man's future is threatened by the demonic perverseness of science and technology that could destroy all that has ever been achieved. This same science and technology beckon us with hope to a future where poverty and physical suffering can be eliminated in all nations forever. In the meantime, we tread an uncertain path in which increasing urbanization and industrialization squeeze the meaning out of life and where manipulation of man to chosen ends makes us less, not more, free. In its program "The Future of Man in a Science-Based Technology," the World Council of Churches is planning to mobilize the resources of concerned people in the professions and in humanistic disciplines to come to grips with all these urgent issues. The goal is a new understanding of integrity where science and technology will not primarily be a threat but will be part of the creative advance of the twentieth century.[21]

Metaphysical Chaos versus Metaphysical Integrity

Professor Joseph Sittler reported that a student interrupted one of his lectures to say, "But look, how can *anything* mean if *everything* doesn't?" [22] How can human life have meaning if there is no meaning to the cosmos? There is an estrangement which a man can experience which is the worst kind of alienation, and that is a sense of separation from the whole scheme of things, not just ourselves or our fellows, not just from the world of nature, but from the total environment of our life. We ask, "Is there any point in existence?"

A sense of separation from the whole scheme of things may be a temporary, though nonetheless poignant, experience after a great grief. Or it may be more permanent as a way of life; for example, the group of students whom Keniston calls the uncommitted or alienated: "These young men find the universe and their own lives lacking in meaning and direction; they live in a 'dead' universe filled with self-seeking men who hide their motives from themselves." [23] Or it may follow the shattering of our childhood and cosy views of the universe by a more mature understanding of the complexity of things. The Sunday school version of God who created the universe and left it except for occasional interventions is about the only image that many people have ever known. They rightly reject it. It is, of course, a miserable concept of God who would have to destroy his creation in order to act. When simplistic pictures are shown to be inadequate, the next easy step is to conclude that there is no satisfactory picture to be had, that the universe and existence are inscrutable. We may opt, as an alternative, for another simplistic picture which is the besetting sin of both science and philosophy, for example, the notion of the universe as a self-made, self-propelling contrivance, with ourselves as cogs in the works. And that is all. The sense of unity we derive from a simplistic view is readily shattered in the modern world. It may require a great intellectual and emotional struggle to replace it with a newfound harmony in diversity. The eminent Victorian biologist Thomas Henry Huxley asked, "Is the universe friendly?" His question implied the possibility, nay the probability, that it was not; contrivance it is, complex to be sure, but nevertheless contrivance—period—contrivance as unresponsive to man's yearnings as any other machine. Camus expresses much the same thought when he speaks of "the unreasonable silence of the world." [24] By contrast, Teilhard de Chardin proclaims this to be a personalizing universe. A universe in which personality is possible requires a different sort of explanation from one in which personality was not possible. [25] A few thousand million years ago there was primeval chaos. And now here we are! I believe that a universe which produced life and consciousness requires an explanation different from the kind that would be demanded from a universe which did not do so and could not do so.

Huxley was overcome by the seeming impersonality of the universe; Teilhard de Chardin can write a "Hymn of the Universe" which bespeaks a meaning to existence that makes sense of his most profound experiences. Without some such meaning, though not necessarily the one that Teilhard found, there is a vacuum in our culture that quickly gets filled with astrology, numerology, and all sorts of prescientific magic. What follows are a series of propositions about the universe that are the basis of my understanding of integrity and purpose in the universe and that I believe are consistent with a scientific understanding of the world.

The Cosmos as Universe, Not Multiverse

The facts of science and human experience cry aloud for an overall view of the unity of creation. "It could be claimed," says White, "that our thinking has got spread over so vast a range of things that it is suffering excess intellectual entropy. Wistfully we yearn for new Aristotles and Leonardos, well knowing that if they could return they would be as appalled as we at the new chaos of what once seemed the mind's cosmos." [26] However, he goes on to say, "The full view of the facts justifies not gloom but exhilaration. . . . The explosion of knowledge and the trend toward specialization have provided a compensatory swing toward intellectual generality." [27] From physics we accept the physical unity of the universe. At least for the cosmos we know the physical building blocks of the outer nebulae appear to be the same as those that make up a human brain. What the poet Francis Thompson wrote is true in physics.

> All things by immortal power
> Near and far
> Hiddenly
> To each other linked are,
> That thou canst not stir a flower
> Without troubling a star.[28]

Every entity "feels" every other entity physically. That was the discovery that Newton made and whereby it was possible for him to explain the movements of the planets and the fall of the apple in one principle. It told us something about the unity of the universe. From biochemistry, we have the unifying concept that life arose out of nonliving matter without the addition of any new entities and that all life is constituted of the same molecules. Biology tells us that all living things evolved over countless ages through the operation of natural selection of random variation. This is the Darwinian principle that ties all living things together in common descent. No new entities were added to the brew to produce the wealth of life through the ages; no vitalist principles were needed. What was there in the beginning was enough for all creation. But what was there? That is the question! It becomes the critical question when we contemplate what evolution flowered into—the human mind that experiences the universe and seeks to interpret that experience. Evolution has produced sentient creatures who know in some sense the universe. George Wald said, "It would be a poor thing to be an atom in a universe without physicists. And physicists are made of atoms. A physicist is the atom's way of knowing about atoms." [29] But there are other sentient creatures besides man. And who is to say where we should draw the line between sentience and nonsentience as we go down the evolutionary tree? There seem to be three possibilities: either we deny the reality of sensation, or we regard it as something added or emerging at some stage in the evolutionary pathway, or we see it as something present in principle in the building blocks of the creation. What we know so clearly by experience we may imply is an aspect of all that exists. I take this to be a central tenet of the process thinking of A. N. Whitehead, Charles Hartshorne, and others. In this idea I find the unity of the universe taken more seriously than in any other concept. We interpret the "lower" in terms of the higher. What we see more fully developed in man gives us a clue to the nature of all the building blocks of the universe. The grandeur and nature of the river of life are revealed not at its source but at its estuary.

A Unitary Actuality

A unitary actuality in the universe embraces all that is and is worthy of total devotion—this is the proposition that the integrity man experiences within his own life, with that of his fellows, with the non-human creation of plants and animals and sunsets and rocks, bespeaks a relationship with something at the heart of all that exists and which has its own oneness. Science describes the outer aspects of things. The inner aspect may elude the laboratory analysis but not my feelings of it. The most complete description of reality would include all that scientific analysis can reveal and all that we feel intuitively, even though vaguely.

The nonrational animals have some sort of unity of response to the world around them. They have their integrity. But their own species is practically all that has value; the rest is largely unknown to them. Man can raise his sense of integrity and wholeness to the conscious level; he makes a conscious unitary response to the universe around him. "Not completeness, but all-inclusiveness, is what is required," says Hartshorne.[30] This conscious unitary response is what the word "worship" means. "It lifts to the level of explicit awareness the integrity of an individual responding to reality." Hartshorne further points out that there are two possible theories of such worship. In the theistic theory, the conscious wholeness of the individual is correlative to an inclusive wholeness in the world of which the individual is aware. This wholeness he calls "deity." According to the nontheistic view, whether there is no inclusive wholeness, or even if there is, it is not what religions have meant by deity. Three great religions agree with this conception of worship: Judaism, Christianity, and Islam. In Christianity, God is that inclusive wholeness to which a person responds with "all his heart, with all his mind and with all his soul and with all his strength." This idea that worship is love with all one's being is in the great religions correlated with the idea that what we wholly love is itself also in the nature of love. In his book *A Natural Theology for Our Time* as well as in many of his earlier writings, Hartshorne has emphasized the logic of this step. How can one love with all one's being an unloving being? "Only supreme love can be supremely lovable," he answers.[31] To worship is to attribute worth to. The view being put forth here is that there is a unitary actuality that includes all and which is worthy of one's total devotion. All-inclusiveness is the integrating aspect. Yet many go for less. Humanism as devotion to that which fulfills human potentiality is a lesser object of devotion, though it is included within the complete object of devotion. Humanism leaves a vast world aside. Furthermore, it has no answer to the question-answer-question sequence: Q. What am I here for? A. To help others. Q. But what are the others here for? Living only for the partly foreseeable but limited human future has something irrational about it. A burning zeal for humanity is one source of integrity. It is not the only one. The discovery of what a man is and is most worthy of becoming leads to the further question of the purpose of existence, not just man's existence. While humanism may cast a bright light on the foreground of morality, it leaves what Whitehead calls "its background" wholly obscure. John B. Cobb [32] has expressed much the same view of the difference between commitment to a humanistic ideal and commitment to the unitary actuality that includes all and to which we can respond with all. He argues that the one who dedicates himself to ideals does so out of the correct judgment that these have objectivity to him, that they lay a claim upon him. Yet he can hardly provide an intelligible explanation of how this is so. The reasons for concern about one's motives and responsibilities for them become obscure. The claim of a neighbor upon me becomes arbitrary and without foundation. But when I discover that my neighbor is part of that total actuality that calls me forward in loving my neighbor (and myself), I am experiencing an at-one-ness with that which is altogether lovable.

If you say that this is all very fine theory, but ask what conceivable reason can a man have for entertaining seriously such ideas, I would reply:

(a) An individual must have integrity in order to exist as an individual, and if the conscious form of integration is commitment to that which matters most in self and others and the rest of creation, then it is illogical for a person to choose deliberately not to be so committed. There is something irrational in choosing not to believe in the integration of the universe.[33]

(b) The reason cannot be one of verification in the empirical sense that all conceivable alternatives have been falsified. Materialism is in the same boat. It, too, is untestable in the empirical sense. So why assert it? Science itself is based not on a series of irrefutable facts, but on faith. Whitehead [34] was correct when he described the scientific revolution as a revolution away from faith based on reason (i.e., the world view developed from Saint Thomas Aquinas) to reason based on faith. It was a faith in the worthwhileness of a passionate concern with stubborn facts and a faith that these were part of what was called the order of nature. Science rested on a faith in the orderliness of nature, that there was a scheme to fit facts into, a jigsaw puzzle to be solved, that it was a real jigsaw puzzle and not just a game of ideas. This is what was new. Of course, people knew that the sun rises regularly. But there were a lot of things that did not occur with any regularity, a lot that was capricious, like the comets that did not seem to belong to any order. The faith of science was that all things, great and small, could in principle be put into an order of nature. If you had asked Galileo or Copernicus or Darwin to prove their faith, they would have been hard pressed to say anything more than that this was their conviction and so far it had not let them down. Each creative advance in science is, in Kuhn's terms, a "revolution" [35] involving the veritable "overthrow" of one order by another in which observable facts take on a new aspect and totally new problems begin to dominate inquiry. In this respect, Kuhn's interpretation of science is the same as Medawar's [36] in that the most important element is the imaginative leap that produces ideas that are fruitful. To trust, even tentatively, in the worthwhileness of an imaginative leap is faith. It is an essential ingredient in science. It cannot be an argument against having broad (and tentative) commitments any more than it is an argument against science. All commitments should have an element of tentativeness about them. What, then, fires the imagination? An essential ingredient is the urge to understand and to relate. But it is more than that. It is an urge akin to that of Eros of Greek mythology, which Rollo May describes as "a desiring, longing, a forever reaching out, seeking to expand, . . . the power in us yearning for wholeness." [37] May quotes that remarkable philosopher of science Charles S. Peirce: "The thinker must be animated by a true Eros for the task of scientific investigation." The scientific venture at its best is a reaching outward to embrace the wholeness of things. Analysis is pointless unless wholeness is its objective. There are plenty of pitfalls in seeking wholeness. We may be guided by Whitehead's [38] proposition that cosmologies are never merely true or false; they are more or less adequate to the full variety of experienced facts. That is the only reasonable attitude to adopt for theories that attempt to be comprehensive. The so-called verification principle is quite inappropriate to them. Simple hypotheses may be subject to it, but broad theories are not verified; they are weighed.[39]

An Ordering Principle in an Ordered Universe

How are we to think of cosmic evolution from chaos (= yawning) some ten thousand million years ago to cosmos (= order) that in one part at least took a path that led to the emergence of life, that in the course of two thousand million years led to life that can know about the universe and knows that it knows? There are some, perhaps most, evolutionists who see in the sequence of cosmic, biological, and cultural evolution an increase in order or levels of organization. Or, at least, they claim that in these historical sequences one sort of order is succeeded by another sort. In a very thoughtful article, Lewontin has recently questioned these propositions.[40] He asks, How can we distinguish order from chaos? Consider a pack of cards which are shuffled a number of times. Let us suppose that on one occasion the cards are grouped by suits. We would say that an order has been created. If the suits were arranged in ascending sequence, we might well say there was even greater order in that set of cards. Yet any particular order of cards has exactly the same probability as any other order. Therefore, Lewontin argues, the appearance of order is the correspondence between the arrangements of objects and a preconception. For the cards, this is indeed the case. However, Lewontin then states, "the demand that an evolutionary process create order, or at least that there be a change from an order to a different order, shows clearly that evolution, in this sense, is neither a fact nor a theory, but a way of organizing knowledge." This is a bewildering statement coming as it does from one of the leading evolutionists of our time. I would put it alongside the proposition of another evolutionist, Sir Ronald Fisher: "It was Darwin's chief contribution not only to biology but to the whole of natural science, to have brought to light a process by which contingencies a priori impossible, are given, in the process of time, an increasing probability, until it is the non-occurrence rather than their occurrence which becomes highly improbable." [41] Any particular combination of cards in a pack is highly improbable; yet all combinations are equally probable. Any particular combination of atoms in a living organism is highly improbable. Darwinian evolution shows us how the improbable is made probable; that is, it increases the probability of a particular order occurring. The shuffling of cards does not do this. Evolution is not just sequence but consequence. At each point of the historical sequence, some events become less likely for the future (e.g., six-legged mammals after the development of the pentadactyl limb) and other events become more likely. Natural selection is continually changing the possibility of the future. Some former restraints are lifted and new opportunities are revealed. This is why it can be called creative. I would therefore argue, against Lewontin, that evolution does create order and that this is a fact and not just a mental construct. Lewontin is onto a much more substantial argument when he questions whether evolution has any direction or linear order. Defining such a direction in terms of increase in complexity or increase in homeostasis is fraught with difficulties. There is nothing in the evolutionary process that puts a premium on complexity of structure and function. There is no reason to suppose that structures and functions might not evolve to simpler states. There is certainly no straight-line arrow in evolution. What there is is change in time as opposed to stasis. Change means sequence and sequence means consequence in the sense described above. The inevitable result is that novel creatures arise in the course of evolution and will yet arise. There are real differences between nonliving matter and a bacterial cell and between a bacterial cell and man, despite the difficulty we might have in defining what they are. They may in essence be differences of degree rather than of kind. But when differences of degree become great, it is reasonable to regard the new productions as having novel characteristics. The most novel characteristics of man as compared with all other creatures are the extent of his consciousness of the world around him, his self-awareness, and his capacity to communicate (through language).[42] Lewontin's article is a timely warning against accepting a too facile interpretation of evolution. But has he not thrown the baby out with the bath water? I believe he has and that he has not given a convincing argument for rejecting the idea that evolution involves the creation of different orders which are real and not just a matter of our way of looking at things. The order of nature is not the order of fixed and determined contrivances. Nature, including man, is a mixture of order and randomness, a point which is strongly made by Hartshorne.[43]

The problem of order in the universe is twofold: how it is that the universe is not just a "shapeless chaos" (Jefferson's phrase) and how it is that the cosmos ever evolved beyond some past primeval state. Objects endure, yet the world changes.

The stuff of the universe is ordered and has the potentiality of being further ordered and reorganized. In modern terms it is "programmed." Materialism takes neither of these two aspects of "programming" seriously. It accepts order at the physical level but does not explain it. "Matter," says Hartshorne, "is just a label for orderly processes of nature, it is not a positive principle to explain their possibility. . . . The mere existence of atoms with definite character, maintaining themselves through time and relative to one another is a tremendous order. Materialism in principle refuses to take order as a problem."[44] Given an ordered physical universe, it is another problem to explain the different levels of order and the evolutionary novelty built historically upon these foundations, from atoms to cells to living organisms. That is in large part a scientific problem, or set of problems. Darwin showed that the principle of natural selection of chance variation explained a lot of the order of the plant and animal world. These principles are not explanations of order per se. Natural selection can produce greater order than exists because it works with ordered systems which have the potentiality of being further ordered. The Darwinian explanation is an account of the outer aspects of things visible to the scientific observer. It leaves open the question of whether there is an inner aspect of things less amenable to scientific analysis but also relevant in seeking to interpret biological order. It does not leave as an open question what Raven called "the doctrine of divine carpentry," in which "the design of nature" is attributed to direct action or intervention by a designer God who is both architect and builder.[45] Darwin showed that this doctrine was contrary to facts.

The existence of an ordered universe implies an ordering principle—not a multitude of ordering principles, but one. There are two sorts of ordering principles: dictatorial and democratic. The "doctrine of divine carpentry" was a doctrine of a dictator God who ruled the universe. The democratic principle is order by persuasion of subjects with a degree of freedom for the subjects. The possibility of anarchy exists. Anarchy is prevented by persuasion or love, which are the same. I recall Professor Hartshorne making this point to an audience of students by telling them that the possibilities of disorder and anarchy in the lecture theater were very great. Such order as existed was, he trusted, the result of self-persuaded discipline. "Order," he said, "is anarchy tamed." The nature of the order in the lecture theater is an appropriate analogy of the nature of the order in the universe. There is an ordering persuasive principle of order which is God (in process thought), and there is the action of the individual entities in relation to the persuasion they "feel." It is not God alone who acts; every entity or individual does. "There is no single producer," says Hartshorne, "one producer is universally influential. Nevertheless, what happens is in no case the product of his creative act alone. Countless choices interact to make a world."[46] They do in a democracy. A dictator cannot bear disorder. Democracy can live with it. The opportunities for good and the possibility of evil are two aspects of just one thing, multiple freedoms. There are no reasons for particular evils; they just happen in a universe where good is possible but not inevitable. It is no argument that a divine creation must absolutely lack evil, be devoid of suffering and frustration. Could good mean anything in a world in which any contrary thing must be totally excluded? I think not.

Hartshorne says, "The order of the world requires a divine orderer, not because the order is perfect, or because there is nothing chaotic or unfortunate in the series of events, but because apart from God there is no way to understand how there could be any limit to the confusion and anarchy implied by the notion of multiplicity of creative agents, none universally influential or wise. And that there are such limits to anarchy is no mere fact; for there would have to be limits in any genuinely conceivable state of reality. But to understand this necessity is to see it as one with the necessary existence of God as cosmic orderer." [47] Without overall coordination there would be chaos in the universe. Peters [48] uses the analogy that, just as it is unlikely that a committee could have produced a Mona Lisa, so too is it unlikely that a multiplicity of events could alone have produced cosmic order. God on these terms provides the limits of freedom such that there is a favorable relation between risks and opportunity. The world is neither a tame and harmless order nor a wild and dangerous disorder.

But, you object, why one orderer of the universe only, why not an orderer of the orderer? To assign two or more cooperating individuals the role of universal interactions is to imply a distinction where there is none. Each cosmic orderer would have to interact with the other to maintain the integrity of the universe, and this seems to me to say that they act as one. "Order is in principle the rule of one." [49] But God as that one is not to be identified with absolute law and nonchance.

Matter and Mind as Two Aspects of One Reality

Dualism carves the universe up into two sorts of entities: matter and mind. Once separated, like Humpty Dumpty who fell off the wall, they can never be put together again; or at any rate, no one has yet succeeded in completing that operation. Materialism reduces all to terms of classical physics and leaves no place for the "nonphysical." Yet between what mind experiences and science describes there is a great gulf. The classical formulas of physics and chemistry give a monocular or one eyed view of things, reliable as far as it goes, but deficient in depth. These disciplines were never intended to provide an explanation of mind and consciousness; yet they are used by materialistic reductionists to this end. To be sure, there is a physical and a chemical component of all experience. That is not the question at issue. The question is whether all experience can be understood in principle in terms of classical physics and chemistry. Materialism answers yes, in principle. The nonmaterialist may still be a reductionist. But he seeks a new physics that allows room for something other than the classical notions of physics in his models of the building blocks of the universe.[50]

The experience of consciousness points, for the nonmaterialist, to a sentient aspect of reality. The immediate facts of experience disclose nothing of a dead, feelingless world. How then shall we account for what we know through experience? If matter and mind are two aspects of one thing, then one major philosophical problem of evolution disappears. We get rid of the necessity of introducing mind into a previously mindless world and the arguments as to when mind first "emerged." There is no direct evidence for asserting or denying the proposition that mind is an aspect of all matter. But if a more consistent and satisfying picture of the universe and its volution can be gained from the assumption that the primary particles are like ourselves sentient in some sense, then physics can have nothing to say against it. There is a place for models that go beyond those of classical physics (metaphysics). Physics itself admits that its concepts of the ultimate particles are models in any case. To go beyond these is to construct imaginative models that may be able to cope with interpreting a wider range of our experiential world. There have been numerous transformations of the physical models of the ultimate particles. Who is to say that we have arrived at any final picture? Certainly, the physicists are not claiming that they have. When an electron is "attracted" to a proton, there is nothing but an emotional reason to refrain from saying that the electron "likes" the proton or that it has particular feelings about a proton. Physics has no argument against that.

In the Whiteheadian view reality is process, the process of experience. This is a feeling universe. There is an outer and an inner aspect to the creatures we know ourselves to be. The proposition of process philosophy is that this model applies all the way down the line to the ultimate particles. As Hartshorne says, "The insentient, dead and mechanical is secondary to or even a mere appearance of a special case of the sentient, living or social. We need an interpretation of experience that will apply up and down the line." [51]

We tend to neglect too readily the seminal concept of the possibilities or potentialities of the universe from the foundations of the cosmos; matter, life, and consciousness were potential or possible, though what became concretely real was a matter of evolutionary history. Possibilities are unseen realities. As far as our human lives are concerned, they are potent causes in guiding and transforming our lives. In the Whiteheadian view, any occasion or event in the universe, be it an electronic event or an event in a higher organism, is an occasion of experience which is in touch with possibilities from which it selects a goal (which is its freedom) regarding its "self-fulfillment." There is an order of relevance to creative advance in the world. Each occasion of experience is partly self-determining and it is part-determined by the possibilities that confront it. The possibilities or potentialities are an aspect of the unitary actuality which Whitehead called God.

The universe has always been and is now in the process of being made. It is incomplete. It is lured to further completion. The order of the universe is well established at the level of electrons and atoms, less so at the level of living cells and organisms, least so at the level of human societies. This last level is where man's conscious groping may meet the persuasive lure of unrealized possibilities that could make a more complete world and more ordered lives. Here is where mankind is challenged to participate consciously in the ongoing creative process. This is a doctrine (panentheism) that recognizes the operation of "efficient causation" or mechanical causes and "final causation" or the effective causation of potentialities, goals, and purposes. Attempts to work out these ideas in detail have been made by Whitehead, Hartshorne, and other process thinkers. Their particular application to biological evolution has been developed by a number of authors, such as, for example, Wright,[52] Overman,[53] and Birch,[54] and by Burgers[55] to physics.

Immortality and the Unitary Actuality of the Universe as Responsive

If the unitary actuality of the universe is characterized by a quality that is best described as love that is inclusive of all that exists, and if the source of this love is worthy of unqualified love, then what is loved must respond to that love. The proposition is that at the heart of the universe there is integrating love that gives and that responds to the response of the creatures. The image is persuasive love transforming the creation and, in the process, itself being transformed or enriched by the creation. "Not a sparrow falls to the ground without your father knowing" is a saying attributed to Jesus and which puts in simple metaphor the concept of a responding love. Certainly for him it was not only man but all living creatures who had this impact on the being of God. If this is a valid image, who is to say that it is not applicable to all entities of existence? As for our own experience, it leaves out most of what is happening in the universe. Is there one who responds to all that exists, who feels the movement of creative evolution, and who saves this experience forever? Perhaps there could be no more daring and all-embracing proposition about our universe than that there is. In some form or another, this concept has appeared in the higher religions. Why? It is a judgment of value about what seems to make sense when we take value experiences seriously. We ask if the contribution each one of us may make is in any way lasting. To some extent, our influence may live beyond the grave in the memory of others. That contribution fades and is very incomplete. As far as our planet and all its works are concerned, its day will end, either in a freeze-up or in a fiery inferno. All will be frozen cold or reduced to ashes.

What then of man and all his works? Has he ultimately no significance in the vastness of the universe? Traditional theology has sought for survival of man beyond the grave. Immortality has

meant postmortem rewards and punishments. That has led to the
unethical notion that we do good for the sake of some future benefit
for us.[56] But there is only one valid reason for doing good, and
that is that it is good—period. The pearl of great price is sought
for its value now. But is that which has been achieved of value
saved in any way in the ongoing saga of the universe? It could be
if the unitary actuality, God, that includes all responds to all.
Created value would then be saved in his experience. That
the world experiences God and that God also experiences the
world and is enriched by it is a familiar image to students of A. N.
Whitehead.

What matters can matter ultimately only if it matters to that
which is itself ultimate and everlasting. What are everlasting in this
view are the value experiences of God. What has been achieved
is saved in his experience. "One personality and one immortality
suffice to save the meaning of existence," says Hartshorne.[57] Ours
can be the satisfaction of knowing that we participate in that.
There is no need for anything else. We, as participants to some
degree in the creative processes of the world, are too inclined to
see ourselves as owners of this and that, albeit temporary owners.
But for the world of the future, this concept of ownership will be
a great obstacle to advance. What matters is not what we as a people or nation seek to own but what we contribute to the whole.
Garrett Hardin has argued very persuasively that in the modern
world the concept of ownership of children is no longer tenable,
if ever it was: "My child's germ plasma is not mine, it is really
only part of the community's store. I was merely the temporary cus-
todian of part of it." [58] And so it is with the resources of the
planet and all that we tend to regard as ours. We are arrogant
because our sights are low. Humanism helps to lift them higher,
but not high enough. Hartshorne suggests that perhaps our culture
will find its way back after a long detour to the original Jewish
insight that only two things matter, creaturely life between birth
and death and the unborn and undying life of God. "The sole
bargain or covenant to make is that we do our best and trust God
to salvage what can be salvaged from our failures, and to make the
most of what can be made of our successes. We write our book of
life," he says, "either for extremely inadequate and ultimately ac-

cording to all rational probability, non-existent readers, or for the one adequate Reader." [59]

> All human forms identified, even tree, metal,
>   earth, and stone; all
> Human forms identified, living, going forth, and
>   returning wearied
> Into the planetary lives of years, months, days,
>   and hours; reposing,
> And then awakening into his bosom in the life of
>   immortality.
> And I heard the name of their emanations: they are
>   named Jerusalem.
>
> [WILLIAM BLAKE, "They Are Named Jerusalem"]

NOTES

1. John Macquarie, *Principles of Christian Theology* (New York: Charles Scribner's Sons, 1966), p. 59.

2. Charles Hartshorne, *Creative Synthesis and Philosophic Method* (London: S.C.M. Press, 1970), p. 317.

3. F. S. C. Northrop, *Man, Nature and God: A Quest for Life's Meaning* (New York: Pocket Books, 1962), p. 20.

4. As quoted in Lynn White, Jr., *Machina ex Deo: Essays in the Dynamism of Western Culture* (Cambridge, Mass.: M.I.T. Press, 1968), p. 39.

5. Matthew Arnold, *Culture and Anarchy: An Essay in Political and Social Criticism* (London: Smith & Elder, 1889).

6. John B. Cobb, *God and the World* (Philadelphia: Westminster Press, 1969), p. 50.

7. Alfred North Whitehead, *Adventures of Ideas* (New York: Macmillan Co., 1933), p. 380.

8. Pierre Teilhard de Chardin, *Hymn of the Universe* (London: Collins Sons & Co., 1961), p. 113.

9. Cobb (n. 6 above), p. 84.

10. Erik T. Erikson, *Identity: Youth and Crisis* (New York: W. W. Norton & Co., 1968), p. 142.

11. Kenneth Keniston, *Young Radicals: Notes on Committed Youth* (New York: Harcourt, Brace & World, 1968).

12. Robert Ardrey, *The Territorial Imperative: A Personal Inquiry into the Animal Origins of Property and Nations* (New York: Atheneum Publishers, 1966).

13. Konrad Lorenz, *On Aggression* (New York: Harcourt, Brace & World, 1966).

14. Jacques Chevalier, *Pascal* (Paris: E. Flammarion, 1936), p. 71.

15. Joseph Sittler, "Ecological Commitment as Theological Responsibility," *Zygon* 5 (1970): 175.

16. Dorothy Lee, "The Religious Dimension in Human Experience," in *Personality and Religion*, ed. W. A. Sadler (London: S.C.M. Press, 1970), p. 35.

17. I. L. McHarb, "The Plight," in *The Environmental Crisis: Man's Struggle to Live with Himself*, ed. H. W. Helfrich (New Haven, Conn.: Yale University Press, 1970), p. 21.

18. White (n. 4 above), p. 75.

19. *Ibid.*, p. 84.

20. Lewis W. Moncrief, "The Cultural Basis for Our Environmental Crisis," *Science* 170 (1970): 508-12.

21. David M. Gill, *From Here to Where? Technology, Faith and the Future of Man* (Geneva: World Council of Churches, 1970).

22. Sittler (n. 15 above), p. 173.

23. Kenneth Keniston, *The Uncommitted: Alienated Youth in American Society* (New York: Dell Publishing Co., 1960), p. 67.

24. Albert Camus, *La Peste* (London: Penguin Books, 1947), p. 36.

25. Pierre Teilhard de Chardin, *The Phenomenon of Man* (London: Collins, 1960), p. 172.

26. White (n. 4 above), p. 134.

27. *Ibid.*, p. 136.

28. Francis Thompson, "The Mistress of Vision XXII."

29. George Wald's introduction to L. J. Henderson's *The Fitness of the Environment* (Boston: Beacon Press, 1958), p. 3.

30. Charles Hartshorne, *A Natural Theology for Our Time* (La Salle, Ill.: Open Court Publishing Co., 1967), p. 16.

31. *Ibid.*, p. 13.

32. Cobb (n. 6 above), p. 62.

33. Hartshorne (n. 2 above), p. 45.

34. Alfred North Whitehead, *Science and the Modern World* (Cambridge: Cambridge University Press, 1926), chap. 1.

35. Thomas S. Kuhn, *The Structure of Scientific Revolutions,* International Encyclopedia of Unified Science (Chicago: University of Chicago Press, 1962).

36. P. B. Medawar, *The Art of the Soluble* (London: Methuen & Co., 1967), p. 138.

37. Rollo May, *Love and Will* (New York: W. W. Norton & Co., 1969), p. 73.

38. Whitehead (n. 7 above), p. 172.

39. Frederick Ferré, "Science and the Death of 'God,' " in *Science and Religion: New Perspectives on the Dialogue*, ed. Ian G. Barbour (New York: Harper Forum Books, 1968), pp. 134-56.

40. R. C. Lewontin, "Evolution: The Concept of Evolution," *International Encyclopedia of the Social Sciences*, ed. by David L. Sills, 17 vols. (New York: Free Press, 1968), 5:202-10.

41. R. A. Fisher, "Retrospect of the Criticisms of the Theory of Natural Selection," in *Evolution as a Process*, ed. J. Huxley, A. C. Hardy, and E. B. Ford (London: Allen & Unwin, 1954), p. 91.

42. Theodosius Dobzhansky, *The Biology of Ultimate Concern* (New York: New American Library, 1967), p. 68.

43. Hartshorne (n. 2 above), p. 318.

44. Hartshorne (n. 30 above), p. 57.

45. Charles E. Raven, *Natural Religion and Christian Theology,* Gifford Lectures 1951, First Series: Science and Religion (Cambridge: Cambridge University Press, 1953).

46. Hartshorne (n. 30 above), p. 59.

47. *Ibid.*

48. E. Peters, *The Creative Advance* (Saint Louis: Bethany Press, 1966), p. 70.

49. Hartshorne (n. 30 above), p. 61.

50. See C. F. von Weiszacker, *The Relevance of Science,* Gifford Lectures, 1959-60 (London: Collins Sons & Co., 1964); and W. Heisenberg, *Physics and Philosophy* (New York: Harper Torchbooks, 1962).

51. Hartshorne (n. 30 above), p. 61.

52. Sewall Wright, "Biology and the Philosophy of Science," in *Process and Divinity—the Hartshorne Festschrift,* ed. William L. Reese and Eugene Freeman (La Salle, Ill.: Open Court Publishing Co., 1964).

53. R. H. Overman, *Evolution and the Christian Doctrine of Creation: A Whiteheadian Interpretation* (Philadelphia: Westminster Press, 1967).

54. L. C. Birch, *Nature and God* (London: S.C.M. Press, 1965).

55. Johannes M. Burgers, *Experience and Conceptual Activity: A Philosophical Essay Based upon the Writings of A. N. Whitehead* (Cambridge, Mass.: M.I.T. Press, 1965).

56. Hartshorne (n. 30 above), p. 108.

57. *Ibid.,* p. 109.

58. Garrett Hardin, "Parenthood: Right or Privilege?" *Science* 169 (1970): 427.

59. Hartshorne (n. 30 above), p. 110.

SUGGESTED READINGS

Charles Birch presents an integrating vision of biology and process thought in his fine little work, *Nature and God* (Philadelphia: The Westminster Press, 1965, paperback). Especially well developed are the notions of chance and purpose. An outstanding comprehensive work is Ian Barbour's *Issues in Science and Religion* (N.Y.: Harper and Row, 1966, paperback). *The Creative Advance: An Introduction to Process Philosophy as a Context for Christian Faith,* by Eugene H. Peters (St. Louis: The Bethany Press, 1966, paperback) and *Process Thought and Chris-*

tian Faith by Norman Pittenger (N.Y.: Macmillan, 1968) provide good introductions to process theology. *Process Theology* edited by Ewert Cousins (N.Y.: Newman Press, 1971, paperback) contains many valuable essays on the process thinkers and on Teilhard de Chardin, together with a comprehensive bibliography. Theodosius Dobzhansky relates biology to Teilhardian perspective in *The Biology of Ultimate Concern* (N.Y.: The World Publishing Company, 1967, paperback). Ralph Wendell Burhoe's "Natural Selection and God" (*Zygon,* March 1972, pp. 30-63) is an illuminating essay on a crucial point in the relationship between religion and evolution. The changeless God of mysticism and traditional Western theology seems to be incompatible with the God of process. Joseph Donceel, S.J., presents a possible avenue of reconciliation in "Thoughts on the Nature of God," *Thought,* Autumn 1971, pp. 346-370. Alfred Stiernotte shows how process thought offers a basis for mysticism in "Process Philosophies and Mysticism," *International Philosophical Quarterly,* Dec. 1969, pp. 560-571. Lastly, the scientific minded reader will be intrigued by the discussion of chance and the central ordering power in the somewhat biographical *Physics and Beyond* by Werner Heisenberg (N.Y.: Harper and Row, 1971, paperback).

Bibliography

WORKS NOT TREATED IN THE SUGGESTED READINGS

Allport, Gordon. *The Individual and His Religion* (New York: Macmillan, 1950, paperback). Although some of the statistical studies are now old, this is still one of the best studies, profound, clear and simple.

————. *Becoming: Basic Considerations for a Psychology of Personality* (New Haven: Yale University Press, 1955, paperback). The concept of self and values, with some discussion of religious sentiment.

Barlow, J. Stanley. *The Fall Into Consciousness: New Accents in Psychology, Therapy and Religion* (Philadelphia: Fortress Press, 1973). The ideas of Freud, Jung, Adler, Horney, Suttie, Klein and others.

Belgum, David. *Guilt: Where Religion and Psychology Meet* (Minneapolis: Augsburg Publishing House, 1963, 1969). On penance or integrity therapy.

Big Sur Recordings: 117 Mitchell Blvd., San Rafael, Calif. 94903. Recordings on many topics related to religion, e.g., Rollo May on the demonic, R. Ornstein and Baba Ram Dass on meditation.

Broad, C. M. *Lectures on Psychical Research* (New York: The Humanities Press, 1962). A balanced, scholarly assessment of the evidence.

Brown, L. B. *Psychology and Religion* (Baltimore: Penguin Books, 1973). A collection of valuable readings, including Argyle's "Seven Psychological Roots of Religion" and Moberg's "Religiosity in Old Age."

Browning, Don S. *Atonement and Psychotherapy* (Philadelphia: Westminster Press, 1966). Three theories of the atonement and a discussion of empathic acceptance in psychotherapy.

Bugental, J. F. T. *The Search For Authenticity* (New York: Holt, Rinehart and Winston, Inc., 1965). An existential-analytic approach to psychotherapy, influenced by Tillich's thought.

305

Clark, Walter Houston. *The Psychology of Religion* (New York: Macmillan, 1958). A classic summary.

Colston, Lowell G., and Johnson, Paul E. *Personality and Christian Faith* (New York: Abingdon Press, 1972). See especially chapter 6, which includes the ideas of Erikson and others on the eight stages of personal development.

Curran, Charles A. *Psychological Dynamics in Religious Living* (New York: Herder and Herder, 1971). The death impulse, selfhood and the validation given by a redemptive community.

Darling, Harold W. *Man in Triumph* (Grand Rapids, Michigan: Zondervan Publishing House, 1968). A survey of major psychologists on guilt, motivation, wholeness and the nature of man.

Doniger, Simon, editor. *The Nature of Man in Theological and Psychological Perspective* (New York: Harper and Bros., 1962). A collection of essays on man's nature, good and evil in man, and his potentialities, including immortality.

Drakeford, John W. *Psychology in Search of a Soul* (Nashville: Broadman Press, 1964). A rather helpful introduction; supports Nygren's position on Eros versus agape.

Erikson, Erik K. *Young Man Luther: A Study in Psychoanalysis and History.* (New York: W. W. Norton and Co., 1958, paperback). An excellent study of Luther's quest for identity.

———. *Childhood and Society* (New York: W. W. Norton and Co., 1963, 2nd ed.). See especially the "Eight Ages of Man," pp. 247-284.

———. *Gandhi's Truth* (New York: W. W. Norton and Co., 1969, paperback). Gandhi's non-violence testing; perhaps not as easily applicable to the present study as *Young Man Luther*: ambivalence toward coercion in Gandhi's non-violence. A study of the ethics of generativity in Gandhi, his reality testing, and the ambivalence toward coercion in non-violence. On Erikson, cf. William W. Meissner, S.J., "Erikson's Truth: The Search For Ethical Identity," *Theological Studies,* June 1970, pp. 310-319.

Fabry, Joseph B. *The Pursuit of Meaning: Logotherapy Applied to Life* (Boston: Beacon Press, 1968). A study of Frankl's method.

Fingarette, Herbert. *The Self in Transformation: Psychoanalysis, Philosophy and the Life of the Spirit* (New York: Harper & Row, 1965, paperback).

Fitzsimons, Allison, C. *Guilt, Anger, and God* (New York: Seabury Press, 1972). The healing power of the Gospel.

Frick, William B. *Humanistic Psychology: Interviews with Maslow, Murphy and Rogers* (Columbus, Ohio: Charles E. Merrill Publishing Co., 1971). Interviews together with synthetic presentation.

Goodenough, Edwin R. *The Psychology of Religious Experiences* (New York: Basic Books, Inc. 1965). The nature of religion, types of experience, and religion as search.

Havens, Joseph, editor. *Psychology and Religion* (Princeton: Van Nostrand Insight series, 1968, paperback). A dialogue between psychologists and theologians, with valuable material on methodology, symbolism, anxiety and transcendence; for advanced students.

Hillman, James. *Insearch: Psychology and Religion* (New York: Charles Scribner's Sons, 1967). Discussion of the unconscious as experience, as moral problem, and the anima reality in religion.

Huxley, Aldous. *The Doors of Perception and Heaven and Hell* (New York: Harper and Row, 1965 ed., paperback). Two works on drugs and mysticism by one of the pioneers in the area.

Jahoda, Gustav. *The Psychology of Superstition* (Baltimore: Penguin, Pelican Books, 1970). Helpful insights and correctives. Concludes that man cannot live without some "superstitions."

Johnson, Paul E., editor. *Healer of the Mind: A Psychiatrist's Search for Faith* (Nashville: Abingdon Press, 1972). Religious autobiographies of ten prominent psychiatrists, each telling of his own lifelong search for a faith to live by.

Kelsey, Morton, *Healing and Christianity* (N.Y.: Harper & Row, 1973). A religious and psychological history.

Kubler-Ross, Elisabeth. *On Death and Dying* (New York: Macmillan, 1969, paperback). A marvelous work with full bibliography, including some religious material. See also Jerry Avorn's "Beyond Dying: Experiments Using Psychedelic Drugs To Ease the Transition From Life," *Harper's,* March 1973, pp. 56-64.

Laing, R. D. *The Politics of Experience* (New York: Ballantine Books, 1967, paperback). Especially chapter 6, "The Transcendental Experience."

Lapsley, James N. *Salvation and Health* (Philadelphia: Westminster Press, 1972). A brief resumé of the literature with a most helpful chapter (IV) on a dynamic process model relating salvation and health.

Lynch, William, S.J. *Images of Hope: Imagination as Healer of the Hopeless* (New York: The New American Library, 1965, paperback). A seminal work on hopelessness, the absolutizing instinct, imagination and the metaphysics of hope.

Maddi, Salvatore, and Costa, Paul. *Humanism in Personology: Allport, Maslow and Murray* (New York: Aldine-Atherton, Inc., 1972). A synthetic review.

May, Rollo. *Power and Innocence: A Search for the Sources of Violence* (New York: W. W. Norton, 1972). Innocence about one's search for power is dangerous. (Cf. *Psychology Today,* Dec. 1972, "The Innocent Murderers," pp. 53 ff.)

Mayerdoff, Milton. *On Caring* (New York: Harper and Row, 1971, Perennial Library paperback). The characteristics of caring as a philosophy of life; excellent, simple work. (Cf. *Psychology Today,* Jan. 1973, pp. 19-20.)

McConnell, Theodore A. *The Shattered Self: The Psychological and Religious Search for Selfhood* (Philadelphia: Pilgrim Press, 1971). Brief surveys of Erikson, Allport, Fromm, Frankl, May and Maslow.

Moran, Gabriel. *The Present Revelation: In Quest of Religious Foundations* (New York: Herder & Herder, 1972). One thesis is that all experience is revelatory and much use is made of psychological insight.

Moustakas, Clark E., editor. *The Self: Explorations in Personal Growth* (New York: Harper and Row, 1956). Valuable essays by Moustakas, Goldstein, Fromm, Rank, Tagore, Sartre, Jung, Rogers, Horney, etc.

Myers, Frederic. *Human Personality and Its Survival of Bodily Death* (New York: Longmans, Green and Co., 1935). Abridged edition of a classic work.

Oden, Thomas C. *The Structure of Awareness* (New York: Abingdon Press, 1969). Guilt, anxiety, boredom and religion.

———. *Kerygma and Counselling: Toward a Covenant Ontology for Secular Psychotherapy* (Philadelphia: Westminster Press, 1967). Acceptance and the theories of Carl Rogers and Karl Barth.

————. *Contemporary Theology and Psychotherapy* (Philadelphia: Westminster Press, 1967). Includes treatment of Bonhoeffer, Teilhard, Tillich, Thurneysen, Hiltner and Bultmann.

Oglesby, William B., Jr. *The New Shape of Pastoral Theology: Essays in Honor of Seward Hiltner* (New York: Abingdon Press, 1969). See especially "The Influence of Psychology on Theology" by Don S. Browning.

Pruyser, Paul W. *A Dynamic Psychology of Religion* (New York: Harper and Row, 1968). A detailed, analytic study for the more advanced reader.

Rudin, Josef. *Psychotherapy and Religion* (South Bend, Ind.: Fides, 1968). A study of theology and clinical psychology, anxiety and freedom, the conscious and the unconscious.

Strommen, Merton P., Jr., editor. *Research on Religious Development: A Comprehensive Handbook* (New York: Hawthorn Books Inc., 1971). Contains valuable bibliographical material.

Strunk, Orlo, Jr. *Mature Religion: A Psychological Study* (New York: Abingdon Press, 1965). A survey of James, Freud, Jung, Fromm, Frankl, plus the author's synthesis.

————. *Religion: A Psychological Interpretation* (New York: Abingdon Press, 1962). A brief but sound work.

————. *Readings in the Psychology of Religion* (New York: Abingdon Press, 1959). A very useful book with many short excerpts.

Thouless, Robert H. *An Introduction to the Psychology of Religion* (New York: Cambridge University Press, 1972, 3rd ed., paperback). Revised edition of a well-known introduction.

————. *Experimental Psychical Research* (Baltimore: Penguin Books, 1963). A thorough survey.

Tournier, Alan. *A Place for You: Psychology and Religion* (New York: Harper and Row, 1968).

Van Dusen, Wilson, *The Natural Depth of Man* (N.Y.: Harper & Row, 1972). An exploration of inner space.

Vergote, Antoine. *The Religious Man: A Psychological Study of Religious Attitudes* (Dayton: Pflaum Press, 1969). An excellent probing analysis.

Watts, Alan. *Behold the Spirit: A Study in the Necessity of Mystical Religion* (New York: Random House, 1971 edition, paperback).

Weatherhead, Leslie D. *Psychology, Religion and Healing* (London: Hodder and Stoughton, 1959). A thorough, detailed coverage.

Zaehner, R. C. *Drugs, Mysticism and Make-Believe* (New York: Pantheon, 1973). A scholar's hard-hitting, semi-popular work which shows the difference between a monistic union with the All and the Christian experience of union with God.

Zunini, Giorgio. *Man and His Religion* (London: Chapman, 1969). Eminently useful, clear and probing, but expensive.

Articles on a given topic may be located by reference to:

Index to Religious Periodical Literature
Readers' Guide to Periodical Literature
Catholic Periodical Index
Religious and Theological Abstracts

Some Journals

Journal of Consulting Psychology
Journal of Existentialism
The Journal of Humanistic Psychology
Journal of Individual Psychology
Journal of Religion and Health
Journal of Transpersonal Psychology
Manas
Pastoral Psychology
Psychologia
The Review of Existential Psychology and Psychiatry
Spiritual Life
Psychology Today